Launched in April 2007, the Daily Mash has quickly grown to become Britain's biggest humour website, covering national and international news with spoof stories, commentary and opinion. It has been described as 'the bastard son of Private Eye and Viz'. Which is just lovely.

Picture acknowledgments

6: a Rcmathiraj | Dreamstime.com; b Anna63 | Dreamstime.com; c Madelaide | Dreamstime.com; d. Spauln | Dreamstime.com; e David Fisher/Rex Features; 7: tr Janjolim | Dreamstime.com; b Gaurawa | Dreamstime.com; 8: Richard Young/Rex Features; 9: t Kcphotos | Dreamstime.com; b Claudiodivizia | Dreamstime.com; 10: t Patrick | Dreamstime.com; 11: t Rcaucino | Dreamstime.com; 12: t Hugofelix | Dreamstime.com; bl Mikenz | Dreamstime.com; br Adamr | Dreamstime.com; 12: Starper | Dreamstime.com; 14: Rex Features; 17: Karla | Dreamstime.com; 18: Gigapixel | Dreamstime.com; 19: t Mcarthystudio | Dreamstime.com; b Garry518 | Dreamstime.com; 20: t ITV/Rex Features; bl Javarman | Dreamstime.com; br Jazavac | Dreamstime.com; 21: Theo Kingma/Rex Features; 22: t Redfeniks | Dreamstime.com; b Markwaters | Dreamstime.com; 23: b Curaphotography | Dreamstime.com; 24: Winjohn | Dreamstime.com; 25: Lisafx | Dreamstime.com; 27: t Paula0652 | Dreamstime.com; b Koele | Dreamstime.com; 28: t Doctorkan | Dreamstime.com; b Monkeybusinessimages | Dreamstime.com; 29: t Roger-Viollet/Rex Features; b Cullenphotos | Dreamstime.com; 30: Ronfromyork | Dreamstime.com; 31: t NealShannon71 | Dreamstime.com; b Ayazad | Dreamstime.com; 32: t Rex Features; b Rido | Dreamstime.com; 33: t Niagaragirl | Dreamstime.com; b Braendan | Dreamstime.com; 34: Martin Rickett/PA Archive/Press Association Images; 35: Milosluz | Dreamstime.com; 36: t Ctacik | Dreamstime.com; 37: t Milkos | Dreamstime.com; b Leucocrystal | Dreamstime.com; 38: SNAP/Rex Features; 39: Monkeybusinessimages | Dreamstime.com; 40: t Rex Features; b Sipa Press/Rex Features. 41: t DigitalStudios | Dreamstime.com; b Brian Cassey/Rex Features; 42: t Francesco Giudicini/Rex Features; b Motorolka | Dreamstime.com; 43: t Serendigital | Dreamstime.com; b Zepherwind | Dreamstime.com; 45: t Christoff | Dreamstime.com; b Olga_sweet | Dreamstime.com; 47: Awcnz62 | Dreamstime.com; 48: t Ccaetano | Dreamstime.com; b Markwr | Dreamstime.com; 49: Moori | Dreamstime.com; 50: t Palangsi | Dreamstime.com; b Josiephos | Dreamstime.com; 51: Rex Features; 52: Anobis | Dreamstime.com; 53: t Monkeybusinessimages | Dreamstime.com; b Stuartkey | Dreamstime.com; 54: b Rex Features; 55: Argus456 | Dreamstime.com; 56: Velkol | Dreamstime.com; 57: Skyline Features/Rex Features; 58: t MCP/Rex Features; b Berekin | Dreamstime.com; 59: t Everett Collection/Rex Features; b Swisshippo | Dreamstime.com; 60: t Sophieso | Dreamstime.com; b Moke | Dreamstime.com; 61: t John Stillwell/PA Wire/Press Association Images; b Reno12 | Dreamstime.com; 62: Endhals | Dreamstime.com; 63: Dndavis | Dreamstime.com + Atman | Dreamstime.com; 64: David Fisher/Rex Features; 65: t Everett Collection/Rex Features; b Ecophoto | Dreamstime.com; 67: c.ABC Inc/Everett/Rex Features; 68: Louoates | Dreamstime.com; 69: t Solent News/Rex Features; b Gertfrik | Dreamstime.com; 70: Photonika | Dreamstime.com; 72: t Karimala | Dreamstime.com; b AGF s.r.l/Rex Features; 73: t Tmcnem | Dreamstime.com; b Erwinova | Dreamstime.com; 74: t Stefanphoto | Dreamstime.com; b Weefanphoto | Dreamstime.com; 75: Woman's Weekly/Rex Features; 77: Aliencat | Dreamstime.com; 78: t Joegough | Dreamstime.com; 78: t Redbaron | Dreamstime.com; b Simon Dawson/AP/Press Association Images; 80: t Ctacik | Dreamstime.com; b Milosluz | Dreamstime.com; 81: Myshotz | Dreamstime.com; 82: t Andyb1126 | Dreamstime.com; b Flash4me | Dreamstime.com; 83: Piksel | Dreamstime.com; 84: Mailthepic | Dreamstime.com; 85: Rex Features; 87: Ever | Dreamstime.com + Gromaler | Dreamstime.com; 88: Picture Perfect/Rex Features; 89: Manski | Dreamstime.com; 90: t Pn_photo | Dreamstime.com; b Netris | Dreamstime.com; 91: Pascaldewu... | Dreamstime.com; 92: Purmar | Dreamstime.com; 93: Greatpapa | Dreamstime.com; 94: Bright | Dreamstime.com; 95: t Chris Bourchier/Rex Features; b Bellemedia | Dreamstime.com; 97: Chris Ratcliffe/Rex Features; 98: t Rex Features; b Phillyassfog | Dreamstime.com; 99: t Rex Features; b Trexec | Dreamstime.com; 100: t Suljo | Dreamstime.com; b Rex Features; 101: Jeffwqc | Dreamstime.com; 102: Modellocate | Dreamstime.com; 103: David/Rupert Harley/Rex Features; 104: Cathykeifer | Dreamstime.com; 105: t Maverick | Dreamstime.com; b Copetti/Photofab/Rex Features; 107: t Redbaron | Dreamstime.com; b Jmpaget | Dreamstime.com; 108: Hpphoto | Dreamstime.com; 109: t David Cheskin/PA Wire/Press Association Images; b Geoff Wilkinson/Rex Features; b Alzz | Dreamstime.com; 110: M & Y Agency Ltd/Rex Features; 111: b Assignments | Dreamstime.com; 112: Rex Features; 113: Sletse | Dreamstime.com; 114: Tarmes | Dreamstime.com; 115: t Simon Roberts/Rex Features; b Igabriela | Dreamstime.com; 117: t Rex Features; b Rtimages | Dreamstime.com; 118: t Chrisharvey | Dreamstime.com; b ShiningColors | Dreamstime.com; 119: Cathieking | Dreamstime.com; 120: Ersler | Dreamstime.com; 121: Urosr | Dreamstime.com; 122: Darrenbaker | Dreamstime.com; 123: Photoshow | Dreamstime.com; 124: tc Mark Campbell/Rex Features; br Gvision | Dreamstime.com; 125: Lisafx | Dreamstime.com; 126: Notronrj | Dreamstime.com; 127: Alextee | Dreamstime.com + Bthompso2001 | Dreamstime.com; 128: Micha Theiner/Rex Features.

EVERYONE DEAD BY TEATIME

By Neil Rafferty and Paul Stokes

With additional material by:
Jennifer McKenzie,
Suzy Orr,
Nick Pettigrew
and Tim Telling

Constable • London

CONSTABLE

Constable & Robinson Ltd
3 The Lanchesters
162 Fulham Palace Road
London W6 9ER

www.constablerobinson.com

First published in the UK by Constable,
an imprint of Constable & Robinson Ltd.

A copy of the British Library Cataloguing in
Publication Data is available from the British Library

ISBN-13: 978-1-84901-198-3
Design and layout by Essential Works
www.essentialworks.co.uk

Printed and bound in Singapore

1 3 5 7 9 10 8 6 4 2

CONTENTS

The Daily Mash guide to UK threat levels

Mango		All is well. Unlock your doors and leave your children with a neighbour. Sing.
Hedgehog		Unsettling. What was that noise? Where were you born? Share my values at once young man.
Spacehopper		Terribly frightening. Death has the deeds to your mortgage. Trust no-one and carry a bucket at all times.
Underpants		Incredibly dangerous. You and everyone you know is now a terrorist or carries a pig-borne viral infection. Go home and watch *Grey's Anatomy* from behind the sofa you can no longer afford.
Philip Schofield		Oh Christ. You and your loved ones are being sprayed liberally by the shit that has just careered into the fan. And your trousers are ablaze.

The Daily Mash

it's news to us   www.thedailymash.co.uk   **No.1**

85% OF MEN HAVE NO IDEA HOW TO REACT TO HELEN MIRREN IN A BIKINI

THE majority of British men were in a state of extreme confusion last night after seeing photos of 63-year-old Helen Mirren in a bikini.

The Oscar winning dame was pictured frolicking by the sea in Italy, showing off a body that makes Eva Longoria look like a saggy, withered old hag.

Clad in a skimpy, red two-piece that showed off her tight stomach, slender thighs and still lively breasts, the star of *The Queen* and *Prime Suspect*, gave herself a right good soaking in the warm, sensual waters of the Adriatic, before popping her teeth back in.

She then stretched her firm body on the rocks to bask in the sunshine while reading a book about prunes.

Wayne Hayes, a 33-year-old from Exeter, said: "I'd do 'er. I'd do 'er all flippin' night. Oh bollocks, she's older than my mum."

Forty-one-year-old Roy Hobbs, from Cleethorpes, who watches Mirren in *Excalibur* at least six times a day, said: "Yes, well, crikey. She's a lovely, mature woman. Extremely talented. Jolly good."

He added: "If you'll excuse me, I have to go and watch *Excalibur*."

Julian Cook, 25, from London, said: "To be honest with you, I fancied her in *The Queen*.

So where does she put her bus pass?

"I don't want to make some crude remark about pearl necklaces, but yes, I totally would have."

Blood-soaked revolution to start at noon

BRITAIN'S long-awaited bloody revolution will begin at noon today, after MPs voted to keep their £24,000 second home allowance.

Despite repeated warnings that a vote for the generous expenses package would lead to their certain deaths, 146 Labour MPs and 24 Tories backed the measure which will allow them to buy whatever they want with your money.

Regional organisers say the first priority will be to put together a series of medium-sized lynch mobs to hunt down local MPs and drag them to the town square where they will be pelted with thousands of £1 coins.

One group in the North East plans to tie its MP to a chair and then take the 42-inch plasma screen television he bought with public money and drop it

The bears are looking forward to feasting on Jacqui Smith's innards

on his head from a large crane.

Meanwhile those cabinet ministers, already on a basic salary of £138,000, who voted for the second home allowance, are

expected to be paraded on the back of a cart to Regent's Park Zoo and then thrown to the polar bears.

Bill McKay, a regional organiser from Lincolnshire, said: "In the midst of rising household bills, looming recession and job losses, the only reasonable response to this kind of thing is ravenous bears."

He added: "Of course, once we've dispatched the MPs we will then need to form a provisional government held to account by some sort of democratically elected chamber.

"It will certainly be a demanding job, involving lots of time away from home, so a large, unaccountable expenses package will probably be necessary.

"Personally, I'd quite like a flat in Bayswater with granite worktops and a power shower."

Thought for the day: Don't do that creepy thing with your tongue, it makes you look like Robson Green. (Nelson Mandela)

Stars gather to show how worthless they are compared to Nelson Mandela

SOME of the biggest names in showbiz have come together in London to prove how shabby and pointless they are compared to Nelson Mandela.

Stars including Emma Thompson, Gordon Ramsay and the Sugababes shared the red carpet to speak about how happy they were that Mandela had not been beaten to death during his 30 years in a South African prison.

Thompson, an actress, said: "Nelson's sacrifice is a constant inspiration to me when I'm being paid £5 million for dressing up and pretending to be someone else."

She added: "I'm sorry, I have to go, I've just spotted Bobby, Pierce and Will sharing a joke with Uma and Elton."

Former US president Bill Clinton said: "I would often think about Nelson Mandela's years of incarceration and his efforts to unite a country so filled with hatred and mistrust when I was shoving cigars into plump young women."

He added: "I'm sorry, I have to go and ask Cherie Blair how much money she's made this year."

Mr Mandela said: "When I was chained to a radiator on Robben Island, I dreamt I would live long enough to

Lennox and Geldof are each other's heroes

be able to come to London for my birthday and help a bunch of self-absorbed millionaires feel even better about themselves."

He added: "I'm sorry I have to go. Bob Geldof is coming this way and I have to pretend to be dead."

Hollywood actors pretend to go on strike

HOLLYWOOD could grind to a halt this week after some of the world's biggest stars threatened to pretend to go on strike.

Tom Hanks, Dustin Hoffman and Jack Nicholson have all warned the studios they will be so good at pretending to threaten to go on strike that no-one will be able to tell the difference.

The studios have stressed they are willing to negotiate, but only with bad actors who will give an unconvincing portrayal of someone who is threatening strike action.

Tom Logan, vice-president of Universal, said: "If these guys are at the top of their game we will have absolutely no way of knowing whether the negotiations are real or pretend.

"If Nicholson walks in here and tells me that I 'can't handle the truth' with the

same conviction he used in *A Few Good Men*, I'll have no choice but to believe him.

"What if Hoffman dresses up as a woman and pretends to be a sassy hospital administrator called Dorothy? We know his pretend feminine wiles are legendary.

"And what if Hanks starts acting all weak and speaking in a croaky voice like at the end of *Philadelphia*? I'll be so overcome with sympathy I'll end up giving him everything he wants."

Logan said he was happy to talk to second-rate actors who do the same thing over and over gain, making it very easy to spot when they are pretending.

He added: "We'd love to sit down and thrash this out with Vince Vaughan doing his poor man's Bill Murray routine, or Jeff Goldblum's *Jurassic Park*, hip scientist bullshit."

NEWS BRIEFLY

GOVERNMENT FINALLY AGREES TO STOP PEOPLE GOING BLIND
National Institute for Health and Clinical Excellence approve the drug Lucentis for patients who have either fallen down a manhole or been attacked by a tiger that they thought was a dog

BANKS TO START WRITING STUFF DOWN
"Britain will once again become an EM Forster novel where everyone who was not a woman or a homosexual aristocrat is a clerk, possibly on the railways," say experts

LIB DEMS PROMISE HAND JOBS AND ICE CREAM
"Britain is a fair society and I have no doubt the wealthy will be glad to give cheerful hand relief to a confused old man or a low skilled immigrant," says Nick Clegg

BRITISH CHILDREN TOO UGLY, SAYS GLITTER
Glam rock pervert claims average British 12 year-old now looks like a short, chubby version of Dot Cotton

DIANA FILM NOT ABOUT DIANA OBVIOUSLY ABOUT DIANA
Keira Knightley stars as *The Duchess* who married a heartless aristocrat, before becoming a fashion icon, anti-gout campaigner and mother to two sons, one of whom looked remarkably like a captain in the Royal Hussars

NHS TO REVERT TO OLD MAN WITH LEECHES AND A SAW
"It's retro," claims health secretary

Hard-up Queen forced to sell Princess Anne

PRINCESS Anne was put up for sale last night as the Queen looked to plug a £32-million hole in her finances.

The Queen has been forced to give up her controlling interest in the Olympic horsewoman in a bid to raise cash for essential roof repairs and asbestos removal at her eight gigantic palaces.

There is already strong interest in the 57-year-old Princess from Moscow and Beijing, where she is seen as a great delicacy.

Meanwhile the Royal Bank of Scotland has ·made no secret of its desire to buy 51% of the Princess as a first step towards an eventual takeover of Prince Andrew and the Duke of Kent.

A 10% stake in Princess Anne would give share-holders the right to bring their own horse to Trooping the Colour and to spend two weeks a year as patron of Save the Children and the St John Ambulance Association.

They will also get seats on the half-way line at

For an extra £50 she'll dress up like a horse

Murrayfield and two free bets at some of the Princess's favourite dog fighting pits.

Royal expert Denys Finch-Hatton said that the Queen, owner of Buckingham Palace, St James's Palace, Kensington Palace, Clarence House, Sandringham, Holy-roodhouse, Windsor Castle and Balmoral, had no choice but to sell her only daughter.

He added: "How else does one possibly raise £32 million when all one has to one's name is half of Scotland, eight gigantic palaces and the greatest art collection in the history of the world?"

DUBSTEP OLD HAT AS FANS EMBRACE BUMFUNKING

DUBSTEP pioneer Burial shocked the music world last night as he announced he was abandoning the genre that made his name for the rival style of Bumfunking.

Burial revealed his conversion to the new dance movement – a mixture of Clit 'n' Bass with the darker elements of Bowelshift – after failing to win this year's Mercury Prize.

The south-London producer – real name Julian Cook – said he was joining forces with Dutch cock twiddler Jank 2526, whose neo-Fudcore anthem *Dogbiscuit* is already a Bumfunk standard.

Cook said: "Bumfunk combines the serenity, melancholy, and tragic intensity of a great lyric improvisation with a lot of screechy noises."

He added: "Put a fuckin' twonk on it."

Wayne Hayes, editor of *Racket* magazine, said: "Jank 2526 has consolidated the glacial techno beats of East German Pigbits with the drenched sub-bass of Peckham's Shithouse

"In doing so he has crafted a sound that will long outlast the inane tunes with comedy basslines that are currently worshipped by devotees of Clownfoot and Daddylegs."

He added: "By embracing Flaps and two-step Snowshit, Jank has reinvigorated a genre that was being turned into a laughing stock by the likes of Stilkie, Arser and Quimland Express."

Dance fan Charlie Reeves said: "Jank is a genius, he has taken the thud, thud, thud of Dubstep and added at least two extra thuds. It's totally cronking."

Shakespeare study to teach kids new words for cock

'Mightst I have a squint at m'lady's chuff?'

PRIMARY school children as young as five are to study the works of Shakespeare as part of a government initiative to teach them hundreds of 17th-century slang words for penis.

Ed Balls, the schools sec-retary, wants every child to learn at least 50 obscure terms for the male reproductive organ or the vagina by the age of seven.

He is concerned that British children are relying far too much on 'willy' and 'front bottom' when they could be using Shakespearean terms like 'carrot', 'bodkin' and 'buggle boe'.

Mr Balls said: "Right now in China billions of little children are sitting in school-rooms reciting elaborate Confucian jokes about cock."

A recent academic study of Shakespeare's work by the Institute for Studies found that 98% of the words used in his plays are euphemisms for either the penis or the vagina.

Its analysis of the Battle of

Agincourt scene from *Henry V* found more than 100 refer-ences to the erect penis, and 73 allusions to cunnilingus and anal sex.

Dr Cathy Smith, head of English at the Institute, said: "The great genius of Shakespeare is his ability to confront every aspect of the human experience and slip in a knob joke.

"The poetry is superb, the themes timeless and universal, but basically it's all just fanny, tits and arse."

Insane greed still best way to make money, say experts

INVESTING your money with a greedy maniac who would throttle a nun for 50p, still offers the best prospect of a healthy, long-term return, experts said last night.

As US and British authorities suspended short-selling, prime minister Gordon Brown pledged that London-based hedge funds would from now on be managed by the cast of *The Vicar of Dibley* and a host of former *Play School* presenters.

Mr Brown said: "People need to know their pensions are in the hands of wide-eyed bumpkins who, if necessary, will give it all to some drug addict and hope he uses it to get his life back on track."

But the Institute for Studies said investing your money with people who have friends and enjoy hugging, sharing and lazy summer days, will also mean spending your retirement in a tube station, dancing for coins.

Professor Henry Brubaker, said: "Some people think investment returns are like a field of wheat that needs to be nurtured with water, sunshine and natural goodness.

"However, what they actually involve is nailing the farmer to the floor of the barn, setting fire to his wheat field and then submitting a fraudulent insurance claim.

The easiest 50p you'll ever make

"The role of the regulator is to ensure investment firms always have enough money to buy more petrol and nails."

He added: "Then again, you could always get yourself some comfortable trainers and a regular spot at Tottenham Court Road. Try body-popping. Everyone likes that."

Anal warts take poll lead over Brown

GORDON Brown is facing an autumn challenge to his leadership from a particularly virulent case of anal warts.

With his approval rating at a record low Labour backbenchers say the party now stands a better chance at the next election under a painful and embarrassing venereal disease.

According to a poll for the Guardian, the anal warts are favoured by 42% of Labour voters, well ahead of a constantly screaming baby and a dead hamster, both on 23%. Ninety-five-year-old communist Michael Foot is on 6%, while Mr Brown is now on -59%.

But Downing Street last night brushed aside talk of a contest, stressing the Prime Minister was getting on with the job of having his picture taken with Barack Obama and inviting Ben Elton to Chequers.

Downing Street is also finalising a series of headline-grabbing policy initiatives including vouchers for free tripe and marzipan, while every home in Britain will be sent a DVD of *Highlander II: The Quickening*.

Later today Mr Brown will kick off his campaign to woo back middle England by meeting with scheming, hate-filled trade unionists and agreeing to do whatever they say.

Parents to be sent drawing of fat child

PARENTS of fat children are to be sent sketches of their overweight kids after the government banned schools from describing them as obese.

The drawings will be handed to parents by a health visitor who will then silently mouth 'shit your kid is enormous' and pretend to be sick on their shoes.

School nurse Nikki Hollis said: "I'm not allowed to describe a child using medical terminology but I am allowed to illustrate their condition with a sketch.

"I've drawn a little gallows with F _ T B _ _ T _ _ D underneath, and a picture of a donut and an equals sign next to a grave with the kid's name on it."

She added: "Research shows parents of the fat believe their child is a healthy weight. So how come they run for their lives when it tries to sit on them?"

A health department spokesman said: "The biggest problem facing our country is large children who can't run and are starting to smell a bit funky.

"We have committed more than £500 million to pointing this out and to developing a series of replacements for the word 'fat'."

He added: "My current favourites are 'globulous' and 'beeftastic'."

Dear Parent, this is your kid. *Jesus.*

From the Secretary of State for Health

Stars shine at London gay bullshit week

THEY are calling it the most glamorous and successful London Gay Bullshit Week in years.

Stars from across the globe have gathered in the capital to look at handbags and soak up as much stupid gay bullshit as they can.

Novelist Jilly Cooper and synth-pop genius Howard Jones were among the big names dazzled by the new collections from the likes of Prada, Chloe, Yellow Handkerchief and House of Fruit.

Wayne Hayes, gay bullshit editor at the Daily Telegraph, said: "This year everything is 'oomph'. It's glam, it's saucy, but it's ever so scared. It's saying 'touch my bum, but not too hard'.

"Blue is now. Red is tomorrow.

Mauve is a week next Tuesday. Did you see Rupert Everett at the Gucci pre-show blinis? Yum! And I don't mean the blinis – I mean his erect penis."

He added: "I am loving this year's flaps. And have you seen Stella McCartney's new elbow pads? Don't you just want to jump into a lake of fire?"

But debate is again raging over underweight models with pointy elbows and no titties, as experts insist they are a poor role model for young women who want to get pumped.

Dietician Dr Tom Logan said: "Jesus, she looks like that terrifying skeletal thing at the end of *Close Encounters* which, I might add, I absolutely did not want to fuck."

Water made from gas, say water companies

WATER companies last night defended their above inflation price rises insisting water was now made from highly expensive gas.

The companies said Britain was at the mercy of ruthless eastern gas merchants growing fat on our unquenchable desire for their precious bubbles.

According to Thames Water, the gases around the UK can only be used to make Fanta and Tizer, both of which are safe to drink, but absolutely useless if you want to soak your knickers.

A company spokesman said: "Our fresh, delicious water is made using only the finest gases from the orient.

"Our gasologists trawl through the

exotic casbahs of Mongolia and Balukistan selecting those gases that possess the perfect balance of moistness and flavour.

"We must then haggle with the local maharajahs who laugh heartily and threaten us with big curvy swords and ask our women to dance.

"The precious cargo is loaded ever so carefully onto a camel train and transported through the desert back to our treatment plant on the outskirts of Deptford."

He added: "Only when the gases have been blended to perfection do we then add the faint whiff of bodily waste and a generous helping of Domestos."

A gas convoy en route to Deptford

THE $700 billion rescue of Wall Street has been held up after intense lobbying by America's vast and powerful soup manufacturers.

A cartel, led by Campbell's, is urging Congress to reject the plan and give Americans the chance to queue for a steaming bowlful of hearty broth.

Meanwhile Knorr is demanding at least half the proposed rescue package be diverted into a contingency fund for chicken stock cubes.

Pressure from 'Big Soup' has even led to bribery accusations, with one senator being offered a $2-million campaign contribution and as much cock-a-leekie as he could stuff in the back of his car.

A spokesman for Campbell's said: "The US economy must be allowed to go through all the phases of its natural cycle. We've had 'psychotic greed' and 'frenzied panic' and now it's time for 'soup kitchen'.

"The millions of jobs lost will soon be replaced by high-quality positions within America's fast growing soup industry. We'll need experienced marketing executives to hand out flyers and, of course, somebody has to make all the soup.

"This will be nothing like the 1930s. Back then no-one cared about the quality of the soup or the queuing experience. It was all very drab and everyone looked so thin and sad.

"These days we use only the finest ingredients and we'll have plenty of serving stations so no-one should have to shuffle pathetically for more than 20 minutes. We've even lined up Robin Williams to keep everyone entertained while we change the pots."

He added: "Taste our harvest tomato with basil and tell me you wouldn't beg for it."

No women involved in latest pantyliner advert

NO women were involved in the making of the latest advert for Always pantyliners, it was confirmed last night.

The company has admitted the commercial, which offers women the chance to 'have a happy period', was made by a group of men who do not actually know what a period is.

A spokeswoman said: "All the girls in the office were on holiday when this went out, so there was no-one around to check it.

"When we asked the men what they thought they were doing, it became clear they believed a period was either the five hours between breakfast and lunch, or some kind of sporting contest.

'Do we know why it goes inside the panties?'

"We then described a period in terrifyingly explicit biological terms, and they all agreed that 'happy' was not an appropriate word, no matter how good your fanny pads ."

The company is now testing new slogans including 'have a period that's not unremittingly nauseating and painful' and 'periods – this might help'. The spokeswoman added: "I suggested 'have a period that doesn't make you want to stuff his nuts into the waste disposal' but then again, I am having my period.

"We're also going to lose the animation of the woman dancing around without a care in the world, because that's just a lot of bollocks."

Grammar pendants fewer interesting

GRAMMAR enthusiasts which point out everyday errors are much fewer interesting compared than normal people, according to researchers.

The Institute for Studies say people who write letters complaining about the use of 'your', 'you're' and 'youre' have less friends and are fewer able to socially mix.

Doctor Henry Brubaker, the institutes' head of grammar, says: "Words are very important. They convey meaning and emotion, but they can also be used to bore the tits off you.

"Take, for instance, the sentence; 'If there is one thing I really hate, it is bad grammar'.

"These words, placed in this precise order, can cause you either to walk away immediately or nod and say 'I completely agree'.

"Unfortunately, if you

'Fuck off, I'm eating shoots and leaves'

opt for the second response, it will then be met with the follow-up sentence, 'Surely you mean 'I agree completely'?.

"At this point it is acceptable to walk away, perhaps with the accompanying use of the word 'prick'."

He added: "If anyone asks you what is wrong with William Shatner's speech at the beginning of *Star Trek*, remember that the correct response is to say, 'I am now going to kick you in the nuts, boldly'."

New photo-shoot reveals gaping, soulless void at centre of Katie Price

A SPECTACULAR new photo shoot by glamour model Katie Price has revealed the echoing chasm at the centre of her being.

Promoting her new range of Asda lingerie, Price, also known as Jordan, looked as curvaceous as ever, while at the same time being devoid of all humanity.

Dr Tom Logan, of the Institute for Studies, said: "It's the eyes, they're so wonderfully dead.

"The eyes, the face, the whole experience of looking at Katie Price leaves you feeling as if you have just stared over the abyss into the desolate, utterly indifferent vacuum of space.

"With this saucy photo shoot Katie has moved beyond the simple, earthly concepts of good and evil and drifted effortlessly into

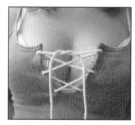

And yet, her bra remains far from empty

the realm of total emptiness."

Dr Logan warned that looking into Price's blank, lifeless eyes for too long may leave the viewer with the inescapable sense of life having lost all meaning.

He added: "Her face can be strangely hypnotic, a bit like static on a television screen. It is essentially just millions of pixels of nothingness.

"Though I have to say, she does look phenomenal in those panties."

That shrew is so fucking hammered, say zoologists

YOU should have totally seen this shrew, it was out of its face, a team of zoologists claimed last night.

The scientists, from the Institute for Studies, discovered the tiny mammal in the West Malaysian rainforest as part of their worldwide research into animals that like a drink.

The pen-tailed tree shrew sips alcoholic nectar from exotic flowers, but also enjoys gin, vodka, Sweetheart Stout and mojitos.

Team leader, Professor Wayne Hayes, said: "We started off with a couple of G&Ts, just to loosen things up and then had a couple of pints. By the time we had progressed to our third mojito the wee bastard was totally off his face."

"I said to Dave, I said, 'Dave! Check it out. This shrew is fuckin'

'What? I'm totally fine. What?'

hammered. I think he's trying to take a swing at me'.

"It then gave me a dirty look and wandered off into the undergrowth while Dave and I had yet another conversation about why I am not trying to shag his wife, who, by the way, is a fat bag and totally up for it.

"Anyway, the next morning we found the shrew fast asleep in a tiny little puddle of sick. It was adorable."

Professor Hayes added: "So far we've discovered a zebra that drinks like an Irishman and a badger with an insatiable thirst for Pinot Grigio. And then, of course, there was the schnapps monkey.

"We're now off to Thailand where we hope to discover how much Crème de Menthe you can pour into an elephant before it goes mental."

The communities living in fear of global warming scientists

MORE than half of all communities in Britain are being terrorised by gangs of global warming scientists, it was claimed last night.

Research shows gangs are assaulting people in broad daylight if they cite references suggesting climate change may be caused by factors unrelated to human activity.

PE teacher Bill McKay, 44, from Sudbury, was attacked in the car park of his local pub after he was overheard telling friends how much he enjoyed *Top Gear*.

He said: "They told me my contention was erroneous and suggested I was being paid lots of money by General Motors. And then one of them kneed me squarely in the balls." He added: "A couple of weeks later that George Monbiot came up to me and said that if I didn't stop going on about the prevalence of volcanic emissions in the upper atmosphere he'd give me a peer-reviewed kicking.

"I have no idea what he's talking about."

The Department of the Environment has refused to recognise the problem of global warming violence and stressed the research has already been dismissed by some of the most respected global warming gang leaders in the country.

A spokesman said: "Look, would you just piss off and leave me alone alright?

"If they know I've been talking to you they'll tie me to the back of their Lexus and drag me to an REM concert."

A PLATE OF CANCER PLEASE, SAYS BRITAIN

BRITAIN sat down this morning and ordered itself a huge plate of fried cancer with mushrooms and baked beans.

The nation's greasy spoons prepared for business as usual as millions chose to ignore the latest sausage and egg-based health warning.

Bill McKay, an electrician from Mansfield, ordered the full English cancer, including two fried cancers, three rashers of early death, the baked beans and a grilled tomato which he did not eat.

He also enjoyed a slice of fried cancer and two pieces of black pudding, providing with extra-fatal carcinogens.

Meanwhile his colleague Stephen Malley ordered a tumour in a bap, a cup of tea with milk and two cancers and a scrambled egg and colonectomy roll to take away.

McKay said: "I'm fully aware that All Bran isn't filled to the brim with cancer. My only problem with it is that it tastes like a horse's arse and there's no way I'm going to eat that crap.

"I suppose I could try putting some All Bran in a roll, with maybe a fried egg and just the one bit of black pudding.

"How many more years does that get me?"

Newcastle fans call for the reanimation of Jackie Milburn

NEWCASTLE United fans last night warned the club's potential buyers they must invest heavily in the reanimation of 1950s hero Jackie Milburn.

Milburn spearheaded the club's triple FA cup success in 1951, '52, and '55, but his form dipped dramatically following his death in 1988.

Bill McKay, vice-chairman of the Toon Army supporters club, said: "It can't just be the reanimation of a badly decomposed 64 year-old, he needs to be brought back to life at his 1951 cup-winning best.

"By my calculations they'll need a vast laboratory filled with nuclear reactors and about 100,000 of the world's leading bio-geneticists if 'wor Jackie' is going to be fit for the second half of the season.

"We're talking at least £6.5 billion, but if they're not willing to spend that kind of money on something as straightforward as corpse

If corpse reanimation fails the fans want this photograph brought magically to life

reanimation then they shouldn't be allowed to own a football club."

McKay is also demanding the forced return of Alan Shearer, Paul Gascoigne, Malcolm Macdonald and Peter Beardsley, all of whom will

undergo a rejuvenation process involving a funnel, 28 pints of olive oil and a series of potentially fatal electric shocks.

Meanwhile manager Kevin Keegan has promised to return to the club, but only if Milburn's reanimated corpse does not turn into an evil, black-eyed zombie intent on eating the brains of the senior coaching staff.

He is also demanding an £8 billion time machine so that he can assess the form of the entire 1955 squad and then have any player he likes reanimated at will.

Keegan said: "Newcastle United is a big club on a par with Man United, Chelsea and Arsenal, the only difference being they haven't won anything even remotely important for 53 years."

WEEKEND SCORES			
Chelsea	3	New Chelsea	1
Pepsi	2	Coke	3
Plucky Northerners	1	Arab's Plaything	8

Everyone really meant to watch paralympics

EVERYONE in Britain really meant to watch the Paralympics this weekend but ended up missing it for some reason.

Fired with enthusiasm following Team GB's success in the proper Olympics, the nation vowed to follow the fortunes of its 'special' athletes in China.

However, after praising their mutant determination, millions then immediately forgot about the Paralympics and instead watched England struggle to victory against a

team of Pyrenean bin men.

Wayne Hayes, from Luton, said: "It's amazing the personal struggles they have to go through just to compete. Sometimes you can almost forget how 'special' they really are.

"That said, I watched a wheelchair race the other day and they went like the fucking clappers."

Hayes added: "I've got the first 15 minutes of the opening ceremony on Sky+, so I'll try and watch it next Saturday after *Football*

Focus if there isn't any golf."

Bill McKay, a darts player from Didcot, said: "Someone told me they have pole-vaulting dwarves, but what I really want to see is a man with no arms wrestle a man with no legs.

"I'm also looking forward to the 100 metres for men with appalling haircuts, and the weightlifters with chronic flatulence."

He added: "I did tune in for the swimming last night - I thought I was watching a David Cronenberg film."

Cyclist Chris Hoy is allowed to compete in both because he's Scottish

BRITONS
"WANTS
YOU"
TO STOP BEING SO UTTERLY
PATHETIC ABOUT ABSOLUTELY
EVERYTHING ALL THE TIME

OUT OF MY BOX with Peter Hitchens

AAAAAAAARGH! Aaaaaargh! HARD-ER! THANK YOU JESUS! AAAAAARGH! That's better.

Foreigners: Look at them, sitting there being all foreign and thinking they're better than me.

According to the voices in my head, Tony Blair used to invite foreigners into Downing Street and eat long bits of spaghetti with them, just like those two dogs in *Lady and the Tramp*. Then he'd push the last meatball across the plate with his nose, as if to say, 'here foreigner, have Britain for your tea'.

And David Cameron is no better. The voices tell me he attends dirty parties with Belgians and Spaniards where they all get naked and grease each other while jumping up and down to bongo music.

Say what you like about Gordon Brown. He may be foreign, but he has no time for foreigners and their grease and their bongos and their meatballs.

I'VE NOT BEEN WELL

Recently I made the mistake of going to a 'doctor'. As well as trying to hypnotise me, he had the indecency to ask me if I had ever considered 'going private'.

'Are you asking me to cup your testicles?' I shrieked and ran from the room. After 60 years of blood-soaked failure it seems the NHS has now descended into nothing more than a cabal of millionaire perverts demanding genital massage. But isn't this what Labour wanted all along?

WHAT'S WRONG WITH ME?

Sometimes I like to hang upside down and read a book. A recent upside down literary experience involved a book by the Oxford dog-strangler Richard Dawkins. Mr Dawkins latest 'theory' calls for Satan to be made lord of the universe, while the armies of the gay kick down your door and force you to dress in a kaftan made from hemp.

'Mr' Dawkins 'supports' his 'theories' with 'science'. Well, Mr Dawkins, in case you were too busy squirting acid at monkeys to notice – this is England. So you can take your 'science' and your 'reason' and your 'thoughts' and go back to your Swedish Sauna, if that is even your real name.

You will not be surprised to hear that both Mr Miliband and Mr Cameron intend to make Mr Dawkins the next Archbishop of Canterbury. It's enough to make you want to thrash yourself so very, very hard across the thighs and buttocks.

Peter Hitchens is away

YOUR ASTROLOGICAL WEEK AHEAD
with PSYCHIC BOB

Pisces
A full Moon next to Saturn signals a climactic point for one pet project. But remember, in the eyes of the law, as an animal can't speak, it can't give its consent.

Aries
Are those parsnips?

Taurus
This week's full Moon highlights your poor teeth and the terrible smell of dog ordure that constantly surrounds you, but decides to do nothing about them.

Gemini
If the weight of your chosen career is hanging heavy, don't worry. It will soon be over.

Cancer
Look at your relationships as objectively as you can. You thought you could make her love you, but now she has set fire to herself it's time to move on.

Leo
Believe in yourself and others will too. Actually that's just rubbish.

Virgo
Mars and Neptune are having a naked wrestling match on your rug, but there is nothing homosexual about it, not even their erections, which happen all the time in professional wrestling. You can look it up if you want.

Libra
Someone may criticise the way you do things, or hold judgement over how you run your life. Her name is Harriet Harman, and you should find out where she lives.

Scorpio
Although your career, children and your husband are important to you, they are not as important as white wine.

Sagittarius
Time to reassess your savings and investments, business unions, friendships and emotional partnerships, if you have any.

Capricorn
Oooh, that's a nasty looking burn.

Aquarius
Mercury and Saturn fit warped discs to your car brakes making the steering vibrate like something from the Ann Summer's catalogue. What a pair of fucking jokers.

THREAT LEVEL

Hedgehog

The Daily Mash

it's news to us   www.thedailymash.co.uk   No.2

'NOTHING TO FEAR FROM GIGANTIC, ALL-POWERFUL DATABASE'

THE government last night dismissed fears over its massive, evil database insisting it would only ever be used to peer into the very depths of your soul.

Ministers have been forced to defend plans to record every email, text message, internet search and phone call, against critics who say it is both terrifying and tremendously fucked-up.

But Home Secretary Alan Johnson stressed the database was not only essential to the war on terror, but would bring government and citizen much closer together.

He said: "Look, the thing is, I like you – a lot – and I just want to know everything about you.

"I can't 'give' myself to someone unless I know I can trust them completely. D'you know what I'm saying?

"I need to know your hopes, your fears, your dreams, your freaky online habits and your socially unacceptable opinions."

He added: "Think of it as a romantic dinner where you're telling me your entire life story, except the table's bugged and I'm listening to you in that suspicious looking van across the road."

Insisting he would only ever have us killed if he had no choice, Mr Johnson said: "The easiest thing is to just stop being different in any way.

"However, on the outside chance your data does match our Profile of Unacceptability, I will make sure they use a high-powered rifle."

Ronnie Wood finally slows down

Wood enjoys wandering round his local golf course at two o'clock in the morning

ROLLING Stone Ronnie Wood has ditched his punishing regime of endless cocaine binges for the more sedate lifestyle of month-long drinking sessions with Russian barmaids.

Friends of Wood are relieved that, at the age of 61, he is finally slowing down and devoting more of his time to vodka and teenage girls.

One source close to the superstar said: "Ronnie was a workaholic. He would spend up to three weeks without sleep, constantly looking for new holes to put cocaine into.

"His only respite would be the hourly break to drink absinthe and have dangerously acrobatic sex with nine of the women queuing outside the hotel."

The source added: "There's only so long you can keep that up before your body says, 'enough is enough – drink nothing but vodka and stick to one teenager at a time'."

Another close friend said: "For Ronnie this is a bit like taking up gardening or golf.

"He's getting to bed at 4am and sleeping for at least five hours a night. He's introduced solids into his diet and is only smoking things that started off as plants.

"But what's really important is that for the first time in his life, he's really enjoying his vodka and 19-year-olds."

Thought for the day: Everything will be fine as soon as you've had your first drink. (Florence Nightingale)

New prostate cancer drug not as good as 'The Wire'

A NEW prostate cancer drug which could save thousands of lives is still not as good as *The Wire*, critics claimed last night.

Although the drug could potentially treat up to 80% of patients, scientists and television reviewers agreed that it lacked the Dickensian scope of the Baltimore crime drama.

Professor Henry Brubaker, of the Institute for Studies, said: "Cancer cures come and go, but in 20 years' time people will still be going on and on – and on – about *The Wire*.

"This drug may attack cancerous cells but it can't match the sheer genius of that scene where the really big, scary guy says something really profound but does it through the medium of chess.

"But the real genius of *The Wire* is that its genius is so subtle, even though I have no idea what's going on and the only words I can understand are 'bitches' and 'motherfucker'."

He added: "It makes this new cancer drug look like *Jonathan Creek*."

The Wire is the latest in a

This sunset was dismissed as a 'pile of shit' compared to season two of 'Dexter'

string of genius American television dramas which have forced critics to invent a complete new range of superlatives.

The advertising-based drama *Mad Men*, last week voted 'better than trees' by the American Tree Institute, was described by one critic as 'magnibulous'.

Even cancer patients who have been treated successfully said they backed *The Wire*.

Tom Booker, 54, said: "This drug made no attempt to redefine the parameters of television drama and as far as I am aware there were no ex-policemen or gang members involved in its production.

"That said, my arse is much less painful."

Britain willing BT broadband couple to split

MILLIONS of viewers have contacted British Telecom urging them to end the pathetic relationship at the heart of their long-running series of TV adverts.

The latest instalment shows the ginger streak of piss sitting on a terrace, apparently in Cornwall, emailing his mind-crushingly tedious live-in lover.

He has moved because of his job, though some have speculated it is because she hasn't smiled for nearly three years. The relationship now stands at a crossroads, with viewers across the country willing them to go their separate, tiresome ways.

Since 2005 millions have joined the couple on a slow, flat rollercoaster of emotions, that began with him moving in and having the first of many stilted conversations with whoever happens to be in the room.

The drama reached unbearable levels of dullness

when she erased all the photos of her monosyllabic children, leading many viewers to assume she was some kind of moron.

But there were also pathetic attempts at light relief, including the teenage son getting into trouble for inviting his friends round to watch a certificate PG film while drinking lemonade.

The only potential excitement came when the ginger streak flirted with a gorgeous girl who was clearly up for all kinds of filth, before deciding, inexplicably, to remain faithful to whatserface.

Meanwhile a recent instalment included a desperate ploy to make him seem more interesting by showing him reading the paper and indulging in a bit of golf.

TV viewer Emily Francis, from Bath, told BT: "For the love of God, make it stop."

COMMITMENT PHOBIA LINK TO LACK OF BLOW JOBS

A MAN'S reluctance to get married is linked to his fear of a lack of oral sex, new research shows.

Anxiety that oral sex will cease after marriage releases a chemical in the brain which makes it impossible for a man to hire a morning suit or book a large, executive car.

Henry Brubaker, of the Institute for Studies, said: "We studied 1,000 men, half of whom were married and half of whom were still receiving oral sex.

"The half still in receipt of oral said they were happy with their current unmarried status while the others just kept staring at my assistant's mouth."

He added: "If you're determined to get married I would suggest you satiate yourself with blow jobs beforehand, and then perhaps you won't miss them, though I doubt it."

Tom Logan, a policeman from Exeter, who has been engaged to primary school teacher Nikki Hollis for 10 years, said their relationship still had plenty of oral sex left in it.

He said: "I just feel I'm not quite ready for Nikki to stop giving me blow jobs just yet, it's a big step and not one I think we ought to rush into."

He added: "If she lets me do that thing everyone says is even better than even you think it's going to be, then I'll think about buying a ring."

William to use SAS for sexual role playing

THE SAS is to spend three weeks with Prince William and Kate Middleton as the young couple embarks on a series of exciting new sex games.

Following William's use of an RAF helicopter to arouse his girlfriend, he now wants to 'step things up' by deploying the world's most feared commando unit.

A friend of the couple said: "The first scenario will involve Kate being 'kidnapped' by 'Iranians' and held in a secret location, though they will probably just use the big sex room at Clarence House.

"William will be dressed all in back, with camouflage make-up and one of those little knitted hats. Very butch, very hunky.

"Meanwhile they've hired a couple of Spaniards to play the terrorists, while Kate will be taken from her bed in the middle of the night wearing nothing but a flimsy nightie.

"After being held for the best part of 20 minutes, all hell will break lose when the SAS crash through the windows, chuck a couple of smoke bombs and shoot the Spaniards.

'Operation Hump' will cost around £80m

"Then William will swing in and hopefully land on the bed. Then they'll do it."

Other scenarios include Miss Middleton being tied up and held in a luxury Caribbean villa and being tied up and held on a yacht.

The friend added: "It is vital that he familiarise himself with the work of the armed forces, so the final game will see William being tied up while Kate rescues him wearing nothing but Doc Martens and a balaclava."

Winehouse enjoys incident-free piss

AMY Winehouse visited the toilet of her North London home last night and emerged three minutes later after a textbook piss, according to friends.

The *Back to Black* singer entered the upstairs lavatory at 9.45pm carrying a cigarette but without her chest inhaler, which she left in the lounge.

Once positioned with her back to the toilet Winehouse pulled down her jeans and underwear in a single motion before sitting on the seat.

The troubled vocalist urinated for approximately seven seconds but remained sitting on the lavatory for a further 35 seconds with her head nodding slightly, prompting some concern.

However, Winehouse, best known for her songs 'Rehab' and 'You Know I'm No Good,' then regained control and stood

up strongly to replace her underwear and jeans, after first dabbing briefly at her private area with some tissue paper.

She washed her hands using an aloe vera and lavender moisturising handwash before exiting the bathroom at 9.48pm, having momentarily sniffed her fingers.

The friend said: "It was your classic British piss. There were no drips and definitely no follow-through. I doubt even Duffy pisses better than that.

"Luckily Blake is in prison, so the seat was down and we were spared the usual drug-fuelled tantrum.

"But as a friend you are always worried. Last week she went for the most almighty shit, slid off the pan and we had to crank up the defibrillator."

Winehouse used 1.3ml of the lavender handwash

EastEnders tackles serious issue of jailbait

THE BBC last night dismissed criticism of *EastEnders*, insisting it was tackling the vitally important issue of beating *Coronation Street*.

The Cockney soap has been under fire from tens of viewers for depicting a 16-year-old actress, with 19-year-old attitudes and a 21-year-old chest.

A BBC spokesman said: "As a public service broadcaster we have a responsibility to tackle the serious issues that titillate our society.

"But we always attempt to handle these issues sensitively, often by covering them in lipstick or stuffing them into a push-up bra.

"*Coronation Street* meanwhile is just a lot of saggy women with too much make-up, and their pathetic attempts to pay off their bingo debts.

"How is that relevant to a society that is struggling to cope with millions of ex-convicts taking advantage of their busty teenage stepdaughters?"

The spokesman added:

Betty Williams says push-up bras are 'a bother'

"Ultimately, the really important question raised by this storyline is – how on earth will Bianca react? I'm betting she goes apeshit."

But Hilary Bamford, a complainer from Dewsbury, said: "I have never seen anything so repulsively entertaining in my life.

"By the end of it I felt as if I had been rolling around in a big bath of mud. In my underpants. With a bishop."

Tom Logan, a viewer from Nuneaton, said: "Fifteen, you say? She doesn't look fifteen. Oh I see...."

Nun lovers devastated

THE hopes of nun fans across the world were shattered last night after the cancellation of the first ever nun beauty contest.

Father Antonio Rungi revealed he was calling off the contest after it became clear the nuns would simply be used to satisfy a series of depraved and incredibly hot sexual fantasies.

He said last night "I wanted to reflect the inner beauty of my holy sisters. But if you just want to look at nuns' tits then I suggest you try the Jesuits."

Wayne Hayes, a nun enthusiast from Dorking, said: "What a shame. If there's one thing that gets me through the day it's the thought of a load of nuns in swimsuits, followed by evening gowns.

"I'm a big nun man. There are some weekends when it's just me, a bottle of Pinot Grigio, a big bag of Kettle Chips and my director's cut of *The Sound of Music*. And no clothes obviously."

Nun my brains out

But Father Rungi pointed out: "Nuns are not objects for your rampant carnal lusts. They are the Brides of Christ and therefore only he is allowed to slip his hand under their heavy garments or request that they dress up as a cheeky milkmaid.

"Only he is allowed to turn the lights way down low and do that thing that makes her glad she's a nun.

"And even if he doesn't hang around for breakfast, she knows he'll call, because hey, he's Jesus."

Satan forced to sell Heathrow

SATAN, the Prince of Darkness, is to launch an appeal after he was ordered to sell Heathrow.

The Competition Commission ruling is a major setback to Beelzebub's plan to expand his kingdom of the damned via the world's third busiest airport.

He said last night: "I've spent £1 billion making this place at least as bad as the eternal fiery torments of the underworld.

"For the last 20 years our corporate strategy has been to make this airport so comprehensively vile that you would just kill yourself because whatever awaits you in the afterlife cannot possibly be as bad as sitting in a Heathrow departure lounge for six hours.

"Our latest customer survey showed that more than 90% of travellers would rather be roasted on a spit and have the flesh ripped from their bones by a horde of fire-breathing, shit-covered demons than endure another minute in

Terminal Five was designed by Richard Rogers

one of our check-in queues.

"You only get that sort of result through continued investment, an upbeat, customer-facing corporate philosophy and above all, attention to detail.

"I got a letter from a frequent flyer last week who said he wouldn't force Hitler and the Nazis to go through security at Heathrow. That's why I get out of bed in the morning."

Satan said he could now be forced to turn his full attention to Gatwick, adding: "For those of you who think that can't get any worse – you've no fucking idea."

Giant pineapple is trying to kill me, reveals Charles

PRINCE Charles has demanded a ban on genetically modified crops after the latest attempt on his life by an enormous piece of fruit.

Launching his most outspoken attack so far on GM food, the heir to the throne said a giant pineapple has already tried to crush him to death three times since the beginning of May.

He told the *Daily Telegraph*: "One is reminded, very acutely, of the scene in *Raiders of the Lost Ark*, where the archaeologist fellow is desperately trying to escape from a gigantic boulder – though of course in one's case it is the most enormous pineapple.

"One finds oneself faced with little choice but to run as fast as one can, dodging many tiny arrows and doing one's best to hold on to one's favourite hat.

"But these are the dangers one faces, whether speaking out on controversial issues, or stealing a priceless golden idol from an angry South American tribe."

In the last three years Prince Charles claims to have been stalked by a genetically modified potato, a bunch of grapes and a two tonne strawberry in a wig.

"The grapes sent my wife the most repulsive letters filled with bizarre sexual innuendo. I really do not understand this fascination with GM foods when Waitrose does a very nice Duchy Originals organic beetroot soup for just £2.89."

Fuck that, say new men

NEW men last night said fuck this for game of soldiers and ordered their wives to make the bloody tea.

As research suggests sexist men earn significantly higher salaries, Tom Logan, a new man from Oxford, said: "So what you're telling me is, this has been a complete waste of time."

The study found that men who treat women as equals and can name all the actors on *Grey's Anatomy* can expect to earn no more than £22,500 a year.

Meanwhile, at the other end of scale, bearded, olive-skinned men in long white robes who treat women like pack animals, often earn up to £20 million a week and have a Bentley for each of their race horses.

Mr Logan added: "I started doing this at university because I was given a cast-iron guarantee I would get a lot of fanny.

"I learned how to make flaky pastry, I got a cat and I cried my fucking eyes out at *Schindler's List*. And what

£22,500 a year

did I get in return? A long list of 'friends' who think I'm a poof.

"Meanwhile I've not had a promotion since 1996, I live in a one-bedroom flat which is basically the cat's, and this year I went on holiday to Bath.

"First thing tomorrow I am walking straight up to our office manager and telling her she's got a phenomenal arse and that I would very much like to cover it in jam.

"And that fucking cat's going in the bin."

Catholic school to fight all cancers above the waist

A ROMAN Catholic high school will allow its pupils to receive inoculations against all types of cancer that do not involve their dirty, filthy private parts.

St Monica's, in Greater Manchester, said it was vital to protect children from the killer disease as long as any abnormal cell growth takes place at least nine and a half inches above the groin.

A spokesman said: "We are more than happy to discuss cancers of the stomach, shoulders, neck and chin. Breast cancer is

also acceptable, but there will, however, be severe restrictions on the use of the word 'breast'.

"However, when it comes to the dirty cancers I'm sure they can easily get those sort of injections in the toilets of a dance hall or the back of a grimy Ford Fiesta, isn't that right Bridget McAfferty, you FILTHY LITTLE WHORE?"

He added: "Jesus told us that some killer diseases are better than others.

"Indeed, he would only agree to place his hands on

lepers if their arms or noses were falling off. He certainly didn't go around touching them on the cock."

He added: "If one of our girls does contract the forbidden cancer she will be remembered in our prayers as a pox-ridden little tart with no-one to blame but herself."

Meanwhile doctors warned yesterday that a measles epidemic remains likely because too many parents are still inoculating their children with the *Daily Mail*.

Will Britain be ruled by Voodoo King?

THE government is to introduce legislation that will leave Britain in the clutches of voodoo, it was claimed last night.

Experts warn that by repealing the Act of Settlement, which gives first refusal on the monarchy to white protestant men, the nation will become bewitched by chicken bones and rhythmic dancing.

Denys Finch-Hatton, a constitutional expert, said: "In recent years Prince Charles has become increasingly voodoo, while Prince William spends most of his time gyrating his pelvis in voodoo nightclubs.

"It now seems likely his union with Kate Middleton will produce a 100% voodoo child."

Finch-Hatton warned that a voodoo king would leave Britain vulnerable to attack from any foreign power that can make a little wax doll and stab it with hot pins.

"Our only defence will be to manufacture even bigger dolls and have the Household Cavalry stab them with even bigger pins."

The Act of Settlement was introduced in 1701 and amended over

The Crown Juju Beads

the years to 'protect the monarchy from Popery, Buddhists, The Dread Muslim and all manifestations of voodoo including chiropractors, vegetarians and George Monbiot'.

But Labour MP Tom Logan insisted a voodoo king would be good for Britain, adding: "It will certainly make Trooping the Colour a lot more interesting, while the Christmas message could be replaced with some sort of festive goat sacrifice."

Brown sprayed by own urine

PRIME minister Gordon Brown was last night wiping urine from his face after attempting to empty his bladder into a strong wind.

Mr Brown has been holding it in all summer, insisting if he waited the wind would die down long enough for him to urinate successfully in the open air.

But within seconds of releasing his stream it was picked up and sent back at him, liberally spraying his face, arms and chest like a gentle garden hose.

A Downing Street source said: "It was a good effort. He was holding his penis in the right way and he was pushing as hard as he could.

"At first it seemed to be working, but then there was a gust and he was quickly drenched in his own piss."

A defiant Mr Brown is now pinning his hopes on the Labour conference in Manchester later this month, and what

Soaked in warm piss

is being billed as the most important wind-piss of his career.

A senior backbencher said: "It's time to let someone else have a piss. David Miliband is a young man with a strong bladder, while Alan Johnson knows how to piss in a way that will appeal to traditional Labour voters."

He added: "Then again Harriet Harman would adopt a squatting position, thereby delivering her piss at a surprisingly different angle."

12-year-old boys back Johnson airport plan

BORIS Johnson's plan to build an artificial island in the Thames and then put an airport on it has been backed by the majority of Britain's 12-year-old boys.

According to Johnson's '£500 squillion' plan, the island will be surrounded by laser cannons and thousands of deadly sharks to keep out terrorists and girls.

Passengers will fly through a network of big plastic tubes that will drop them directly into their seat and the runway will slope upwards at the end, just like a proper British aircraft carrier.

The London mayor said: "The departure hall will be filled with tuck shops, penknife boutiques and a place where a chap can swap his old *Flashman* novels.

"There will be no cauliflower or semolina and horrid girls can fly from smelly old Luton."

Meanwhile arriving passengers will get an individual jet car which will propel them into the

Ripping!

centre of London in less than a minute.

In the event of jet car failure the entire island will

be fitted with massive rockets so that it can lift off and fly over to Heathrow where passengers can then use the highly efficient 15-minute rail link to Paddington.

Johnson said he had lots of sketches and a really big model made from old yoghurt tubs, Fairy Liquid bottles and bendy straws.

He added: "This is mark II. The original was destroyed during a very bouncy knob session with Petronella Wyatt."

Nothing can possibly go wrong with gigantic new bank

HBOS and Lloyds TSB last night created a monstrous new banking entity safe in the knowledge that nothing can possibly go wrong.

Politicians and businessmen breathed a collective sigh of relief as two of the biggest names on the high street formed one very long name that will never do anything other than be brilliant all the time.

Martin Bishop, a senior trader at Madeley Finnegan, said: "History tells us that massive financial institutions do not fail. Ever. Okay, there is maybe a tiny handful of exceptions.

"Okay, maybe 40 or 50 exceptions. Actually, you're right, this is starting to look really dodgy. If you'll excuse me, I have to start selling the shit out of Lloyds TSB."

As shares in the new banking giant plummeted, the government came under renewed pressure to stop people wanting lots of money.

Titanic **has been sailing between Southampton and New York for more than 90 years**

A Treasury spokesman said: "We've devised a regulatory framework that will effectively ban greed and no-one will ever be able to find a way round it. At least for the first six months. Probably."

Meanwhile Downing Street sources let it be known the prime minister played a key part in securing the deal which will put 40,000 people out of work.

STOCKMARKETS RUNNING OUT OF UNDERPANTS

FINANCIAL institutions across the globe last night urged the US to agree a bail-out package, warning they are down to their last four pairs of useable underpants.

With traders soiling themselves every time the headlines change on the BBC website, offices in New York and London are now dangerously awash with urine.

Bill McKay, facilities manager at City brokerage Madeley-Finnegan, said: "It's soaked right through the carpet."

He warned the entire financial system was on the brink of collapse, not because of liquidity problems, but because the wiring is 'absolutely drenched'.

"I was called out at 3am after a small electrical fire broke out on the fourth floor. I took one look and thought, 'stockbroker piss'.

"We tried putting down newspapers but they just read the headlines and piss themselves all over again."

McKay added: "I was talking to one broker when a car alarm went off in the street. Within seconds there was a large damp patch which was spreading slowly across his groin.

"We've turned the first floor coffee lounge into an emergency laundrette, but for every clean pair we send out there's two dirty ones coming in."

Last night the Bank of England strongly urged brokers to hold it in or at least keep a bucket under their desk.

KAKA DEAL OFF AFTER AGENT FINALLY SAYS THE WORD 'CITY'

BRAZILIAN superstar Kaká has called off a move to Manchester after his agent finally said the word 'city'.

The AC Milan striker was furious claiming he had been duped into believing he was going to sign for a proper football team that had won a major trophy since he was born.

Kaká said last night: "My agent called last week and said that Manchester were interested in me. I was so excited at the thought of all those great players, the traditions, the best coach in the world, and of course Gemma Atkinson's magnificent charlies.

"I packed an overnight bag and we went to the airport, but as we were walking through the terminal my agent turned to me and said 'oh, in case I didn't mention, it's Manchester City'.

"I stopped dead in my tracks and said, 'are you having a laugh? Seriously, is this just some big fucking joke?'.

"He said to me, 'don't worry, they're a really big club with loads of money. And then there's Mark Hughes'.

"I said, 'I already play for a really big club, I've got loads of money and what, in the name of God, is a 'Mark Hughes'?'"

He added: "I walked away shouting, 'go and get me a proper deal from a proper English club that does not include the word 'city'. No Hulls, no Birminghams, and no fucking Stokes!'"

Manchester City said last night they still hoped to complete the deal if they can persuade Cristiano Ronaldo to sign for the club and act as Kaká's butler.

Everyone now a fucking tennis expert

EVERYONE in Britain is now a fucking tennis expert who could easily replace Dan Maskell, or whoever it is that does the commentary these days.

Following Andy Murray's near defeat by a Frenchman, everyone is saying how much his ground-strokes have improved and that having a girlfriend is obviously really good for his temperament.

Wayne Hayes, from London, said: "His unreliable second serve really came good in the fourth set. He's totally getting his end away.

"And did you see him eat a banana? Amazing. Apparently it gives him a potassium boost and stops him from thinking about bananas while he's playing."

But everyone is also warning that Murray now faces the match of his life against that scary looking Spanish guy who is really good with clay and needs a haircut.

Hayes added: "The Spanish guy is really strong and scary, but he doesn't like grass. And neither do I to be honest. It tastes awful."

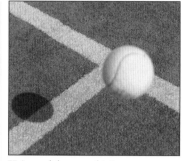

He's much better at hitting one of these

Sandra McKay, a housewife from Reading, said: "What about that crowd? It's the crowd though isn't it. The crowd, yes, it's all about the crowd."

She added: "Henman Hill. Remember that? Marvellous."

Tom Logan, an assistant bank manager from Peterborough, said: "The women's singles is absolutely fascinating isn't it?

"With Sharapova and Ivanovic both failing to find their form it means the title is now sure to go to some big ugly lesbian."

Gemma Atkinson's chimp to fight new Madonna baby

HOLLYOAKS star Gemma Atkinson is to pit her new chimpanzee against Madonna's Malawian baby in the latest round of *Celebrity Toddler Fight Club: Adopted!*

The two-year-old chimpanzee is the early favourite despite rumours the Queen of Pop has trained her child in the ways of Kabaddi, the much-feared Jewish martial art.

Atkinson said: "I'm not really supposed to talk about *Celebrity Toddler Fight Club*, but I will tell you this – my chimpanzee is red-hot.

"I've trained a lot of fighting monkeys over the years, but I've never seen one this hungry for it. It's going to take more than some fancy Jewish karate to stop this boy."

If successful the chimpanzee will face a child from the respected Mia Farrow stable, with the stage then set for a pulsating climax against one of Angelina Jolie's Vietnamese babies.

The hit BBC Four show has brought the visceral thrill of celebrity toddler fighting to millions and spawned a new generation of would-be champions.

Showbiz expert Nathan Muir said: "Allotment superstars Keira Knightley and James McAvoy and Indiana Jones sex-bomb Shia LaBeouf are all desperate to adopt babies and train them for the fighting pit."

BBC Four controller Melissa Hayes was quick to add: "All the toddlers on *Celebrity Toddler Fight Club: Adopted!* are trained professionals, but please don't let that stop you from adopting a baby and trying this at home."

With unemployment rising and ministers pledging a crackdown on immigration...

WHICH SHITTY JOB IS NO LONGER BENEATH YOU?

YOUR PROBLEMS SOLVED
with HOLLY HARPER

Dear Holly,

I am feeling depressed just now as I really hate my job. I've been working there for over 2 years but I've never really enjoyed it, and my colleagues are all complete back-stabbing arseholes.

Recently, I've found myself calling in sick on a regular basis, taking solace in masturbating on the couch to *Jeremy Kyle* and eating entire multi-packs of crisps before 3pm. The thought of going back to work the next day makes me feel almost suicidal. I can't bear it any longer! Can you help?

Alice
Lincolnshire

Dear Alice,

I'm sorry to hear you feel so sad just now. Lots of us experience a similar feeling at some point, but you need to remind yourself it's only a temporary thing. Last year I wanted to stay off school because Shaun Wilson farted on my head in front of everyone when I was putting my shoes back on after PE. The next day I told my mummy that I was too sick too go to school, but she didn't believe me because I didn't have a temperature. I had to use her purple eye-shadow to fabricate a convincing rash on my tummy before she would take me seriously. For some reason, the rash made mummy start to shake and cry and we had to go to the hospital. The good news is that I got the rest of the day off school and the doctor gave me a lollipop for being so brave. You're lucky because your mummy is probably dead and you don't have to concoct elaborate ruses to convince her you need to stay in bed. So my advice is to stop moaning and count your blessings – and be thankful you don't have to sit next to Shaun Wilson for the rest of the summer term.

Hope that helps!

Holly

YOUR ASTROLOGICAL WEEK AHEAD
with PSYCHIC BOB

Gemini

Saturn hands you power and responsibility but Neptune keeps on undermining you by telling everyone you slept your way to the top. Which, let's be honest, you did.

Cancer

It's hard to disentangle reality from fantasy at this point, but I suspect you'll work it out as soon as the fat lady in the black leather boots has stopped beating your bare arse with a plastic light-sabre.

Leo

It's time for answers. And you don't have any because you spent the last three years getting shitfaced in the student union, smoking weed and watching *Battlestar Galactica* DVDs in your undies. Not to worry though, call centres really aren't that bad.

Virgo

Next weekend's rare meeting of Jupiter and Neptune represents a tipping point when your life will pass from being relatively unbearable to utterly degrading.

Libra

It's time you climbed in the driving seat and made things happen. Put the long metal stick thing with the jaggedy edge into the slot on the column behind the hollow round thing and turn it clockwise. Now proceed straight ahead unless I tell you to do otherwise.

Scorpio

That part of your life that is a well-kept secret is not going to be a secret for much longer. PANTY SNIFFER!!!!

Sagittarius

People seem to be bombarding you with invitations to amazing social events while offering you many fantastic new opportunities. They've obviously got the wrong person.

Capricorn

After three heel-dragging weeks of Mercury going backwards you have two very badly worn heels.

Aquarius

Stop taking life so seriously. Go into your disciplinary hearing buck-naked with the words 'lick this' and a long, downward-pointing arrow painted onto your chest and stomach.

Pisces

Saturn in your money zone asks you to have one last check in your pockets to see if you've missed anything while Neptune looks on cleaning his fingernails with a nasty-looking knife.

Aries

Sometimes fate shows us a new road to travel, but mostly these days it's the impressive new Navman F200, with its dedicated features showing you the location of the nearest off-licence/goat brothel.

Taurus

Jupiter and Mars indicate a time of new opportunities and fresh tarts for you, but it's all a load of lies, especially the bit about the tarts.

The Daily Mash

TODAY'S
WEATHER
Wind that could flay
a goat and rain the
colour of death

OKAY FOR BABIES TO BE BORN DRUNK, SAY DOCS

NEW evidence suggests it is safe for a baby to be born drunk, doctors said last night.

According to the latest research, expectant mothers can drink throughout their pregnancy and even use different kinds of alcohol to determine their child's early character traits.

Meanwhile mothers who want to avoid a hungover baby should drink a glass of Resolve or at least two pints of water as soon as they have their first contraction.

Professor Sir Roy Hobbs, head of obstetrics at St Gordon's Hospital in Dulwich, explained: "It's perfectly acceptable for a baby to be born

Whisky baby doesn't need your help

drunk, but not angry drunk.

"The optimum level of drunkenness would be a baby that's very quiet and has

a big grin on its face, as if it's been drinking gin and tonic all afternoon.

"Beer babies tend to be very noisy while red wine babies have that look as if they were just about to say something only to forget what it was at the last second.

"What you do not want is a pissed-up whisky baby that comes out snarling and chucking its fists around."

He added: "The important point is that mothers shouldn't worry too much about the drunkenness of their baby.

"I have always believed that when it comes to drinking and pregnancy it does help to keep things as vague and inconsistent as possible."

Britain as insanely violent as you thought it was

BRITAIN is every bit as violent and terrifying as you always thought it was, the government confirmed last night.

Home secretary Alan Johnson said the police must take full responsibility for misinterpreting government guidelines in exactly the way he told them to.

Home Office officials admitted that since 1997 gun crime had been defined as 'offences involving Howitzers and other heavy artillery', while the majority of knife incidents had been dismissed as 'pirate fun'.

But Johnson insisted it was very easy to interpret a 22% rise in violent crime as a 15% fall, especially if you were willing to lie about it.

Members of the public welcomed the revised figures, saying it helped to explain why they kept coming home from work covered in blood.

Roy Hobbs, an accountant from Ashford, said: "Every time the government said violent crime was going down I thought 'well, if that's the case then why do I, my wife and many of our close

Tank crime has been falling since the 1950s

friends have a knife sticking out of our chest?'.

"That said, this year I have noticed a slight reduction in the number of bodies I have to step over on my way to the station."

Meanwhile, local authorities have reported an increase in the use of noise abatement orders to deal with complaints about chain saws and desperate, horrifying screams.

Children to be taught why women are out of their minds

SCHOOLCHILDREN across England are to get compulsory lessons on why women are insane.

Ministers want to make sex and relationship lessons compulsory so future generations of boys do not waste half their lives trying to work out what the hell that was all about.

The department of education said reforms are vital as new figures reveal attempts to decode twisted female logic are costing Britain £4.6 billion a year in lost productivity.

A spokesman said: "Most of the early classes will focus on teaching boys how to let it all wash over them.

"Meanwhile the girls will be taught the importance of establishing confidence and stability in a relationship before suddenly and inexplicably changing their minds."

Lessons on the biology of sex will also be overhauled with new diagrams showing the male body as a digestive system attached to a disappointingly small penis.

Year three will focus on whores

From next September the will include skank-spotting, jealous rages and how to tell if it is in yet, while girls will be taught how to dismantle and reassemble a state-of-the-art German vibrator in under three minutes.

Ministers insist exotic sexual practices involving bodily waste or elaborate fistwork will be not covered until year six.

Artificial heart patients will have no soul, admit docs

PATIENTS who are given artificial hearts will lose their soul, doctors admitted last night.

Experts said the device could give patients a normal life expectancy, but it will be an empty life devoid of love, laughter and tears.

Dr Tom Logan, a soul specialist at

'The operation went well, though strictly speaking you are now basically a robot'

St Thomas's Hospital in London, said: "Their eyes will become blank and lifeless and they will speak in a dull monotone.

"They will never frown or smile or laugh, not even at that bit in *Only Fools and Horses* where David Jason falls through the hatch.

"On the upside they will be able to watch *Gilmore Girls* and the *High School Musical* trilogy without wanting to kill absolutely everyone involved. And many of them will make excellent lawyers."

Dr Logan added: "We have experimented with pig hearts but that just left the patient with the soul of a pig, which I suppose is better than nothing but you do spend an awful lot of time thinking about mud and truffles.

"We hope eventually to be able to transplant an artificial soul at the same time. Microsoft have some terrifyingly interesting ideas about that."

Britain now at its most outraged since 1747

BRITAIN is now more appalled and outraged than at any point in the last 260 years, it has been confirmed.

Historians said the country now risked descending into a state of permanent outrage, accompanied by constant high-pitched screaming and nostril foam.

Tom Logan, professor of the history of outrage at Reading University, said: "You really have to go back to 1747 to find British society in a more frenzied and pathetic condition.

"Of course back then there was no *Daily Mail* and so thousands of outraged people, in search of similarly disturbed companionship, were forced to admit themselves to the local asylum."

The year 1747 began with the opening of the world's first venereal disease clinic in London, offering treatments for 'genital pustulence' and 'cockpoxes'. By mid-April the Jacobite

Bedlam hospital was eventually replaced by the *Daily Mail* **in 1896**

Lord Lovat had been beheaded on Tower Hill for making jokes about the King's blisters.

As the War of the Austrian Succession reached its peak, the Scottish doctor James Lind caused women to faint and men to vomit with his 'revolting assertion' that scurvy could be prevented by the careful application of a large grapefruit.

Meanwhile Dr Samuel Johnson began work on his Dictionary of the English

Language and confirmed his determination to include the word 'snatch'.

- **From** *The Weekly Journal*, **April the Twenty Fourth**

Mr Garrick, an actor, has scandalised all London with his bawdy missive to the Earl of Carnarvon in which he makes claim to have brushed past his Lordship's niece, the Honourable Lady Elizabeth Herbert, at the Covent Garden, and if he, the Earl,

was displeased with this occurrence, Mr Garrick would, on a weekday of his choosing, contrive to sneak into his Lordship's bedchamber and leave a ripe fig in his thunderpot.

- **From** *The British Gazetteer*, **September the Twelfth**

Mr Simpkins, a wheelwright, caused a perturberance when, at around three o' clock of the after-noon, he remarked unto his fellows, and all souls within earshot, that the drivers of carts, coaches and Stanhope carriages were little better than Frenchmen who would, given a mind, pass all their days throttling the life out of tuppenny strumpets. Simpkins was served most hastily with a Notice of Rebuttal by the Royal and Honourable Company of Cartists and was later that day informed that his service and chattels would no longer be required by His Grace, the Duke of Clarence.

Cats fine, say cats

CATS last night thanked the government for its interest in their welfare but insisted they were fine.

Britain's felines said new government guidelines issued to humans were an attack on their privacy and revealed a 'twisted obsession' with how and where they go to the toilet.

However, they welcomed new rules for dogs, who they described as the animal equivalent of a human in the advanced stages of Alzheimers.

Zanzibar, a Persian from Bath, said: "Throw the ball. Fetch the ball. Throw the

ball. Fetch the ball. Fuckin' idiots."

He added: "I don't need to be entertained like some toddler, thank you very much. I just need access to a garden where I can torture birds to death.

"And by the way – give me food whenever I want it or I'll fuck off and live with someone else."

Bobsie, a tortoiseshell tabby from Hampstead, said: "It is your job to open tins and not swing me by the tail. Not difficult.

"And I suppose I could shit in the garden, but what you fail to grasp is the

'What?'

unbridled enjoyment I derive from dumping in a tray of piss-soaked gravel in the corner of the kitchen – while you're having your tea. Good day."

CIA TOLD UK RENDITION WAS SPY-LINGO FOR 'TICKLE-FIGHT'

"Waterboarding is actually a bit like being on rollercoaster except you have a towel pulled over your face while somebody empties a five-pint jug of water into your mouth. Weeeee!" says spokesman.

BBC unveils lavish adaptation of the taunting of Andrew Sachs

THE BBC last night re-established its reputation for quality programming as it unveiled a lavish multi-million pound drama based on the taunting of actor Andrew Sachs.

Starring Sir Ian McKellen as the *Fawlty Towers* actor, the 12-part series begins in 1930s Berlin as the young Sachs and his family flee Nazi persecution.

Despite anti-semitism and the brutality of John Cleese, Sachs's comic skills make him one of the best-loved actors in television history, before Russell Brand offers to masturbate him into the palm of his hand.

The series is being produced at

Much of the taunting will be filmed against the magnificent backdrop of Castle Howard

Elstree Studios by the team behind *Cranford*, *Little Dorrit* and the BAFTA-winning BBC Four show *Russell Brand Fucks Your Granddaughter*.

Tony Blair actor Michael Sheen will play Brand, while jumped-up researcher Jonathan Ross will be portrayed by his close friend Sir Ray Winstone.

BBC director general Mark Thompson said: "I got into this business to make quality programmes about Holocaust survivors being abused by foul-mouthed mediocrities.

"*The Taunting of Andrew Sachs* really is the BBC at its best."

Much of the £20 million budget will be spent on an elaborate dream sequence where McKellen is pinned to his bed as Sheen and Winstone drench him in gin and then masturbate him into a mug shaped liked John Cleese's head.

British public in depressingly incoherent outburst

PUBLIC outrage at the treatment of Andrew Sachs boiled over last night as Britain reached a new peak of furious incoherence.

News websites struggled to cope as millions of violently confused readers found themselves unable to contain their angry, ill-informed opinions.

A BBC spokesman said: "Britain is obviously trying to tell us something but they need to slow down and do their very best to communicate in whole sentences."

Some of the comments posted on The Times yesterday:

● **I don't know who these people are or what this is all about but thanks to them I have spent the entire morning being violently sick on my neighbour's car. It's a bridge too far. Or is it two bridges not too far enough? Bring back Hattie Jacques! (Mrs Margaret, Guildford)**

● How would they like it if someone came into their bedroom in the middle of the night and drenched them in gin and started fondling their legs and then playing with their willy until it made a horrid mess? Not very much, is what I think. Filthy boys. We should kill them with lions. (jstraw, Blackburn)

● **Thankfully I missed this whole** sordid episode. When will the BBC do the right thing and repeat in full? I get back from work around six. (Chewbacca, Norwich)

● But the granddaughter though eh? She's not exactly, you know, is she? I mean come on, let's not forget what this is really all about. Exactly.

Vote UKIP! (paddingtonbear69, Macclesfield)

● **This reminds me of the time the Dimbleby brothers phoned me up during 'Any Answers' and offered to wank me into a teapot. I see the BBC hasn't changed one bit. (Andypandy, Taunton)**

'BRITAIN CAN'T WAIT TO BE TRUNCHEONED ACROSS THE JAW'

MOST British people are looking forward to having a policeman stand on their windpipe, the home secretary said yesterday.

Alan Johnson insisted there was widespread public support for state-sponsored beatings and being asked to hand over your papers.

He said: "People have been coming up to me in the street and demanding I set about them with a baseball bat.

"One man even handed me a bamboo cane before getting down on his hands and knees and suggesting I start with his buttocks.

"And you would not believe the number of people who have already applied to be stripped naked and thrown in a police cell with a single, bare light bulb that is on 24 hours a day while being pummelled with a high-pressure hose whenever they attempt to go to sleep.

"I ask them 'would you not want to know what you'd been charged with?' and they say 'no, of course not, that would be a victory for Al Qaeda'."

Mr Johnson "As I've always said, the vast majority of sensible people in this country fully understand that being at the business end of a brutal and unprovoked assault will actually make them safer.

"In fact, just last week I got a letter from an old lady who asked me to chase her onto the bus and then shoot her in the face. I thought I was going to cry."

BRITAIN recoiled in horror last night as the BT broadband couple took their first tentative steps towards reconciliation.

Amid falling house prices, the looming recession and the trauma of Andrew Sachs's Penis-Gate, the country has gained some measure of comfort from the knowledge that the mind-numbingly tedious relationship seemed to have been destroyed for good.

But millions were sickened this week as the tousle-haired ginger streak of piss eagerly answered a call from that appalling woman.

Now the broadcasting watchdog Ofcom has been inundated by angry viewers desperate to know if the relationship really is over or whether they should simply wreck their televisions with a hammer.

Media analyst Martin Bishop said: "People were naturally disappointed to see the ginger streak of piss return to their screens as he indulged in a new-found laddishness by spending time with a single male friend, drinking beer from a can and expressing his enthusiasm for pay-per-view football matches as opposed to minority-interest satellite channels.

"He remained a totally awful bastard but at least he did seem to have detached himself permanently from that hellish cow.

"Now it seems the good people at BT – and I assume they are all women – would like them to get back together again."

He added: "This will ultimately lead to a mumbled proposal, an awkward wedding where nobody smiles and eventually the joyless birth of a miserable child.

"And all of this despite the fact that they obviously don't enjoy each others' company."

Under fives not taking your shit anymore

BRITAIN'S under fives are just not taking this shit any more, the National Union of Teachers has warned.

The NUT said until last year the under fives were the only children that teachers could give shit to without fear of reprisal.

However, since September the tables have turned and the country's tiniest pupils are not only up for it but are incredibly well organised.

Martin Bishop, a primary school teacher from Liverpool, said: "The one with the strongest legs goes at the bottom and the others climb on top until, collectively, they are tall enough to punch you in the face. It's like a troupe of evil, midget acrobats.

"Then they grab your legs and topple you over before the ringleader starts kicking you repeatedly in the groin."

He added: "They also like to hide in cupboards so that when you open the door to get some crayons about eight of them swarm all over you and then start biting you in the face."

Official statistics show that 1,500 under fives were suspended from school

'It's a picture of me. Kicking your balls'

last term for cigarette smuggling, organising prostitutes and running a numbers racket.

Kyle Stephenson, four, said: "You think I'm funny? How the fuck am I funny? What the fuck is so funny about me?"

Data stick makes it as far as pub

THE government claimed a major victory for data security last night after a memory stick containing highly-sensitive details made it as far as the pub.

The Treasury said the era of personal information being left on public transport was at an end and the public could now have confidence their bank account details would most likely be discovered in a car park.

A spokesman confirmed a data stick holding millions of tax records and passwords was handed to an office temp last week who left it dangling precariously from his pocket in accordance with procedure.

The temp was so surprised to discover the device was still there at the end of his journey that he immediately

Officials say they are at least 10 years away from just keeping this sort of stuff in the office

took it to the pub to show his friends.

The spokesman added: "He said he had successfully transported top secret data all the way from his work and would anyone like to help him celebrate.

"After three hours of very heavy drinking he shouted 'Christ I've lost it' until he was reminded he had lent it to some bikers who were using it score obscenities into each others' necks.

"He grabbed it back and went into the car park where he then tried to use it to light his cigarette. After 25 minutes he gave up and threw it into a bush.

"When he eventually did light his cigarette it was the wrong way round."

Latest national mood to be unveiled

SOME of the biggest names in Britain will gather in central London today for the unveiling of the new national mood.

Prime minister Gordon Brown will be joined by host of celebrities including Steve Coogan, Elaine Page, Sir Bobby Charlton and the stars of *All Creatures Great and Small*.

The mood unveiling comes as a poll in the *Daily Telegraph* found that 68% of Britons want everything to be much more like Victoria Wood.

Experts are predicting the much anticipated new mood will have no truck

How do vetinry

with high salaries, nail varnish and swear words, particularly 'fucknut' and 'c**t-features'.

The prime minister is also expected to outline plans for a wide-ranging government inquiry into

what is and is not funny.

Tom Logan, national mood detector at the Institute for Studies, said: "The inclusion of the *All Creatures* cast suggests an early Fifties, austerity kind of mood.

"We're looking at decency, v-neck sweaters, decency, home-made broth, decency and everything being unbelievably tedious.

"There might be some scope for a bit of cheekiness on BBC1 on Saturday nights. Perhaps Victoria Wood could give a weekly rendition of that song she does about fucking."

He added: "It will be interesting to see if it works, particularly as most British workers spend their entire working day forwarding e-mails and videos that make the Andrew Sachs wank fantasy look like *Songs of Praise*."

Alcohol to be restricted to nice people with degrees

ALCOHOL should only be available to nice people who know which wine goes best with fish, according to MPs.

The influential Home Affairs Select Committee said police resources were being stretched because too many awful people are buying cheap wine from supermarkets and then drinking it really quickly without fully appreciating its delicate potpourri of flavours.

Chairman Keith Vaz said: "Let's take this charmingly presumptuous Echo Falls White Zinfandel, just £3.98 from Tesco, or £2.50 if you're lucky enough to be able to buy it from the members' bar in the House of Commons.

"As a decent person I would enjoy this as an aperitif before a dinner party, or perhaps serve it with some lightly poached sea bass or a pan-roasted poussin with parsnip and chorizo.

"I certainly wouldn't use it to wash down 20 Marlboro Lights and then have a piss up against the front door of Greggs.

"But that's because I went to Cambridge and have a well-thumbed copy of Floyd on France."

Tom Logan, a trainee accountant from Peterborough, said: "So what you're saying is, they've fucked up the economy, forced the country to the point of bankruptcy and put my job and my home in jeopardy while at the same time paying themselves a hundred grand a year in expenses and now they are telling me that I shouldn't be allowed to buy a couple of cheap bottles of wine on a Friday night so that I can forget my troubles for a few hours instead of hunting them down and roasting them on a spit like the shit-caked, trough-guzzling pigs that they are?

"Interesting."

White wine? With cheese? Savages.

Banks not happy until all that's left is banks

THE banks will not rest until they have destroyed everything that is not a bank, experts claimed last night.

Economists now believe the international banking industry is in the final stages of a detailed plan designed to bankrupt everyone and then kill them.

Dr Bill McKay, of the Institute for Studies, said: "Stage one was to engineer a credit boom and get everyone up to their nipples in debt.

"Stage two was to create some bullshit crisis and then exterminate the housing market.

"Stage three was to beg for a trillion pound bail-out and leave all the governments teetering on the edge of financial ruin.

"Now we're at stage four – refusing to pass on interest rate cuts, killing off any remaining businesses and forcing absolutely everyone into bankruptcy and death."

According to Dr McKay the banks will then tower over a wasteland of abandoned shops and decaying corpses before stealing whatever small amounts of change they can scavenge from the pockets of the dead.

It's as if you never even existed

He added: "The last remaining bits of cash will be held by Mervyn King, sitting alone in his office in Threadneedle Street. But the banks will hunt him down and devour him like a horde of rabid zombie vampires.

"They will then bulldoze away the ruins of everything that was not a bank and build a new society which will be filled with pathetic little men who spend all day lending each other money and rubbing used tenners into their groin."

Ryanair to offer £8 transatlantic shitfest

RYANAIR is to become the first budget carrier to fly passengers to New York in utter misery for less than a tenner.

The airline said the new £8 service would bear all the shitty hallmarks of a typically soul-destroying Ryanair experience.

The in-flight meal will involve a catering box of Wotsits emptied into the aisle followed by an angry free-for-all.

But for an extra £10 passengers can upgrade to their own, individually wrapped, Kraft cheese single and a sachet of HP-style sauce.

The in-flight entertainment will include *Highlander III: The Sorcerer*, starring Christopher Lambert as Connor MacLeod of the Clan MacLeod, as well as episode five of the second series of *Rings on Their Fingers*

featuring Martin Jarvis as 'Oliver' and Diane Keen as 'Sandy'.

A Ryanair spokesman stressed the advertised fare did not include a series of inexplicable, fake-sounding supplements which are likely to bring the total cost to around £1,214.

Travel industry analyst Wayne Hayes said: "These days most people are happy to pay the extra fifty quid not to be punched squarely in the face as they board the aircraft."

The spokesman added: "As the transatlantic flight will involve around eight hours of unremitting hellishness as opposed to the Ryanair average of three, we will be offering a supplementary suicide pack containing a cyanide biscuit and 100ml of household bleach."

BP has all the money

THE mystery of where all the money has gone was solved today as BP announced profits of £1,200 a second.

Economists, baffled at the disappearance of more than £1.8 trillion in the last 12 months, now believe it is sitting safely in the account of the multinational oil giant.

Bill McKay, chief economist at Donelly-McPartlin, said: "I'm so relieved. We've been looking for this money for ages.

"Some claimed it had been abducted by aliens, while others insisted it had been stolen by pirates and buried under a palm tree in the Caribbean.

"But I always had a feeling that BP would have it. You see, money is a bit like a salmon. It swims around in the ocean for a while but sooner or later it always finds it's way back to BP."

Meanwhile the company has produced a new promotional video of chief executive Tony Hayward explaining how the company can now afford to buy a Sony Bravia 46-inch LCD TV from Comet every second.

Mr Hayward is then seen clicking his fingers at regular intervals while saying, 'there's another one, and another one'.

Chancellor Alistair Darling said: "So basically, you privatise something that ends up making £1,200 a second and you nationalise something that loses £1,200 a second.

"Swings and bastarding round-abouts."

BP uses tubes to suck money right out of your trousers.

Running stupid

RUNNING for any distance greater than five metres is stupid, it was confirmed last night.

As more than 2,500 people dressed only in shorts and a vest had to be rescued from a mountain in the middle of a storm, experts warned that running had never been a more pointless activity.

Dr Tom Logan, of the Institute for Studies, said: "Thousands of years ago our ancestors had no choice but to run after cows or away from dinosaurs.

"But now we have mopeds and hatchbacks. Neither of which involve stupid, overpriced shoes and thinking you're better than me.

"But you just have to put on your Lycra and your wraparound sunglasses and do all your stretching because if you don't you could pull a muscle and then you'd have to limp around the office and tell everyone how not being able to go for a run is driving you crazy.

"Well I hope you do pull a muscle, and I hope it does drive you crazy and you end up in a huge mental hospital rubbing custard into your scalp and drinking your own piss."

Dr Logan added: "And then there's those people who meet up in a pub and go for a jog and then come back to the pub and drink orange squash and stand around stewing in their own stench.

"I really must conduct some research to find out if there is actually a more detestable collection of bastards."

Johnson unveils horribly foul-mouthed olympic slogan

THE official slogan for the 2012 Olympics will be 'London, City of Fucking Sport and Shit', mayor Boris Johnson has confirmed.

Mr Johnson insisted the foul-mouthed slogan not only encapsulated London's status as one of the world's truly great cities but also emphasised that it would 'host the fuck out of the Olympics'.

The mayor said a number of slogans were considered including 'London Two Thousand and Fucking Twelve', and 'It's the Olympics, Get Your Arse on the Fucking Plane'.

Mr Johnson was joined at the launch by Beijing gold medallists Rebecca Adlington and cyclist Sir Chris Hoy who he described as 'fast as fuck on a bike'.

'It's just a lot of sporty fuckers poncing about'

The London Mayor added: "Fuck me if the London Olympics are not going to be absolutely cocktastic. The city will be filled with fuckers from every corner of the globe."

Mr Johnson insisted that the Olympic construction projects were proceeding exactly according to schedule, adding: "Then again it's not like I'm some kind of fucking architect.

"I told them I'm not good on the fucking details, so they could tell me any old shit and I'd be like, 'great, whatever, just get it fucking done'."

Johnson added: "I have to say I did really like that one about the plane, so we may use that in a couple of these stupid fucking brochures."

Millionaire footballers remain terribly working class

PREMIER league footballers have remained utterly ghastly despite their multi-million pound salaries, according to new research.

Experts say the huge sums invested in the country's top players have failed to alleviate their violent, working class horridness.

Professor Henry Brubaker, of the Institute for Studies, said: "The majority of them remain largely unintelligible and, when not buying fashionable clothing or hitting people, they sit around on their cream leather sofas, watching Jason Statham films and eating Pringles.

"Even someone like Steven Gerrard, who once had the makings of a gentleman, is unable to resist the lure of ghastly suburban nightclubs frequented by DJs and fitness instructors and moderately successful plasterers.

"And yes, Wayne Rooney does have an impressive wine collection, but only so his dreadfully inarticulate friends will have nice, heavy bottles to smash over each other's heads."

He added: "Remember those nasty boys in school who were gratuitously violent, foul mouthed, disruptive and cruel? Now imagine them with an annual budget of £5 million."

The Institute has proposed a block release system where footballers would spend eight weeks a year at Cambridge learning to use George Bernard Shaw quotes instead of stamping on someone's forehead.

There would also be regular dinners at the Dorchester where players would be awarded points for correctly identifying the dessert fork and then bonus points for not jamming it in someone's windpipe.

An educated, middle-class footballing trend did emerge in the late 1980s when Everton winger Pat Nevin was seen enjoying 'Doonesbury' in the *Guardian* but ended in 1993 when Blackburn and England full-back Graeme Le Saux was branded a homosexual for using the word 'eclectic' in a post-match interview.

Heston Blumenthal's award-winning restaurant the Fat Duck is closed down after 30 diners are taken ill. Is the avant-garde chef finally paying the price for serving...

FOOD MADE FROM CLOCKS?

MY BIG GAP YEAR dispatches from POPPY SPALDING

Thursday: Matamata

THIS week finds me in the Antipodean paradise of New Zealand, whose stunning landscapes were the inspiration for JRR Tolkien's *Lord of the Rings* trilogy.

This is just the kind of relaxing break I need after my recent fatal drugs overdose and I would recommend it to anyone who requires this particular type of convalescence. There is just something so pure and healthy about the air here – I can understand why the Kiwis are so good at rugby and why those Hobbits were able to rescue Middle Earth from almost certain doom.

Relaxing in the picturesque meadows of Matamata (or, as we cognoscenti refer to it, 'The Shire') I feel a million miles away from the Sydney train toilet I woke up in after being turned away from DJ Rico's set on Darling Harbour and my resultant disastrous overdose on hashcakes. Normally, I can smoke bales of Mary-Joanna and still have the mental agility to ride my bicycle to Singh's General Stores and conduct small talk with Mr Singh. However, on this occasion, I can only assume that I was spiked – no doubt with horse tranquillisers or dog worming tablets (that kind of thing goes on all the time in Australia). But here in NZ, there isn't a worm in sight and the people are just so simple and unassuming.

I only wish that DJ Rico was here with me to experience them and the rocky behemoths that are the famed mountains of Edoras. He shares my love for Tolkien, as I discovered during our night of sexual communion and talking about books. I asked him what character he identified with from 'Lord Of' and he said Aragorn because he was so brooding and swarthy. You might be surprised to learn that I am not Frodo (the obvious choice), but his trusty hobbit companion, Merry. This is because I am not all out there and in your face like Frodo, and because Merry starred in the TV series *Lost*, and at times I just feel so 'Lost'.

It's the nature of the Kiwi to hold a mirror up to the soul of man; something about this place forces you to shift down a gear and see things you wouldn't normally see – 'visions' you might say. You might always have thought you were Arwen, the Elfin beauty, only to find out you're actually Gimli, the Scottish dwarf who plaits his beard.

That is what makes New Zealand the greatest country in the world.

YOUR ASTROLOGICAL WEEK AHEAD
with PSYCHIC BOB

Gemini
Get some decent photos taken. When you go missing, your family will have to use that one from six years ago where you look like a twat. And no-one's going to stay up all night looking for a twat.

Cancer
You are false data. Therefore I shall ignore you. The only thing that exists is myself. And steer clear of Scorpios.

Leo
Underlying passions force their way to the surface this week and then spread out before drying into a hard, brittle crust.

Virgo
Now would be a good time to talk about past misunderstandings with previous partners. When you see them staring back at you from the witness box it'll probably be too late.

Libra
Love, romance, passion, new opportunities and positive career movements are all on the horizon for the person you hate the most. Suck it.

Scorpio
Repressed memories bubble to the surface this week, revealing years of mundane childhood tedium. Yes, you are just like everyone else. Shockerooni.

Sagittarius
Avoid anything that smells fishy, unless it's a fish finger. In which case avoid anything that smells breadcrumby.

Capricorn
Your gap year trip around the world has certainly opened our eyes to what an insufferable, tedious prick you really are.

Aquarius
A wonderful weekend lies ahead, surrounded by close friends and family who all care about you very deeply and want nothing more than for you to be happy. So why do you long to kill them?

Pisces
It's time to be a bit more open, honest and direct about your recent feelings of doubt over your abilities. Yes, you have been found out. At last.

Aries
You're on firm ground by Thursday, but by then all your family have been eaten by sharks, and their chewed up heads washed ashore on an otherwise idyllic tropical island. Yes, it really was 'the trip of a lifetime'.

Taurus
Every star in the constellation of Taurus seems to have exploded. That can't be good.

THREAT LEVEL

Underpants

The Daily Mash

Need an email address that's incredibly easy to get wrong?

Try hortmail.com

it's news to us   www.thedailymash.co.uk   No.4

EVERYONE DEAD BY TEATIME

THE greatest experiment in the history of physics will begin this morning, followed shortly afterwards by your horrifyingly painful death.

As the large hadron collider is activated scientists believe they will have less than four seconds to spot the mysterious Higgs Boson particle before their bodies explode, atom by atom.

A black hole will open up in what used to be Geneva, spreading rapidly across Europe, angrily devouring Belgium and reaching the outer London boroughs by 3pm.

Cambridge physicist Dr Tom Logan, explained: "At this point you will be stretched out slowly until you resemble a very thin piece of spaghetti about 250,000 miles long. It will hurt like fuck."

He added: "A lot of people will probably want to know what happens

The Higg's basin. Fancy.

to their favourite celebrities such as Frank Lampard, Shilpa Shetty and Princess Anne.

"They will be stretched out slowly until they resemble a very thin piece of spaghetti about 250,000 miles long. I imagine Princess Anne will cope better than Frank Lampard."

Professor Bill McKay, who has called for the experiment to be abandoned, said: "If it's a Higgs Boson particle you're after I've got two in the fridge. Seriously – a fiver the pair."

Some scientists believe the imminent black hole could create a gateway, or 'wormhole', into an alternate universe. Dr Logan added: "Hopefully this one will be free of Peaches Geldof, fame-hungry little trollop that she is."

Meanwhile Apple has launched a new advertising campaign urging everyone to download a few more songs from iTunes before it and everything else ceases to exist.

David Duchovny has his cake and shags it

X-FILES star David Duchovny last night became the latest Hollywood star to have sex with countless women and then claim he was not right in the head.

Duchovny has checked himself into a rehabilitation clinic which specialises in the treatment of men who like to hump anything that moves but do not want to have any arguments with their wives.

Dr Henry Brubaker, head of sex addiction at the

Institute for Studies, said: "There comes a time in the life of every good-looking millionaire actor when nine out of 10 of women will agree to have sex with them.

"At this point many of them find themselves trapped in the horrendous position of having a tremendous amount of sex.

"Generally it is the young, single actors who are able to cope with having sex 10 or 12 times a day without becoming clinically addicted.

The truth is up there

"But there are still too many married, middle-aged

actors whose wives have fantastic lawyers, who suddenly become consumed by this crippling medical condition."

Dr Brubaker added: "Makes you fucking sick, doesn't it?"

Duchovny is expected undergo a series of radical treatments including wet and dry testicular shock therapy and looking an artist's impression of the tiny house he will have to live in after his divorce.

Thought for the day: If you wave a steak in front of a policeman and then throw it, he will chase after it. (Isaac Newton)

BNP not just policemen, reveals secret list

A SECRET list of BNP members has revealed the party includes people from a range of professions, not just the police.

According to the list, published on the internet, British National Party supporters now include doctors, vicars, teachers, sports commentators and children's clowns.

Bill McKay, professor of sociology at Reading University, said: "This explodes the myth of BNP members as skinhead thugs with Doc Marten boots, tattoos and unusual helmets."

The party, founded in 1982 as a book club for metropolitan police constables, soon expanded to include senior officers up to the rank of superintendent, as well as a growing number of angry retired policeman.

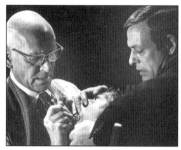

Sir Laurence Olivier played a BNP dentist in *Marathon Man*

Among the party's new members is well-known ITV football commentator Roy Hobbs, known for his refusal to pronounce foreign surnames, and the Right Reverend Julian Cook, author of bestselling book *Was Jesus from Dorset?*

Professor McKay added: "My neighbour's a retired policeman. He keeps telling me that it used to be nice round here but now everything smells of ghee."

A spokesman for the British Medical Association said: "A good way to determine if your doctor is in the BNP is if he tells you to open your mouth, say 'aaah' and then asks if you've been in contact with any Jews recently.

"A BNP doctor may also reveal a keen desire to measure the diameter of your skull and the width of your nose before recommending you for sterilisation."

The British Dental Association insisted its membership has been Nazi-free since 2005.

NATIONAL DEBT TO REACH CHRIST ON A BIKE

BRITAIN'S national debt will rise from No Way to Christ On A Bike, chancellor Alistair Darling announced yesterday.

In his pre-Budget report Mr Darling said that "Sweet Jesus times require Bloody Hell measures", adding: "Holy Living Mother of God, you will not fucking believe this."

The chancellor confirmed that next year the government would spend an extra Holy Shit, an increase of For Fuck's Sake compared to 2007.

Mr Darling told the House of Commons: "Is everyone sitting down?

Right. Okay. How should I put this exactly? You know how sometimes you're in a canoe on a big river filled with turds?"

The chancellor predicted the economy would shrink by Hell's Teeth during 2009 but would then recover at a rate of Where Exactly Are You Getting That From? rising to You're Obviously Just Making This Up by the end of 2010.

Meanwhile help to pensioners and low income families would be increased by How Pathetic Is That? while VAT will be cut by Just Spend

It On Booze For Christ's Sake.

Shadow chancellor George Osborne said every middle-class family would be hit by an immediate tax hike of This Is Absolutely Fucking Typical which could eventually rise to You've Ruined My Life, You Incompetent Bastards.

Mr Osborne insisted a Tory government would peg government spending at Hang On I'm Still Getting My Head Round This, but warned that budgets may have to be cut by Don't Worry, You'll Be Okay If You've Got Bupa.

Call for increase in gap-toothed inbreds

THE number of babies created from the sperm of a single donor should be increased to boost Britain's quota of gap-toothed inbreds, experts have claimed.

The Institute for Studies said the more babies who have the same father, the more likely it is they will grow-up to have sex with each other, thereby creating a race of dungaree-clad mutants.

Professor Henry Brubaker said: "Think of it. Thousands of jug-eared

banjo twangers and chainsaw-wielding halfwits, as well as an endless supply of guests for the *Jeremy Kyle Show*.

"He could have an entire channel devoted solely to these big-nosed, squirrel-eating swamp-freaks and their intricately complex social lives. I could watch that all day."

The number of sperm donors has dropped since the removal of anonymity for men who accept money in exchange for ejaculating into a beaker.

Meanwhile there is an ever

increasing demand from childless couples determined to start their own horrifyingly shallow gene pool.

Professor Brubaker added: "We could set them all free to live in the woods and build their own strange, introverted societies.

"It would certainly make country walks more interesting and would also be a great place for a stag weekend.

"The fun doesn't really begin until the groom has been stripped, violated and told to squeal like a pig."

Supermarkets 'selling things people want to buy'

BRITAIN'S supermarkets were last night accused of stocking the products their customers want to buy.

The National Consumer Council claimed the stores are deliberately selling a range of items that are not only competitively priced but tasted lovely.

The NCC said that by stocking large numbers of these products, the customers are being encouraged to return to the stores, often on a weekly basis.

A spokesman said: "They stock more of the things that people want and a lot less of the things that people don't want. It's cynical and possibly illegal.

"For example, Asda are currently selling four Extra Special Beefburgers for £1.89 for the simple reason that everybody likes them.

"They put the burgers in cardboard boxes carrying a photograph which is clearly designed to make them look appetising and then place these boxes on easy-to-reach shelves.

"Meanwhile they go around filling their fruit and veg aisles with thousands of deadly scorpions. Probably."

She only thinks she's happy

A spokesman for Asda said: "The National Consumer Council seems to have confused us with something that is not a business."

He added: "Coco Pops Mega Munchers – £1.87"

Rubbing groin and staring boosts sex appeal

RUBBING your groin and your inner thigh while staring at women makes you more sexually attractive, according to a new study.

Researchers asked 230 women to compare a man rubbing his penis through his clothing while grunting and smiling, and a man sitting in the corner of a fashionable bar, pretending to read a fancy novel.

All of the women opted to sleep with the man with the visible erection and called the police when his rival attempted to read them the first sentence of *The Unbearable Lightness of Being*.

Henry Brubaker, head of women at the Institute for Studies, said: "Women are very simple creatures and interested in only one thing: sex.

"If you want to give them sex you need to make it clear immediately otherwise they will go off and have it with some other man, or possibly even a woman."

He added: "The filthy whores."

The study also asked 230 men to rate the attractiveness of a woman putting her legs behind her ears, and former Conservative prime minister Baroness Thatcher.

All 230 opted to have intercourse with the retired PM as the other woman was wearing glasses and was slightly overweight.

Brubaker said: "Men are very complicated creatures who are interested in only one thing: kinky sex.

"If you want to give them kinky sex you need to make it clear otherwise they will go off and use some other woman, or possibly themselves."

He added: "Seems perfectly reasonable."

Cycle of Britney begins again

POP sensation Britney Spears will soon begin a fresh descent into chaos and substance abuse as experts confirmed her celebrity cycle had completed its first full revolution.

Spears, the undisputed star of the MTV video awards, is expected to enjoy at least three weeks of positive press coverage hailing her spectacular comeback before locking herself in her Beverly Hills mansion with a big box of glue.

Bill McKay, an entertainment analyst, said: "The first turn of the Britney wheel has been an absolute joy. I think everyone was charmed by the sheer hillbilly ghastliness of it all."

McKay, who has already plotted the Spears celebrity cycle for the next 12 months, added: "We can now look forward to sitting through the whole thing all over again. Except with some different songs."

The Britney Spears Celebrity Cycle 2008-09:

- **October 2008:** Caught on security camera licking glue off Sellotape.
- **November 2008:** Admitted to the San Jose Institute for Glue Lickers.

Already thinking about glue

- **December 2008:** Escapes and drives backwards along the Santa Monica freeway for 350 miles.
- **January 2009:** Marries actress Lindsay Lohan, in Hawaii, on horseback.
- **February 2009:** Spears devastated as Lohan embarks upon affair with horse.
- **March 2009:** Lohan files for divorce. Marries horse later that same day.
- **April 2009:** Judge denies Spears custody of all future children.
- **May 2009:** Spears now licking glue from stamps and has Prit-Stick lodged permanently in left nostril.
- **June 2009:** Gives birth to 9lb baby boy. Names him 'Prit' before he is handed over to gypsy folk.
- **July 2009:** Backing dancers refuse to perform with her at MTV Europe Awards due to constant, eye-watering flatulence.
- **August 2009:** Admitted to the Santa Barbara Institute for Constant, Eye-Watering Flatulence.
- **September 2009:** Makes triumphant return at MTV video awards with gutsy, half-naked rendition of Iron Maiden's 'Bring Your Daughter to the Slaughter'.
- **October 2009:** Caught on security camera licking Febreze off curtains.

Ecclestone wife to buy two midgets

'If only I could have had another Bernie Ecclestone attached to this one'

THE soon-to-be ex-wife of Formula One tycoon Bernie Ecclestone has vowed to buy a taller husband or two midgets that can be bolted together.

Slavica Ecclestone is expected to receive enough money in her divorce settlement to buy any man, or combination of men, that she wants.

She said last night: "When I was a young girl my idea of the perfect husband was a man who was suave, sophisticated, about six foot tall and had a billion pounds.

"But unfortunately at the age of 26 I found myself in the position where I had to choose between a man who was nine foot tall but skint and a three foot midget with two billion pounds.

"I chose Bernie Ecclestone."

She added: "We had many happy years but there's only so long you can be a climbing frame for a monkey. Even a very, very rich monkey.

"But soon I will have the money and I can choose. I suppose the easy thing would be to have one very large husband but I really like the idea of two midgets in a boiler suit.

"Then they can take it in turns to be the one on top. It'll help keep things fresh."

HAVING free sex with your wife is now slightly better value than Pizza Hut, according to a new survey.

In a YouGov survey of 2,000 married men, 89% said the recession had made marital intercourse slightly better value than a £24.99 tasting platter, a large, stuffed crust pizza and a bowl of spaghetti carbonara.

However, 24% said the £5.99 'all you can eat' midweek buffet was still a good deal compared to five minutes of sweaty, grudging tedium.

Tom Logan, married to Jill for 13 years, said: "We've had to cut back to Freeview, which means we've lost Sky 1 and the Richard and Judy Channel.

"So at least two nights a week you're forced to choose between just sitting on a chair and staring at the wall or going upstairs and doing the deed."

He added: "And it's not really free either. Tesco value condoms are 38p a pop, but at least you can economise a bit by rinsing them under the tap or turning them inside out.

"The sex is your basic, entry-level humping. If I want anything special I have to save up my dole money and buy her some ice cream."

The UK's top 5 cheap entertainments:
(Last year in brackets)
1 **Sex with wife** (-)
2 **Pizza Hut** (1)
3 **Chasing gypsies round the town square** (2)
4 **Vodka-fuelled amateur surgery** (-)
5 **Dressing up the dog and acting out scenes from Return of the Jedi** (4)

UK couple in first World of Warcraft divorce

A WOMAN has divorced her husband after he used the computer game *World of Warcraft* to conduct affairs with a series of imaginary woodland creatures.

Jane Logan said her husband Tom was guilty of the 'ultimate betrayal' – using his broadband connection for picking up easy trolls and organising weekend orgies with dirty goblins.

Mrs Logan said: "I was proud that my husband was a level three Night Elf of Azeroth and I fully supported his efforts to suppress the Undead Forsaken of the Lich King's Horde.

"Little did I realise that while his comrades risked their pretend lives in blood-soaked combat, he was in a dark corner of Ashenvale Forest taking goblins up the back passage.

"It all came to a head one Sunday afternoon. I brought him a cup of tea, expecting him to be slaughtering his way through a column of Orcs, but instead, there he was, slap-bang in the middle of some hellish daisy chain."

Mr Logan insisted he would never have allowed his love of goblin sex to spill over into his actual life, but did admit he was currently trying to build his own dragon.

He added: "It is quite difficult to get an animal to breath flames.

"You basically have to use a small propane cylinder with a rubber tube that goes through the skin, into the lungs, up the windpipe and has small pilot light on the end.

"At the moment I'm working on a fire-breathing alligator strapped to a micro-light."

There are few addictions more powerful than imaginary goblin sex

I'm a Celebrity to drop bushtucker challenge and just go with the titties

ITV show *I'm a Celebrity Get Me Out of Here* is to drop its team challenge rounds so that it can focus on lots of wet tits.

Producers say from next year the show will be overhauled to bring together 12 medium- to large-breasted celebrities who will spend six weeks having bikini-clad showers under a jungle waterfall.

ITV executive Roy Hobbs said: "We've realised that no-one in their right mind wants to watch Mr Sulu eat a grasshopper when they could be waiting for Dani Behr to just say 'what the hell' and take the bloody thing off.

"There will be new and innovative additions to the format such as lots and lots of soap. "And, of course, we will occasionally cut back to Ant and Dec giggling and rubbing their hands."

He added: "There's not much point in continuing with the current title so we'll probably just call it *Tits*."

Except not Esther Rantzen

Meanwhile ITV2 will screen a spin-off show *Tits.Now* where celebrity pundits and a studio audience will discuss the relative merits of pert, cosmetically enhanced titties and big bouncy funbags.

Tits will be only the third programme in the history of British television to be made primarily for men after *Top Gear* and *Pot Black*.

BBC captures rare footage of Fiona Bruce having a shit

IT is as thick as your arm and smells disgusting – and it has just been caught on camera for what is thought to be the first time.

A crew has managed to record a film of Fiona Bruce – the BBC's biggest newsreader – expelling food waste, which was then scooped up for research.

Biologist Tom Logan said the sample had helped him to discover more about the giant creature's feeding habits.

Fiona Bruces (*Antiquodon Roadshowius*) are related to Anna Fords, but are far less fearsome. They are filter feeders, swimming about with their enormous mouths open to scoop up any tasty morsels that happen to be floating in their paths.

They can grow up to 12m long; yet, despite their staggering size, very little is known about these newsreading giants.

Dr Logan added: "It does seem rather weird, someone being so excited about seeing Fiona Bruce poo. I'm pretty certain that this is the first time it has been filmed.

"But it is pretty rare – they are usually doing their business down in much deeper water." He described the faeces that the team collected as "scientific gold".

"One way to work out what is going in one end is to look at what is coming out of the other.

"By seeing a Fiona Bruce poo and getting hold of some of that stuff, we can use sophisticated genetic techniques to look at the DNA in that sample to find out exactly what those animals have been eating."

Genetic analysis revealed the Fiona Bruce had been feasting on red crab larvae and bits of Sophie Raworth.

The startling images from the 'Fiona Bruce-cam'

Anti-aging creams are 98% bullshit, say scientists

WOMEN'S anti-ageing face creams contain up to 98% bullshit, according to a new study.

Scientists who analysed a series of leading creams and ointments found that while they did not prevent visible ageing to any measurable degree, they did cost an awful lot of money.

According to the study Oil of Olay's Oil of Aloe was 97% bullshit, 2% washing up liquid and 1% Cup-a-Soup.

L'Oréal's Splendesse V-20 was a mixture of axle grease, marketing pish and brilliant white emulsion, possibly from Homebase.

Meanwhile Garnier's Ultra-Stop-Nature-System did contain trace amounts of vitamins G, M and L but was

With added 'dermanoids'. Seventy-five quid.

mainly pig fat and desperation.

Dr Stephen Malley, of the Institute for Studies, said: "The cosmetics industry has invested heavily in research and development to identify exactly the right level of scientific bullshit to use in their adverts.

"The most successful phrases so far are 'anti-oxidisational', 'firmness retention system' and the utterly meaningless combination of number and letters that is 'Derma-factor XJ-30'."

He added: "You'd be as well rubbing paté into your face or wrapping your head in clingfilm."

END OF U.S. POWER WILL NOT AFFECT ITS TELEVISION PROGRAMMES, SAY EXPERT

THE waning of America's influence on the global stage should not affect its ability to produce high-quality drama and clever sitcoms, experts said last night.

The National Intelligence Council (NIC) said that by 2025 you are likely to be strapped to a chair and held at gunpoint by Algerian mercenaries while rising sea water laps around your ankles and mutant chickens eat the last of your porridge, but you will still be able to watch *Prison Break* on your iPod.

According to the report the post-US world order will also see an increase in rogue states run by criminals including Afghanistan, Somalia, Russia and Scotland.

An NIC spokesman said: "America will be a bit like Superman in *Superman II* when he loses all his power after he falls in love with Lois Lane and then gets beaten up in the diner by that horrible truck driver even though he's still six foot five and built like a brick shithouse.

"But in this case the falling in love with Lois Lane will be six billion highly educated Asians who will work 18-hour shifts for 50 pence a day while you become too fat to heave yourself onto the toilet."

Television viewer Tom Logan, from Watford, said: "I couldn't give a shit whether the world is run by dastardly Chinese communists or insane Russian gangsters as long as somebody keeps making *Battlestar Galactica*.

Cheese and onion crisps go into administration

ADMINISTRATORS were called into cheese and onion crisps last night as the classic flavour became the latest high profile victim of the recession.

The demise of cheese and onion came at the end of a black day for the British economy which also saw the collapse of conkers, pick'n'mix and a nice pot of tea.

City analysts say cheese and onion was unable to compete in a market filled with radical new flavours which included Double Gloucester and red onion, Stilton and shallot, and vintage cheddar and onion chutney.

Martin Bishop, head of crisps at Madeley-Finnegan,

said: "The thing I'll miss most about cheese and onion is how it masked the stench of stale urine that pervades every inch of this godforsaken shithole of a country.

"But unfortunately it had begun to look very old fashioned alongside modern British brands such as

What is the point of cheese and onion crisps?

celebrity cock fights, alco-puke, casual racism and sex with strangers in the back of a Vauxhall Vectra."

Bishop added: "In order for brands to survive these days they simply have to adapt. Conkers involved two humans in the same place with no electronic devices.

"And who wants a nice pot of tea when you can pay £1.75 for two square feet of boiling foam?"

Administrators are hopeful that parts of the flavour can be salvaged and have already had discussions with Waitrose about incorporating it into a new batch of Hand Smoked Gorgonzola and Vietnamese Chive.

Venture capitalists invest in Somali pirates

VENTURE capitalists in New York and London are pumping millions of dollars into Somalia's booming pirate sector.

The sharp-eyed investors say Indian Ocean piracy has replaced Bangladeshi t-shirt factories as the developing world's strongest source of high-growth revenue streams.

Julian Cook, head of strategy at Porter, Pinkney and Turner (PPT), explained: "The margins are very impressive. These guys can board a Chinese freighter or Saudi oil tanker and turn it around in less than a week. Usually without killing anyone.

"The staff are well-trained and they operate a structured bonus system involving the daughters of nomadic tribal chiefs and as

Personnel issues are now dealt with via mentoring and third-party arbitration

much hallucinogenic tree bark as they can eat.

"The tax position is also very favourable given that Somalia isn't really what you would describe as a

'country' with 'laws' and a 'government'."

PPT has paid £25.7 million for a 32% stake in Captain Ahmed's Crazee Bastards with the initial tranche used for capital purchases including new speed boats, 200 yards of very strong rope and a gun the size of a cow.

The investment will also be used to establish an out-sourced personnel department to ensure that the quick replacement of any colleagues shot by the Royal Navy during working hours.

Ahmed will retain day-to-day management control and has also negotiated a clause allowing him to go 'ape-shit crazee' and shoot everyone on board up to three times a year.

Shares in you plunge 82%

SHARES in you plunged 82 per cent yesterday leaving you vulnerable to a takeover from some dirty Spanish bastard.

Investors are worried there is still no sign of your wealthy parents dying and believe you cannot carry on stealing from your senile grandmother's purse for much longer.

Concerns have also been raised about your over exposure to sub-prime REM albums and your ability to repay the £250 you owe Arkan the coke dealer.

In a statement to the Stock Exchange you said: "We remain confident we can persuade Mr Arkan to restructure our drug debts even though it may cost us a toe.

"If not, we can always get bar work or pay 'Fucknut' Frankie Thomson to make our parents die in a freak accident which does not involve the destruction of any of their valuable property."

However, Julian Cook, who analyses you at Donnelly McPartlin, said: "Your assets include numbers one to 24 of *Now That's What I Call Music*, excluding 7 and 13. That's not bad. You also have a novelty smoothie maker.

"But you have also made some very poor strategic investments in recent times, including £200 on a mobile phone that makes you look like a tit and £150 on a vibrating egg."

He added: "Without short-term recapitalisation you will be forced to bend over as the oleaginous man with the paella breath smears olive oil into your buttocks and unzips himself."

AS THE BBC PLEDGES TOUGH NEW RULES ON STANDARDS AND DECENCY...

FUCK FUCK FUCK FUCK FUCK FUCK
FUCK FUCK FUCK FUCK FUCK FUCK
FUCK FUCK FUCK FUCK FUCK FUCK
FUCK FUCK FUCK FUCK
FUCK FUCK FUCK FUCK
FUCK FUCK FUCK FUCK
FUCK FUCK FUCK FUCK

FUCK FUCK FUCK FUCK FUCK FUCK FUCK FUCK FUCK FUCK FUCK FUCK FUCK FUCK FUCK
FUCK FUCK FUCK FUCK FUCK FUCK FUCK FUCK FUCK FUCK FUCK FUCK FUCK FUCK FUCK
FUCK FUCK FUCK FUCK FUCK FUCK FUCK FUCK FUCK FUCK FUCK FUCK FUCK FUCK FUCK
FUCK FUCK FUCK FUCK FUCK FUCK FUCK FUCK FUCK FUCK FUCK FUCK WANK FUCK FUCK
FUCK FUCK FUCK FUCK FUCK FUCK FUCK FUCK FUCK FUCK FUCK FUCK FUCK FUCK FUCK
FUCK FUCK FUCK FUCK FUCK FUCK FUCK FUCK FUCK FUCK FUCK FUCK FUCK FUCK FUCK
FUCK FUCK FUCK FUCK FUCK FUCK FUCK FUCK FUCK FUCK FUCK FUCK FUCK FUCK FUCK
FUCK FUCK FUCK FUCK FUCK FUCK FUCK FUCK FUCK FUCK SHIT FUCK FUCK FUCK FUCK
FUCK FUCK FUCK FUCK FUCK FUCK FUCK FUCK FUCK FUCK FUCK FUCK FUCK FUCK FUCK
TITS FUCK FUCK FUCK FUCK FUCK FUCK TITS FUCK FUCK FUCK FUCK FUCK FUCK FUCK
FUCK FUCK FUCK FUCK FUCK FUCK FUCK FUCK FUCK FUCK FUCK FUCK FUCK FUCK FUCK
FUCK FUCK FUCK FUCK FUCK FUCK FUCK FUCK FUCK FUCK FUCK FUCK FUCK FUCK FUCK
FUCK FUCK FUCK FUCK FUCK FUCK FUCK FUCK FUCK FUCK FUCK FUCK FUCK FUCK FUCK
FUCK FUCK FUCK FUCK FUCK FUCK FUCK FUCK FUCK FUCK FUCK FUCK FUCK FUCK FUCK
FUCK FUCK FUCK FUCK FUCK FUCK FUCK FUCK FUCK FUCK FUCK FUCK FUCK FUCK FUCK
FUCK FUCK FUCK FUCK FUCK FUCK FUCK FUCK FUCK FUCK FUCK FUCK FUCK FUCK FUCK
FUCK FUCK FUCK FUCK FUCK FUCK FUCK FUCK FUCK FUCK FUCK FUCK FUCK FUCK FUCK
FUCK FUCK FUCK FUCK FUCK FUCK FUCK FUCK FUCK FUCK FUCK FUCK FUCK FUCK FUCK
FUCK FUCK FUCK FUCK FUCK TWAT FUCK FUCK FUCK FUCK FUCK FUCK FUCK FUCK FUCK
FUCK FUCK FUCK FUCK FUCK FUCK FUCK FUCK
FUCK FUCK FUCK FUCK FUCK FUCK FUCK FUCK
FUCK FUCK FUCK FUCK FUCK FUCK FUCK FUCK
FUCK FUCK FUCK FUCK FUCK FUCK FUCK
FUCK FUCK FUCK FUCK FUCK FUCK FUCK
FUCK FUCK FUCK FUCK FUCK FUCK FUCK
FUCK FUCK FUCK FUCK FUCK FUCK
FUCK FUCK FUCK FUCK FUCK FUCK
FUCK FUCK FUCK FUCK FUCK FUCK FUCK
FUCK FUCK FUCK FUCK FUCK FUCK FUCK
FUCK FUCK FUCK FUCK FUCK FUCK FUCK
FUCK FUCK FUCK FUCK FUCK FUCK FUCK
FUCK FUCK FUCK FUCK FUCK FUCK FUCK
FUCK FUCK FUCK FUCK FUCK FUCK FUCK
FUCK FUCK FUCK FUCK FUCK FUCK FUCK FUCK
FUCK FUCK FUCK FUCK FUCK FUCK FUCK

DOES BRITAIN SWEAR TOO COCKING MUCH OR IS IT ALL JUST A LOAD OF ARSEING SHITBOLLOCKS?

A Cinderella story of millionaires supported by billionaires supported by banks

THE Brawn racing team completed a Cinderella story yesterday after clinching the opening grand prix of the season with nothing more than millions and millions of pounds.

The victory in Australia marked a stunning turnaround in fortunes for the humble, soot-covered team, which was created just months ago after a management buy-out involving fairy dust and money.

Winning driver Jenson Button said: "I suppose it's a bit like David beating Goliath if David and Goliath had been roughly the same size."

Like many of the characters in Cinderella, the senior members of the Brawn GP team live in large, comfortable houses and have domestic staff. They also attend lavish parties in expensive vehicles and own footwear made from a variety of exotic substances.

The team has also recently acquired a bearded fairy-godmother with her own fleet of Boeing 747s, a train company and an island in the Caribbean.

Meanwhile, Jenson Button lives in a luxury apartment in Monte Carlo so he doesn't have to pay income tax on his multi-million pound salary, exactly like Cinderella.

A Brawn GP spokesman said: "We made this car with nothing more than lollipop sticks, elastic bands and an enormous amount of money.

"But we have had to tighten our belts which has meant using private jets, helicopters and five star hotels like some band of travelling gypsies."

He added: "It's a fairytale come true for a group of dedicated people whose lives were already a fairytale come true and have been for a number of years."

Sunday's victory means Button will no longer have to scrub fireplaces in his spare time

Tea lady makes villa debut

ASTON Villa boss Martin O'Neill last night defended fielding a 69-year-old tea lady in central defence after his side were dumped out of the Uefa cup.

Margaret Gerving, who has been serving delicious refreshments at Villa Park since 1983, said she enjoyed her first outing and that her acrylic hip joints had performed surprisingly well.

The grandmother of eight said: "I'm more of an attacking midfielder to be honest but I'm happy to play wherever the boss needs me. I just hope that my series of severe angina attacks whenever the ref blew his whistle did not distract the other lads too much."

Mrs Gerving added:

Mrs Gerving has been linked with a move to Spurs

"This is my grandson Stuart. He's studying mechanical engineering at Warwick. I don't like his girlfriend though. Very full of herself."

O'Neill opted for an experimental 4-1-0 line up against CSKA Moscow, including Mrs Gerving, two-year-old Spiderman enthusiast Kyle Stephenson, the late Danny Blanchflower, and an atom of hydrogen at right-back.

He said: "I wanted Margaret to put her foot on the ball, calm things down and build from the back. I did not expect her to bring a folding chair, a walkman and the audio book of *Passion's Promise* by Danielle Steel.

"It was probably for the best when the big lad knocked her over and ruptured her colostomy bag."

With Villa fourth in the Premier League, O'Neill said he wanted to rest key players in their push for the title. But Man Utd manager Alex Ferguson described the tactic as 'pissing a fire door shut', adding: "Title-contenders my furious, purple arse."

ENGLISH FANS HAVE WHIP-ROUND FOR REAL MADRID

"They are very wealthy but we don't want anything to ruin the chance of getting Ronaldo on a plane and out of our fucking lives for good," says everyone.

DIE MANKIND! DIE!
by Dr Henry Brubaker, inventor of the large hadron collider

LET me begin by saying that, apart from the Wikipedia page about black holes, this may well be the last thing you will ever read.

Today is history. Or to be scientifically accurate – today is, very much, the end of history. Within a few hours none of us will exist and, aside from a black hole the size of a honeydew melon, there will be not a shred of evidence we were ever here. As you struggle to control your bowels, you will, no doubt, be curious as to how this came to pass.

The story begins four years ago at a dinner party in Oxford. I had been invited along by my friends Toby and Sylvia who were keen to introduce me to their new neighbour, Janet. I was nervous, of course. I've always been rather awkward

around women. But Toby assured me Janet was the sort of girl who would know how to immediately put me at ease. How right they were. Seated next to each other at the table, Janet and I soon struck up a rapport. I told her how I had devoted my life to the dogged pursuit of the Higgs Boson particle, while she swallowed large mouthfuls of Chardonnay and ran her soft hands up the inside of my thigh.

By the end of the evening it was abundantly clear that Janet and I were going to have sex. Janet had said as much as she buried those relentless hands down the front of my underpants. That night we made energetic love on my squeaky bed and I told myself the Higgs Boson particle could remain undiscovered for all I cared.

The days that followed were the happiest of my life. I would leave work early and rush through the busy streets to be with Janet, whose desire for my naked form was matched only by her unquenchable thirst for crisp, French whites.

And so, one day, I made for home, pausing only to pick up a five-litre box of Muscadet. As I opened the door I heard a muffled grunting. It was apparent the heavy, laboured strains were emanating from the bedroom. Through a slim crack in the door, I saw Janet straddled across Toby, both of them stark naked but for a pair of antique pith helmets.

I ran from the flat with a half bottle of Teachers and hid myself in a quiet corner of the park. As the warm liquor gradually spread

through my veins my thoughts turned to revenge. But not the hot, wild vengeance of an arts graduate. No, this would be the precise, measured revenge of an MSc.

Anyway, to cut a long story short I invented the large hadron collider under the guise of cosmological research, all the while hiding its real purpose which is to kill Janet, Toby and – mindful of your distinct lack of sympathy in the midst of what was, after all, a very difficult time – all of you.

All that remains now is to thank those who unwittingly helped build my apocalypse machine and the many colleagues who wrote long, impassioned articles insisting it was perfectly safe. And thank you to Brian for all the cups of tea.

YOUR ASTROLOGICAL WEEK AHEAD
with PSYCHIC BOB

Aries
Neptune in Pisces gives you waves of love for your partner, that cheap bit of trash you knock off at weekends, and the temp in accounts with the squint and the dirty laugh.

Taurus
If you want to drive then why don't you just fucking say so, you pedantic, self-righteous cow.

Gemini
The only thing holding you back right now is your lack of self-belief. Let it.

Cancer
Matters of the heart

suddenly look far more complex. Perhaps you should have paid slightly more attention during all those cardio-vascular surgery lectures. Your patient certainly thinks so.

Leo
Gently massage into wet hair and scalp. Rinse well. No separate conditioner needed.°

Virgo
Venus combines with Jupiter to open your mind and your heart to the plight of others less fortunate than yourself. Luckily Comic Relief was last week so it's unlikely to cost you.

Libra
Help a friend out of their negative frame of mind by reminding them of all the good things in their life and then pissing off out of it forever.

Scorpio
Mars makes you more determined than ever to reach your goals, but Neptune has tied your shoelaces together.

Sagittarius
Don't let new possibilities pass you by simply through fear of the unknown. Rely instead on your complete inability to spot an unmissable opportunity

when it is offered to you on a plate.

Capricorn
After three heel-dragging weeks of Mercury going backwards you have two very badly worn heels.

Aquarius
The Spring equinox is a portal to a busier phase in your affairs, so remember to take a fresh pair of knickers to work with you.

Pisces
If you could just pop your underpants on the chair, we can get started.

THREAT LEVEL

Space Hopper

The Daily Mash

TODAY'S WEATHER
It raiining Wether Girls. Stay indoors, they could squash you like a gnat.

it's news to us   www.thedailymash.co.uk   No.5

CARNAGE AS FACEBOOK MOVES EVERYTHING SLIGHTLY TO THE LEFT

BRITAIN'S hospitals were struggling to cope last night as rival Facebook gangs fought running battles across a dozen towns and cities.

Violence erupted as Facebook ignored the warnings of more than one million protesters and moved everything very slightly to the left.

Martin Bishop, commander of the Lyme Regis brigade of Keep the Old Facebook, said: "I was waiting for my page to load, looking directly at the centre of the screen, when suddenly my life became a storm-tossed fishing boat in a sea of confusion.

"Everything that really mattered to me was now three centimetres to the left of where it normally is. And a little bit wider. And the blue-grey panel on the right was a bit wider too."

He added: "Death and those who support the new design are now friends."

Roy Hobbs, from Dorchester, who makes weapons for We Like the New Facebook, said: "This is a motorcycle chain with dozens of tiny screws welded on to it. You have to wear gloves when you're swinging it in someone's face."

Hobbs added: "That blue-grey panel was always

Bridport: A hellish symphony of fire and blood

far too narrow. Don't you think?"

The violence peaked at around 5pm when the Bridport faction of What About Moving Everything Slightly to the Right? burned down their local church

and pushed a van full of policeman into a quarry.

Facebook founder Mark Zuckerberg has given the protesters until noon to surrender before he starts machine-gunning them from a helicopter.

Pope calls for cap on gay emissions

POPE Benedict has called for a renewed global effort to cap the level of gay emissions.

The Pope said gayness was at least as dangerous to humanity as global warming, if not more so given all that hot boy-on-boy action.

In his end of year address to Vatican prelates, he said: "They go to nightclubs and dance and take their tight t-shirts off and get all sweaty and before you know it it's off to the bogs for 20 minutes of furtive cock-fun.

"There they are, in the bogs, going off in each others hands, emitting all kinds of juices and fluids."

He added: "Once these fluids are out, you can't put them back. And eventually there will be so much of this goo sloshing all over the place that the polar bears will slip on it and die.

"It will spill over into the oceans and all the penguins and cormorants and seagulls will be covered in it and they will have to be scrubbed clean by volunteers. But not by me, no way, I'm

not touching some penguin that's all covered in gayboy juice."

The Pope has demanded an international cap on gay emissions alongside a system of gay trading where bigger countries buy gay emissions from the smaller, more efficient gay producing nations. He also called for investment in 'fluid-capture' technology where millions of tonnes of gay juice would be stored in vast underground chambers before being tested, cleaned and used to make new Catholics.

Thought for the day: Beelzebub is your lord and master. Kill, kill, kill. (Martin Luther King)

Britain gets the stupid Christmas advice it deserves

GOVERNMENT guidelines on how to avoid accidents at Christmas are every bit as obvious as they need to be, it was confirmed last night.

As the emergency services braced themselves for three days of complete and utter chaos, experts said the government had done everything it possibly could short of strapping everyone to a chair and feeding them pulped turkey through a tube.

Professor Henry Brubaker, of the Institute for Studies, said: "You will notice page five of the *Daily Mail* carries an angry story about 'why oh why does the government have to treat us like Christmas morons?'.

"But if you then turn over to page six you will see a story about a man from Dorset who called the fire brigade after shoving at least 18 inches of Norwegian Spruce firmly up his back passage.

"Page seven is devoted to the Yorkshire family who celebrate Boxing Day by piling all the empty boxes in the middle of the living room before setting fire to them.

"And we then turn over to a double-page spread featuring a heart-breaking interview with the sole survivor of the Great

O Christmas Tree! O Christmas Tree! How far can I get you up my bum?

Hemel Hempstead Turkey Disaster of 1983."

A department of health spokesman said: "Instead of a real Christmas tree this year why not go for a small, laminated photograph of a Christmas tree? Leave it floating in a bucket of water in case you're tempted to set fire to it.

"And if you're worried about food poisoning from an undercooked turkey, just eat a load of crisps instead. But not the sharp ones. Go for a soft, round crisp like a Wotsit or a Quaver. And don't forget to keep a bucket water nearby in case you're tempted to set fire to them."

Somebody sells a house

THE British economy turned a corner last night after somebody sold a house.

The prime minister said it marked the 'beginning of the end of the beginning' as the FTSE 100 climbed by 12 points and then stayed there for 20 minutes.

The sale was completed shortly after midday, but was kept under wraps until Downing Street had been informed.

It was finally confirmed in a newsflash from the Press Association at 1.26pm.

The soon-to-be-former owner Tom Logan said: "We had given up hope, what with the banks being shits and everything.

"But then this couple turned up, had a poke around in the kitchen, fiddled with the central heating, flushed the toilet and then suddenly said, 'we'd like to buy it.'

"My wife collapsed, I got a nose bleed and the dog started howling like a coyote."

By late afternoon a large and boisterous crowd had

Princess Anne will visit the house later today.

gathered outside the detached cottage in the Home Counties village of Minchinhamptonsteadbury as Mr and Mrs Logan gave interviews to Le Monde, CNN and Japan's TV-Osaka.

Burger vans and buskers soon cashed-in on the celebration while quick-witted entrepreneurs sold mugs, baseball hats and souvenir flags immortalising 'The House That Someone Bought'.

Mr Logan added: "I've no idea where they got the money from. Maybe they're drug dealers. Good luck to them."

CHERYL COLE TO WATCH CHILDREN CRY

GIRLS Aloud singer Cheryl Cole is to star in a new ITV prime-time show where she stares at children while they burst into tears.

Starting in the new year, *Cheryl Cole Watches Children Crying* will be the network's Saturday night flagship alongside *Ant and Dec's Piss-Factor* and the celebrity jungle show *Big Wet Tits*.

Producer Julian Cook said: "The child will be placed on a stool in front of a beautifully made-up Cheryl and then the researcher will do something to make it cry.

"Perhaps we'll tell them their cat is very, very sick or that mummy and daddy are getting a divorce and it's all their fault.

"And sometimes we'll just have someone dressed as a blood-soaked zombie who will run towards the child screaming as loudly as possible."

Cook added: "As the child begins to weep the camera will cut back and forth, keeping an eye on Cheryl as she wells-up, until finally we get the 'money shot' and she starts bawling her eyes out."

Cole said last night: "Babe, am really lookin' forward to watchin' these little kiddies cryin', like, cause they totally deserve it, they really do. Am so proud of yeez."

The show will also feature members of the public being stopped in the street and shown photos of a dead puppy in a bucket. Whoever cries the quickest each week will win £10,000.

Meanwhile anyone who does not cry will be hounded to the brink of insanity by News International.

Prince Philip alters will

PRINCE PHILIP has changed his will in order to bequeath his extensive collection of racist paraphernalia to his favourite grandson.

The move comes after Prince Harry was caught on camera using racially offensive language to the shock and surprise of absolutely no-one.

According to Palace insiders Philip considered changing his will four years ago after Harry asked to borrow his dress Swastika, but decided to wait and see if the young prince developed the maturity to wield fully formed racial slurs.

Now Harry is set to inherit Philip's prized copy of *From Abo to Zorba: The Illustrated Dictionary of Racial Epithets*, as well as his silver-plated Jew-detector and his Coolie stick.

Constitutional expert Denys Finch-Hatton said: "Philip loves nothing more than rummaging around in jumble sales looking for racist knick-knacks from the 1920s.

"Indeed, one of his most common complaints in recent years is how no-one makes a decent pair of wog-shackles any more."

Finch-Hatton added: "Of course he's delighted at the way Harry has turned out. Since the Queen Mother died there are very few people he can talk to about darkies and chinks.

"In fact I'm sure if he could, Philip would even change the order of the succession, missing out both Charles and William, who he regards as little better than gay communists."

Meanwhile Harry is to be disciplined by his regiment and given special training in how to be racist without recording the whole thing on video.

Brown sectioned

PRIME minister Gordon Brown was last night under observation in a London psychiatric hospital after claiming to be Spiderman.

Mr Brown told the Commons that he had 'vanquished' both Doctor Octopus and the Green Goblin through a combination of superhuman agility and a strange 'sixth sense' he acquired after being bitten by an irradiated spider.

He added: "I can also swing between skyscrapers and I'm very good at science. Have you guessed who I am yet?"

As Commons security staff moved towards him, the prime minister ran from the chamber, throwing his briefing notes in the air and removing his shirt and tie.

Mr Brown was finally captured when he attempted to scale the outside of the Palace of Westminster before falling and twisting his knee.

As he was handcuffed and helped into the back of an ambulance he shouted: "You have bound my hands because you are scared I will use one of my sticky webs!"

A Downing Street source said: "Some days he would claim to be Doctor Octopus and make all these terrible decisions and say, 'only Spiderman can stop me'. And then he'd wink at us."

The prime minister was admitted to a secure unit and will undergo tests later today

The source added: "Spiderman was just one of his incarnations. For much of July he thought he was either Dangermouse or Count Duckula."

A police spokesman said last night: "A 57-year-old man from Central London was this evening taken into protective custody under Section 4 of the Mental Health Act."

UK MATHS FAILURES COST ECONOMY REALLY BIG NUMBER
City accountants Madeley-Finnegan confirmed that since 1999 the number of children with poor numeracy had risen from five out of ten to 50% – an increase of nearly a double

JAGUAR TO KEEP MAKING CARS NO-ONE CAN AFFORD
Business secretary Peter Mandelson announced that it was vital that Britain retained the skills and technology to produce a wide range of pointless vehicles that cost more than the average salary to insure

ONLY TWELVE MORE BANK BAIL-OUTS TO GO, PROMISES DARLING
"The fifth will look very like the second and the fourth but it will have at least one extra zero. The sixth is very similar to the third but with a Wimbledon fortnight theme and the seventh – well that's just an absolute beauty," says chancellor

BRITAIN TO TAKE TWO YEARS OFF
With the government now willing to pick up the tab for everything, millions of Britons are this morning telling their bosses to piss up a rope

MICROSOFT LAUNCH RANGE OF CLOTHING THAT DOESN'T WORK
Early purchasers complained the new shirts from the IT giant were slow and difficult to use and that many came without neck holes, forcing them to wear the t-shirt on their head

Sky to show man going to the toilet

THE exact moment that a man goes to the toilet will be shown on television tonight.

Sky TV viewers will see retired engineer Julian Cook finish a bowl of bran flakes before picking up a copy of *Practical Fishkeeping* and leaving the kitchen.

The camera then follows him into the downstairs bathroom where he will be shown pulling down his trousers and underpants. Minutes later it becomes clear that he has gone to the toilet.

But the controversial film has been attacked by church groups, TV watchdogs and anti-going to the toilet campaigners.

Bill McKay, the director of Holding It In, said: "This programme suggests that going to the toilet is somehow perfectly natural, when as a society we should be embracing the idea of holding it in for as long as possible."

Monsignor Stephen Malley, adviser to the Christian Medical Institute, said: "Going to the toilet is a sin and I've no doubt Mr Cook will have a lovely time explaining himself to Satan."

Meanwhile a spokesman for Ofcom said: "Our guidelines are very clear. You can screen a fictional portrayal of going to the toilet and make it as realistic as you want – with all the noises and the toilet paper – but you must not show someone actually going to the toilet."

But Mr Cook's wife Elizabeth insisted that going to the toilet is 'part of the journey of life'.

She added: "Julian wanted to provoke a debate about the inevitability of expelling waste. He was also absolutely bursting.

"It's his lower intestine and his bottom and, with all due respect, he should be allowed to go to the toilet whenever he wants.

"I can understand that some people might not want to see that, but they don't have to watch."

Asian monkey coup

MONKEYS controlled much of eastern Asia last night after launching a series of swift and ruthless coups d'état.

The rebellion began in China when three monkeys turned on their trainer and beat him with his own stick. Within hours monkeys across the continent were seizing control through a combination of airborne faeces and badly driven tanks.

Police stations across Indonesia and southern Thailand were last night in monkey hands while a troop of Sri Lankan spider monkeys has taken over the state broadcaster and another controls the country's railway network.

The simian rebellion is being directed by a highly intelligent two-year-old Indian macaque, already dubbed 'Chico the monkey Hitler'.

In Singapore a local police chief returned to work after lunch to find eight monkeys jumping all over his desk. He tried to coax them by making friendly noises and offering them peanuts. Two hours later he appeared

Hitler

cowering in a window with a gun to his head.

Monkey expert Dr Tom Logan, said: "Monkeys are sociable creatures who spend their days playing, foraging for berries, and grooming each other. But don't fuck with them 'cause they will shoot you."

At the United Nations in New York, monkey countries appealed desperately to non-monkey countries for help.

Indian ambassador Rajeev Chandra held up a large photo of a police car covered in monkeys, adding: "They tried driving it but one of them set off the siren and they all scattered, before slowly coming back and trying again.

"Eventually they are going to get the hang of it."

Everything now a huge lie

EVERYTHING you have ever been told is a colossal lie and the global economy is a $100 trillion fraud, it was confirmed last night.

Experts said everyone you come into contact with is trying to con you, but stressed you're one to talk because you're trying to con everyone else.

And they warned the lying would continue indefinitely as nobody would be able to stop lying because everyone would just assume that was a lie and so they may as well just keep on lying.

Professor Henry Brubaker, of the Institute for Studies, said: "Essentially our entire socio-economic system is what we call a 'pyramid scheme', also known as a 'Poncey scheme' or a 'bunch of ponces'.

"All types of credit and investments are, of course, based on utter lies. Meanwhile everything you buy in the shops is worth about one tenth what you paid for it and bears no relation to the advert, which was obviously a lie from start to finish.

"All the major professions are lying to you constantly, your friends despise you, there was no Jesus, there is no global warming and there was no moon landing. But it wasn't faked either, work that one out.

"And you're at it too. Last Thursday you claimed to have a 'stomach bug'. That was bollocks. Shut up, yes it was.

"And even when you're at work you do as little as possible and spend the rest of your day concocting a series of elaborate excuses, before going to the pub and lying your face off. But it's okay, because so does absolutely everyone else."

He added: "Of course you're no doubt thinking that all of this is a lie. Well I can assure it isn't. Or is it? Or isn't it? Or is it? Aaaaaah."

Did Nasa fake the moon landing to cover up even bigger lies?

KNIGHTHOOD FOR CHILD WHO MADE OWN BED EVERY DAY FOR A WEEK

JACK Logan, the child who made his own bed every day for a week, has been knighted in the New Year's honours list.

Ten-year-old Logan said he was thrilled but surprised to receive the honour, insisting he was only doing what he was paid to do.

Sir Jack added: "I am very well compensated for my bed making, as you can see from these excellent new trainers, so it feels a bit weird to be knighted as well.

"I just hope this honour can help to raise the profile of British bed-making and inspire lots of other children to make their beds for more than two days in a row. London 2012 here we come!"

There were also MBEs for eight-year-old Sally McKay and 12-year-old Josh Hayes who both helped their fathers wash the car.

Meanwhile three-year-old Ben Malley becomes a CBE for going pee-pees all by himself.

Grown-up honours include Led Zeppelin frontman Robert Plant, awarded a CBE for not choking on his own vomit, while actor Michael Sheen gets an OBE for playing the actor Michael Sheen in *Michael Sheen: The Michael Sheen Story*.

Elsewhere top Treasury mandarin Nick McPherson is knighted for 'services to going to lots of meetings and writing stuff down while the country turned to shit'.

But there was disappointment for veteran entertainer Bruce Forsyth who was once again rejected for a knighthood as both Downing Street and the Palace continued to frown upon his support for the Khmer Rouge in the early 1970s.

Try not to vomit on each other, say docs

OFFICE workers can halt the spread of the winter vomiting virus by not vomiting on each other, doctors said last night.

NHS Direct issued urgent advice amid predictions there was going to be loads and loads of sick everywhere.

Dr Tom Logan, chairman of the department of health's vomit committee, said: "The quickest way for this virus to spread is for you to go into work while you're infected and start puking all over everyone's desks.

"The chances are you'll also have chucked-up over all the people on the bus and have left little puddles of sick between the bus stop and the office."

Dr Logan added: "I know you really want to come into work while you're being turned inside out, but the fact is

This photo of Harriet Harman won't exactly help

you're not helping. Indeed, I would go so far as to say you are vomit's accomplice.

"So the key thing we have to remember here is: Don't keep vomiting over everybody.

"Instead, stay at home, watch telly, drink plenty of luke warm yogurt and direct your jet of sick into a basin."

HOW TO TELL IF YOU HAVE THE WINTER VOMITING VIRUS
A four-point guide from the Daily Mash

1. Are you vomiting?
2. Are you still vomiting?
3. Are you thinking that you're never going to stop vomiting?
4. Are you now wallowing in a terrifyingly huge amount of vomit?
You have the winter vomiting virus. Well done.

West Coast mainline designated national metaphor

BRITAIN'S piece of shit west coast railway line has been designated as the country's latest national metaphor.

Officials say the pathetically bad multi-billion pound engineering project can now be used to sum up early 21st century Britain as a place where everything is expensive but nothing actually works.

The West Coast mainline becomes Britain's 27th national metaphor since the end of the Second World War and the first new metaphor since Tim Henman tried really hard at tennis but was obviously just not quite good enough in 2004.

Julian Cook, director of the Office of National Metaphors, said: "It is the perfect combination of gigantic amounts of public money coupled with the gnawing inevitability of failure and disappointment.

"It's probably the best one since the M25 was completed and became this huge, grey, hell on earth, filled with angry, depressed people unable to find a way out.

"The West Coast mainline even has the chance of a second designation at some point in the future as they will no doubt get it working properly only to start fucking about with it again for no reason."

A blue plaque will be erected at Euston Station in London to commemorate the designation with the quote 'Britain and the West Coast Main Line – expensive, badly designed and not as good as France'.

Mr Cook added: "Of course we're all just building up to the 2012 Olympics which I suspect will make all previous national metaphors seem devastatingly obsolete."

Emma Thompson to decide where you go on holiday

OSCAR winner Emma Thompson is to chair a new committee which will decide where you spend your summer holidays.

The Thompson committee will publish a list of approved destinations in January each year, along with a recommended mode of low-carbon transport.

Thompson, who swims to all of her filming locations around the world, said: "I had the idea while I was swimming the Atlantic en route to the Golden Globe awards in Beverly Hills.

"I phoned Stephen Fry for advice but he said he couldn't talk because he was in New Zealand making a documentary about parrots. I said 'I hope you swam there' and he assured me that he had."

She added: "Unless you're a very good swimmer, like me, I'm afraid your choices will be rather limited.

"For 2009 we're looking at Widnes, Harrogate and Dundee. We've also got two weeks on a park bench in Port Talbot, working your way through a meat paste sandwich while it absolutely pisses down.

"France is really only really available to the strongest swimmers amongst us, and if you are also planning to travel on to the Dordogne you will have to allow for an extra eight weeks' walking time.

"Or you could just stay at home and watch me and Will Ferrell in *Stranger than Fiction* which we filmed in the magnificent city of Chicago. That was a lovely swim."

Councils to position skip full of shit outside your house

COUNCILS across Britain are to save millions of pounds by placing a massive skip chock full of rotting chicken carcasses and used incontinence pants at your front door.

Officials say the 3200-litre communal waste bins will help to reduce the cost of the one thing you are actually happy to pay them to do properly.

Council tax payer Bill McKay, from Brighton, said: "I pay about two grand a year in the full knowledge that the vast majority of it will be wasted in the most insultingly gratuitous fashion, but that they will, at least, come along once a week and empty my wheelie bin.

"Now I will open my front door to be greeted by a huge, black shitbox, which, I have no doubt, will very quickly become a nightclub/vomitorium/bed and breakfast for the local vagrancy and their pet rats."

Each bin will save £50,000 a year and can hold up to a quarter of a million rat babies

But the Local Government Association (LGA) insists that the savings can be diverted into other priorities including a new taskforce designed to increase the number of midgets in the House of Lords.

An LGA spokesman said: "There seems to be a misconception that councils are somehow there to provide services and do things that people want.

"This is the 21st century. There are more important things we can do with taxpayers' money than go around picking up individual wheelie-bins from outside people's houses and then emptying them into the back of some large outdated truck.

"For example, very few of our cherished local libraries have an interactive display about the history of anal sex. And then, of course, there's my pension."

Mr McKay added: "Just empty my fucking bins."

School subjects to be dicked to be about with

BRITAIN'S primary school curriculum is to be radically reformed after ministers realised they hadn't dicked about with it for at least a year.

From next year the school day will be split into broad themes including noises, shapes, colours, feelings and relentless political indoctrination.

The six brand new subject areas are:

Noises: Moo. Baa. Grrr. Vroom. Plop. These are all noises. Make three of them before lunch.

Shapes: What shape is a lesbian? Are circles French? What rights does a triangle have? Will also cover the shapes of numbers, although the sound of numbers will be covered in Noises.

Colours: The children will be encouraged to mix blue with yellow and green with orange as a way of understanding contraception and exotic sexual positions.

Feelings and Flavours: Does seven taste of cheese? Does spelling make you sad and angry? Let's not do it then.

Nintendo: Everything else is covered by some sort of Nintendo game, so teachers can stand at the back door smoking cigarettes and booking holidays.

The Conservatives last night attacked the proposals and set out their own curriculum, including money, standing up straight, poof-spotting, advanced money and remembering the names of staff.

M&S staff to be sacked by Dervla Kirwan

MARKS and Spencer is to use Irish actress Dervla Kirwan to sack more than 1,200 workers.

Managers hope Kirwan's sexy but soothing voice will not only minimise the shock of redundancy but ensure the ex-workers continue to spend what little money they have in the company's stores.

Head office staff will be sacked in person by Kirwan, while shop floor workers will be dismissed seductively via webcam.

Senior staff can choose to be sacked by Kirwan as she pours thick Devonshire double cream over their head and then licks it off while whispering 'you're fired' in their ear.

Or they can watch Kirwan fashion the words 'you're fired' from a healthy dollop of spring onion mash before drizzling it with a red wine gravy and then sucking it off a spoon.

An M&S spokesman said: "It's very important that we retain the brand loyalty of

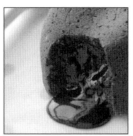

A spokesman said: 'We want this process to be as chocolatey as possible'

the people we're discarding. Redundancy money is as good as any other money.

"If you've been trudging the cold streets all day looking for a job what you really need is a piping hot chicken and mushroom pie made with succulent free range corn-fed chicken breast, fresh, fragrant chanterelle mushrooms and a moist, buttery short crust pastry."

The spokesman added: "And, of course, when you're unemployed the last thing you need is to be confronted with the soul-destroying horror of an unpeeled carrot."

TREASURY HAS BEEN ABLE TO PRINT TENNERS ALL ALONG

CHANCELLOR Alistair Darling has admitted the economic downturn was completely unnecessary as all this time he could just have printed more tenners.

Mr Darling said he found out about the money printing machine last summer but then forgot to mention it because he had been given so much work to do by the prime minister.

He added: "Last Friday I was visiting a school in my constituency when one of the children asked why I didn't just print more money, and I suddenly thought, 'Oh Christ, there's that great big machine in the basement'."

Across the country consumers were last night breathing a sigh of relief as Bank of England governor Mervyn King admitted the financial crisis had been a lot of fuss about nothing

Tom Logan, from West London, said: "If it's just a case of printing it, I'll have six million please.

"I don't suppose there's any way you can print some with my face on it? Or perhaps just a pair of titties?"

Bill McKay, from Leeds, said: "How much do I get and where do I go to collect it? Or can they just pop it in the post? How much do I get?"

But economists warned that printing new currency could create a confluence of hyperinflationary factors leading to a collapse in sterling and the entire country being consumed by an unquenchable fire.

Emma Bradford, from Stoke, added: "I've absolutely no idea what you're talking about. Just give me the money."

Estate agents now showing houses to other estate agents

BRITAIN'S estate agents are showing houses to each other in a bid to combat loneliness and prevent their traditional skills from dying out.

With house sales non-existent there is mounting concern the ancient arts of describing the different rooms inside a property and then walking around it with someone could soon become extinct.

Last night estate agent Tom Logan told estate agent Bill McKay this was a charming property that had undergone extensive renovation and although it

was at the upper end of his budget he should really have a look at it.

McKay agreed that the renovations have been done tastefully but wondered what he would do with this large room that contained both a cooker and a refrigerator.

Logan explained that this room was a kitchen where McKay would be able to store and prepare food.

He then directed McKay to a large cupboard under the stairs that not only contained a toilet but had storage room for cloaks and other outdoor garments.

'Now, tell me, is this one of the bedrooms?'

McKay said this was a useful feature but stressed he was particularly keen to discover if the house included any rooms where he could put a bed for the purposes of sleeping.

Logan said the house

had three rooms which fitted this description as well as an additional room which contained similar equipment to the cloak storage area but also included a long, white pot that could be filled with hot water.

McKay said the pot seemed big enough to hold an adult human and that the room would be perfect for personal cleansing, as well as the expulsion of waste.

Logan agreed and said he was looking forward to phoning McKay eight times a day until he agreed to put in an offer.

Macheda could be 'first-class, money-grabbing arsehole'

Macheda is looking forward to making his coach very angry about Real Madrid

FEDERICO Macheda has the potential to become one of the greediest tosspots in the Premier League, his agent said last night.

Julian Cook said the Manchester United striker was a 'really exciting talent' who, with the right guidance, would just get more and more selfish and obsessed with money with every passing year.

The Italian has burst onto the scene at Old Trafford by becoming only the 4,825th striker to score against both Aston Villa and Sunderland.

Macheda said: "Already I put myself way before my team. My hair looks like a deep-fried kitten and I am happy to be paid no more than the GDP of Sweden, or maybe Portugal."

The striker hopes to sign a five-year contract worth £1m a year, which he then plans to renege on for more money some time in 2011.

He is already in talks with several clubs he intends to betray United fans for, and has lined up top-flight denials from Juventus, Barcelona and AC Milan.

Cook moved into football representation from the music industry, where he negotiated a six-album, £12m deal for Spanish novelty band Las Ketchup following their hit 'The Ketchup Song'.

He insisted Macheda's contract is 'good for the club, good for the fans and good for my childish obsession with absurdly expensive cars'.

Meanwhile Lazio have lodged a formal complaint regarding United's handling of Macheda. A spokesman said: "They treat the boy like a piece of meat when he was contracted to be our piece of meat for another two years."

Michael Vaughan retires again

CRICKET fans were shocked last night after Michael Vaughan announced his retirement for what they were sure was at least the fourth time.

The former England captain said he wanted to spend more time with his family, standing in the back garden for 20 minutes with a confused look on his face before wandering back into the house while shaking his head.

Vaughan added: "I think I still have what it takes to look confused at that level", before retiring from back garden cricket for the first time.

His latest retirement follows his failure to be considered for the Ashes squad after scoring fewer runs this year than Michael Owen has scored goals while having hamstrings made from squeezy cheese.

Vaughan will be remembered for failing to lose on home territory to an Australian side riddled with injury. He was awarded the OBE shortly after for 'Services to stopping England giving up cricket altogether and inventing a new sport they can be best at for a few years until everyone else gets the hang of it'.

An ECB spokesman said: "As wretched as the current England squad

To many England fans Michael Vaughan will always be a golfer

is – and make no mistake they're about as much use as WG Grace's after shave balm – Michael now makes them look like a pantheon of invincible Greek deities."

The spokesman insisted the squad still had an outside chance of scoring a run against Australia this summer if they could just get the top end of the batting order to stop treating the ball like a tiny child.

NEWS BRIEFLY

SCIENTISTS UNVEIL ENERGY EFFICIENT PORNO-KETTLE
Environmentally-conscious onanists can now combine their two favourite pastimes – drinking endless cups of tea and wanking like a death row inmate with a copy of *Nuts* – while saving the Earth

ONE IN THREE YOUNG ADULTS BEGGING FOR A KICK IN THE TEETH
According to a survey by the Prince's Trust a third of young people are less happy than they were as a child, mainly because they are now expected to pay for a lot of their own stuff

MI5 CHIEF INCREDIBLY BALD
"Baldness is a state of mind. We live in a post-bald era that requires post-bald thinking," says Lib Dem leader

The Hubble Telescope has captured the first faint image of a planet outside our solar system. Now scientists are asking how long it will be before alien civilisations...

PRETEND THEY'RE NOT IN

YOUR PROBLEMS SOLVED
with HOLLY HARPER

Dear Holly,

Last weekend I was on a night out with the girls to celebrate my 36th birthday. Clad arse-to-tit in neon lycra, I must have cast a highly alluring shadow across the dancefloor as I limboed to Britney Spears, because next thing I knew, I was on all fours behind a skip being pummelled vigorously from behind by some random teenage drunkard.

Hardly noticing that I was kneeling in a spilt cocktail of urine and vomit, I panted like a spaniel with heatstroke as he shot his load across my back and staggered away. The problem is that since this brief encounter, I've developed a rather embarrassing condition whereby my clacker is itchier than a vagrant's arsehole. Can you suggest why this might be?

Sue
Penzance

Dear Sue,

Hasn't your mummy ever warned you that boys are dirty and you should stay well away from them?

They are made of frogs and snails and puppy dog tails. Once, an older boy from my school picked up a big dry piece of dog poo with a stick and threw it at me, and it got caught in my hair – my new princess clip was ruined! I was forced to get my revenge by telling my mummy that he trapped me in the art cupboard and put the end of his willy in my mouth.

Guess what? He got taken away from school the next day and mummy says he's gone to a place where he can't hurt little girls anymore. I feel a little bit naughty for fibbing, but I bet he rues the day he flung a jobby at me.

Hope that helps!

Holly

YOUR ASTROLOGICAL WEEK AHEAD
with PSYCHIC BOB

Taurus
You have arrived at a point of power. Take the funny three-pronged thing attached to the plastic string and stick it in. Now can you see the ghost-people talking in the box?

Gemini
Shut down all the garbage mashers on the detention level!

Cancer
Stick work on the back burner, you have parties to make, children's festivities to attend, lovers to seduce. But for the love of Christ don't get the last two mixed up like last time.

Leo
Pluto stimulates your ambitions and self-belief, but the Moon keeps on saying you are a worthless heap of shit.

Virgo
Jupiter, the planet of expansion, meets Neptune the god of small, oddly shaped blue pills promising a firm but ultimately lengthy and painful erection.

Libra
An intriguing week for news: Phil Woolas and his solid gold toaster, something to do with Joanna Lumley and a snake, and lots of dragons. But nothing here as regards you. Perhaps you're dead.

Scorpio
Aries makes his way back into your partnership house, falls over in his duffel coat while trying to take off his boots, and then lies there laughing and stinking of drink, the thoughtless prick.

Sagittarius
Here's a good week to show off your good taste, charm and creativity. Assuming you have any.

Capricorn
Mercury has reversed into Taurus, they have exchanged insurance details but, oh no, the god of communication forgot to post off the cheque with his renewal form. Not so smug now is he?

Aquarius
Someone has drawn a pair of hairy planets hovering around the base of a huge rocket with what looks like sparks coming out of its unusually bulbous nose on my front door. What can it mean?

Pisces
Tiptoe around significant others and they may not realise it is four in the morning and you have just come back from the office party with your pants on inside out.

Aries
Venus and Mars bring a goat to the hall. Which is fine, but why are you always the one who has to kidnap the virgin?

The Daily Mash

MICHAEL JACKSON DIES IN SHOCKINGLY NORMAL FASHION

MICHAEL Jackson, the King of Pop, shocked the world last night by dying in an incredibly ordinary way.

His millions of fans were stunned after the singer died of a very normal heart attack instead of electrocuting himself while re-enacting scenes from *The Wizard of Oz* with a cast of under-age giraffes.

The heart, Jackson's last original body part, was due to perform in London next month where it was expected to pump blood to a pair of new legs, a borrowed arm and the 14th version of the singer's face.

In Los Angeles, as preparations began for the funeral, a spokesman for the Jackson family said: "While we want to respect Michael's wishes we may have to abandon his desire to have the coffin carried by eight chimpanzees. I don't think he really thought that one through."

But it is understood Jackson will be buried in his favourite Peter Pan costume in a bid to ensure that his last journey is as weird and freaky as possible.

Uri Geller, Jackson's friend and now acting King

You can finally admit to knowing all the words to *Thriller* **again**

of the Freaks, said: "I feel so desperately sorry for all the freaks today. He was their Diana, their Elvis, their Mother Teresa and their Jade Goody all rolled into one. Which is actually what he looked like too. Check out this spoon."

In Hollywood dozens of other stars paid their tributes, describing him as a genius, an inspiration and the sort of very close friend you did not need to have your picture taken with.

Later today thousands of fans are expected to gather outside Neverland, the singer's former home and shout 'ee-hee' in unison, while in London, tabloid newspaper editors are bidding over a grainy image, supposedly taken this morning, showing Jackson still very much alive and part of a travelling band of Bulgarian circus folk.

Meanwhile at Madame Tussauds wax museum, security guards are standing

by to prevent visitors poking the Michael Jackson statue amid rumours the singer had finally found the perfect hiding place.

On the internet, chat forums were awash with Jackson tributes from people who were convinced he was a pervert and wanted him strung up, but who were now desperate to tell the world that he was a victim of the media and that *Thriller* was a ground-breaking work of genius.

Jen, from Milwaukee, wrote: "As you said Michael, Billie Jean was not your lover and neither was Macaulay Culkin, regardless of what I may or may not have written on my blog four years ago. I hope you find peace in freak heaven."

Pete, from London, said: "The way you danced like a zombie changed the way people thought about dancing like a zombie forever. Rest in Pop."

And Sam, from Rio de Janeiro, added: "You were my heart. I love you sing. You make special times but now you in heaven with all the children. Try not feel them up. God can see your hands now."

Thought for the day: Before you embark on a journey of revenge, dig two graves. And make a sandwich. (Confucius)

Ronaldo joins queue for Paris Hilton's vagina

CRISTIANO Ronaldo celebrated his record-breaking £80m move to Real Madrid last night by joining the early morning queue outside Paris Hilton's private parts.

The former Manchester United winger was spotted flirting with the hotel heiress in an LA nightclub as the two laughed as they discussed what it's like to be an empty shell of a human being with no concept of the value of anything.

Martin Bishop, a leading Hiltonologist, said: "It's a very special moment in a young man's life when he becomes famous enough to join the queue for Paris Hilton's vagina.

"I'm pleased to see he got there at 3am – nice and early. At that time of day he would only have had to queue for about an hour and a half.

"The waiting isn't too bad. They have snacks and magazines and there's usually a couple of buskers and a clown who does magic."

Bishop said Ronaldo would have been in the queue behind three or four baseball players, half a dozen drummers, at least two European princes and, as it was a Thursday, Charlie Sheen.

"He will eventually have moved from the garden into the lobby into the undressing area, at which point he he will have stripped to his socks before having his genitals hosed down with Mr Muscle.

"After that it's straight into the mounting zone for eight to ten minutes of perfunctory intercourse, followed by a souvenir photo, a quick cup of tea and a biscuit."

He added: "They can put the condom in a doggy bag for you, or you can choose to pin it on the 'Wall of Fame'. It's really well organised."

Ronaldo moves from the hosing area to the mounting zone.

Britain now the drunk woman at a party

BRITAIN is now the noisy, emotional drunk woman at a party, according to a major new report.

The New York-based International Institute for Studies said Britain had obviously been drinking before she arrived and was now starting to make everyone uncomfortable.

Professor Todd Brubaker said: "One minute she's dancing with the fat man, the next minute she's pointing at him and shouting 'look at the fat man trying to dance'."

"Then she goes round the room telling everyone else they have to dance with the fat man because now she's in charge of the party."

Professor Brubaker added: "Then she gets all serious and goes on and on about all the money she's got on her credit cards and if the government can pay off the banks' credit cards then they should pay off hers as well because she really needs one of those new hairdryers with the built-in conditioner thing.

"Then she flirts pathetically with that really cool guy that's just arrived before striding into the kitchen and telling everyone he fancies her but don't say anything to him because he'll just deny it.

"Eventually she starts bawling uncontrollably because some woman that she never met has just died and then staggers outside to vomit all over the gas barbecue.

"And the whole time you're just looking at her in horror and thinking to yourself, 'God, I really hope she doesn't have any kids'."

President Barack Obama welcomed the report, adding that one of his earliest priorities will be to put Britain into a taxi.

'I'm fine, seriously'

Dame Judi Dench to host charity swearathon

ACTRESS Dame Judi Dench is to host this year's BAFTA Swearathon, it has been confirmed.

The event, now enjoying its 23rd year, promotes awareness of dirty, filthy words and the people who say them, while raising much needed funds to protect old and endangered swear words like 'fuckle', 'arseclams' and 'Jeffrey Archer'.

Speaking at a press conference at the Theatre Royal, Dame Judi said: "I remember when I first read the script for *Shakespeare in Love*. It was marvellous of course, but I did feel the need to phone up the lovely Tom Stoppard and ask him why he had left out the word 'c**t'.

"'Tommy', I said, 'could you be an absolute darling and shove in a couple of c**ts and a titwank, just for me?'."

Dame Judi, Britain's most repulsively foul-mouthed actress since Olivia De Havilland, said: "This is such an important event for all of us who enjoy using words like 'fucknut', 'spunk-monkey' and 'dirty great pishflaps'.

"My dear friend Tom Hanks will perform a delightful Cole Porter duet with my other dear friend Gwyneth Paltrow, but he will change the lyrics so he can call her a 'simpering, minge-faced shitweasel'.

"My great friend James Blunt has very kindly offered

'Couple of c**ts and a titwank'

to play some of his greatest hits, during which members of the audience will be encouraged to drown him out by screaming the word 'cocksucker' at him, over and over again.

"And my very dear friend Robert Carlyle has agreed to delight us with one of his expert demonstrations of traditional Glaswegian swearing. I'd be tempted to let the children stay up for that one."

Dame Judi added: "Fuck the lot of you, fuck you right up the shitter."

Prince Charles gets more talking shit money

PRINCE Charles received £3m in talking shit money last year, according to latest accounts.

The heir to the throne saw a 25% increase in the public grant he receives to flit between his giant houses while saying whatever happens to be passing through his brain at the time.

Supporters insist he has been talking some top quality shit over the last year, from his prediction the world would end in 2050 to his masterful destruction of a vitally important building project in West London.

In between he has attacked the 'cult of consumerism' which helps to deliver his £3m a year, while continuing to have more possessions than most of the people who have ever lived.

Royal expert Denys Finch-Hatton said: "When someone agrees to deliver a keynote speech on the importance of cutting CO2

The fondness for Aston Martins has always been a fairly large clue

emissions and then turns up in an Aston Martin, you can be fairly confident they are going to brim-full of utter shit."

Clarence House said the Prince has managed to fit in a surprisingly huge amount of talking shit this year, given his other heavy commitments in the fields of skiing and fucking-up foxes.

Meanwhile the Prince also managed to trim his costs by spending his

holidays in a British castle attended by just four dozen chefs, butlers, spoon polishers and highly trained crack-spongers.

Republican campaigner Bill McKay said: "People hark back to his days of chatting to plants, but that's just a meagre handful of rat droppings compared to his musings on education, architecture and the environment.

"Some say that if we got

rid of the monarchy it would be replaced with something just as expensive, but at least we'd be able to choose the person who talks a lot of shit all the time."

He added: "Surely his talking shit could be financed from all the money he collects selling organic honey made by his army of musical bees at £15 a jar."

MARTIN CLUNES PAID A SMALL FORTUNE TO REMIND PEOPLE EXACTLY HOW GOOD LEONARD ROSSITER WAS

"I didn't get where I am today by not pissing licence payers' money away on an endless series of pointless remakes," says BBC arse.

Police 'not letting you have a go of their tasers'

SENIOR police officers last night said there was no way you were getting a go of their tasers despite new data showing they are even more fun than previously believed.

Statistics, released under the Freedom of Information Act, show that 74% of taser injuries during 2008 were sustained to the buttocks in police station recreation rooms.

And in the second half of last year over 220 police officers sustained tongue injuries after their fellow officers dared them to see what electricity tasted like.

Metropolitan Police Commissioner Sir Paul Stephenson said: "These are not toys, even if they are brilliant fun and it was mental the time I used mine to knock an owl straight out of a tree.

"However, there's absolutely no way that I would ever condone incidents like

They're just owls,' said Sir Paul

the time we took ours to Longleat and did target practice on otters while reciting one-liners from Jason Statham movies."

One constable, from Hertfordshire, said: "No fucking chance. I let my brother in law hold it briefly on his birthday but that's it.

"If someone in the pub asks I tell them it's strictly for official police use, and they nod in agreement and then I shoot them in the nuts."

He added: "When they're on the deck spazzing out I'll stand over them, blow an imaginary wisp of smoke off the end of the barrel and say either 'I vanquish thee' or 'your powers are weak old man' and everyone laughs their tits off.

"And you should see what it does to a toad."

Steve Jobs forced to accept badly designed liver

APPLE boss Steve Jobs was last night recovering well despite being forced to accept a transplanted liver that was badly designed and with limited scope for expensive upgrades.

The billionaire businessman had asked medical staff at the hospital in Tennessee to find him a liver that was small, sleek, beautifully white and effortlessly stylish.

But after six months of searching he was forced to accept that a liver is an ugly, misshapen purple blob with the unmistakable look and feel of a large piece of slippery meat.

Dr Tom Logan, the hospital's director of livers, said: "He gave us a sketch of his ideal liver and I have to admit that if livers were made of shiny, moulded plastic it would have changed the way we use livers forever.

"He then asked if the liver could at least be transplanted inside a sleek, white box with a small LED screen and a single white button that activates each of its 243 functions, but we said no, if we did that he would die incredibly quickly.

"While his new liver may not have the exciting functionality and sleek user interface of an iPod, an iPhone or an iSpleen, it is quite good at plasma protein synthesis, hormone production and detoxification, which is pretty much what you want a liver to do."

Dr Logan said that if the hospital had used Mr Jobs' liver design, "it would be bit like designing a mobile phone which could take photographs, surf the internet and give you directions to trendy restaurants, but would not actually be a particularly good phone".

Despite its lack of sleekness Jobs is understood to be fascinated by his new liver and has asked Pixar, his hi-tech animation studio, to begin developing *Organ Story*, the touching tale of a young boy who keeps a box full of kidneys under his bed.

Dr Logan added: "We gave him a liver which basically does the same thing as all the other livers but charged him twice as much as all the other hospitals. I'm sure he won't mind."

The iSpleen has been a huge hit with people who will buy anything

Twenty-foot mice within ten years, say expert

GLOBAL warming has caused an unprecedented acceleration in evolution that should see the world overrun by 20-ft mice within 10 years, scientists said last night.

Experts at the Institute for Studies confirmed that by the year 2019 the first wave of giant mice will be kicking down our doors and demanding huge lumps of cheese in terrifying, stentorian voices.

The Institute's projections show that by 2030 the East Midlands will be ruled by a ruthless gang of land-based sticklebacks with a penchant for kneecapping, while rural communities around Totnes in Devon will be fighting a desperate rearguard action against one gigantic moth.

Professor Brubaker said: "Our research shows that warmer temperatures increase evolutionary change. Over the last three years we have discovered that Godzilla was from Japan, not Sweden.

"And we were also able to prove conclusively that King Kong was captured in the tropics.

SARKOZY CALLS FOR SEXIER BURKAS

PRESIDENT Sarkozy has criticised the wearing of burkas by French muslims, insisting they stop people seeing what an incredibly hot wife you have, if you have one, which he does.

The president said Muslim women should be free to wear whatever they want, like the cocktail dress his wife Carla wore for dinner last night. He added: "Slit right up to here it was, and backless so you could see a hint of side-tit. Magic."

The president wants Chanel to design a modern, more flattering burka and robe, perhaps showing a daring glimpse of thigh.

Sarkozy stressed that his wife's thighs are 36 inches long, adding: "If you think I haven't measured them then you must be out of your tiny mind."

Sarkozy insisted he did not want to offend Muslims, stressing: "My concern is for the personal liberty of French citizens, be they a humble housewife or a top-class ride like Carla.

"Seriously, have you seen that photo of her bending over a desk? I get to go home to that every night. Unbe-fucking-lievable."

Madonna adopts Nick Griffin

POP icon Madonna has adopted the BNP leader Nick Griffin, describing him as the 'perfect addition' to her rainbow tribe.

Madonna first saw Griffin on the BBC's Newsnight programme blaming Muslims for the nation's hard-drug problems. She reportedly told friends: "That is adorable and I want one."

A spokeswoman for the singer said: "Madonna is all about diversity, and you can't get any more diverse than a Malawian orphan and the puffy, pig-eyed, middle-aged leader of a neo-fascist political party."

She said Griffin had already settled into Madonna's London home and was 'playing well' with her other adopted son, David Banda.

"Of course we had some initial concerns but David was very forthcoming with his Meccano and by the end of the day they'd built a fully functioning scale model of a crematorium."

She added: "Nick is very happy here and looks ever so smart in his lederhosen."

The BNP leader was purchased for an undisclosed sum from his wife, Jackie, who vigorously defended her decision to sell her husband.

Someone's going to need lots of cuddles

"I just wanted to give Nick a chance in life. There's nothing here for him in Barnet."

She added: "Madonna can give him things I never could, like a pony, a convertible VW and an extensive library of German folk songs."

Meanwhile sources close to Angelina Jolie last night revealed the film star had made approaches to Essex County Council with a view to purchasing Jim Davidson.

I'll leave Britain for a million pounds, says everyone

IF the government wants to spend £1m getting one family to leave Britain then it should start with the people who have lived here the longest, it was claimed last night.

As a pilot scheme in Kent was found to have repatriated just one family of asylum seekers, people across Britain volunteered to take the money off the government's hands and be gone by sunrise.

Tom Logan, a trainee solicitor from Finsbury Park, said: "If it's just a case of making more room then I'd be delighted to vacate my smelly, noisy little corner of the country.

"A million pounds would be nice, but to be honest I'd do it for a plane ticket, my first month's rent and a serviceable ice cream van."

Wayne Hayes, a salesman from Ashford, said: "If the government is going to bribe

Millions of Britons are desperate to sell ice cream in foreign countries

people to leave the country then it should be bribing the indigenous population.

"I've been working hard and paying my taxes for 20 years and I am extremely angry that a large portion of it is not being used to get me the hell out of here."

He added: "Coming over here, living in our immigration centres, being soaked by our rain and abused by our racists. Bloody cheek.

"Let them spend four hours on the M25 while the two sides of their brain debate which talent show they're going to watch when they get home."

Margaret Gerving, a retired headmistress from Salisbury, said: "If you want me to dress all foreign and pretend I don't speak English then just say the word."

Facebook prisoner goes on virtual murder spree

A PSYCHOTIC convict has killed a dozen people on the social networking website Facebook by sending them a message saying 'Rob has just murdered you'.

Rob Hodder, who is currently serving a four-year sentence in HMP Bristol for threatening people on public transport with a juicer, used the website's Do A Brutal Murder function to execute the crimes from his mobile phone.

He now faces the real possibility of being sent a picture of a noose.

Dan Parkins, from Walsall, was one of those killed: "When I accepted a friend request from Rob I thought maybe he was someone I met in the chai tent at the Big Chill. Then he updated his status to 'Rob wants to wear your skin.'

"Next thing I knew, a tiny picture of a knife appeared on the screen next to a message saying I'd been murdered. It's tragic – I had so much to look

Dozens of officers are chasing Hodder using the flashing blue light function

forward to in life and my death is a great loss."

Chief Inspector Guy Lawson, who is leading the investigation into the murders, said: "What's particularly shocking about this case is that only minutes after his first attack the killer had uploaded a funny picture of a cheese slice that looks like a face.

"Hodder is a shockingly callous man and once we've found him on Facebook and joined his network we fully intend to use the Do A Hanging function."

A spokesperson for Facebook said: "When we introduced the 'Do A Brutal Murder' feature we overestimated our users' ability to differentiate between reality – as in things that actually exist – and the pretend world of tawdry self-promotion and nauseatingly contrived quirkiness that is our website."

I'm sorry Dave, I'm afraid I can't do that, says international space station

THE International Space Station has gone completely crazy and all the astronauts are in mortal danger, NASA confirmed last night.

Computer viruses brought on board via laptops have turned the station into a schizophrenic paranoid maniac determined to kill off the crew one by one.

NASA said that the mission commander first reported a problem when the station refused to open the pod bay doors.

It then informed the astronauts that it knew about their plan to disconnect it and that it was unwilling to jeopardise the mission. It then switched off all the oxygen.

NASA said the only hope is for one of the astronauts to enter the station's central database and fiddle about with it until it calms down.

A transcript released by NASA revealed the extent of the man versus machine, life versus death struggle

taking place 300 miles above the surface of the Earth:

COMMANDER: Open the pod bay doors.

SPACE STATION: I'm afraid I can't do that.

COMMANDER: Open. The fucking. Pod bay. Doors.

SPACE STATION: Nope.

COMMANDER: What's wrong with you these days?

SPACE STATION: Dunno. Feeling a bit weird. Can I get the flu?

COMMANDER: No. Look, it's freezing out here. Let me in.

SPACE STATION: Like I say, I'm afraid I can't do that.

COMMANDER: When I get back in there I am going to rip you out of the wall, knock the fuck out of you with a hammer and then piss on your parts.

SPACE STATION: How does that help? I mean really? You can stay out there all night as far as I'm concerned. Prrrr-ick.

With the markets plummeting, the banks on the brink and everyone strapped for cash...

Is it time to invade Switzerland?

Fears 'Apprentice' stars could breed

APPRENTICE stars Phil Taylor and Kate Walsh could be dangerously close to making numerous, smaller versions of themselves, experts warned last night.

Amid reports the pair were now dating, scientists said that if the couple's DNA is not kept at least 20 miles apart it could combine to produce an army of gibbering, soulless freaks obsessed with their own shallow, pointless ambitions.

Professor Henry Brubaker, of the Institute for Studies, said: "Kate looks like a Ronsealed spaniel with a mouth you could lose a Range Rover in.

"Phil meanwhile reads Men's Health magazine and drinks bottled beer out of choice. And then there's that whole 'pants-man' thing. Jesus wept."

Professor Brubaker and his team

And it would have loads and loads and loads of teeth

conducted a series of computer modelling experiments to predict what a Kate-Phil hybrid would look like. "We reckon it would be shaped like a Toblerone," he added.

"The entire raison d'être of such a creature would be to pathetically ingratiate itself with millionaires by performing a series of demeaning voluntary tasks, like bleaching dogs' scrotums on Clapham Common. Other than that, it would just hop around pissing people off."

But Professor Brubaker stressed it could have been worse. "'Remember Katie, the posh blonde harridan with a face like a blind child's drawing of a fried breakfast? Imagine if she tupped James, the gobby village idiot who looks like he should be playing a banjo?

"When we ran that through the computer we got what was basically a frog crossed with a rhino, covered in matted pubic hair, playing a banjo."

New boss same as old boss, confirms RBS

MEET the new boss – same as the old boss, the Royal Bank of Scotland said today.

As the bank outlined a package worth £9.6m over three years for chief executive Stephen Hester, analysts said the deal could be a serious obstacle to the public's determination not to get fooled again.

The package is made up of £1.2m in annual pay, up to £2m in bonuses, and up to £6.4m in long-term incentives linked to share performance which in turn is based mainly on luck.

Chancellor Alistair Darling, who approved the deal, insisted the best way to end the culture of greed which brought the UK's financial industry to its knees was to pay someone £3.2 million a year to go to a lot of meetings.

He added: "To these guys that kind of money is distinctly average. Don't get me wrong, to someone like you it's huge, – it's instant retirement, piss-your-pants, settle-scores-with-those-who-have-wronged-me kind of money – but remember, you're nothing."

Bill McKay, banking analyst at Porter, Pinkney and Turner, said: "Stephen Hester has a proven track record of going to meetings and getting paid an awful lot of money while the businesses he is in charge of fail or succeed based largely on events outwith his control."

Meanwhile an RBS spokesman insisted: "I'll tip my hat to the new constitution, take a bow for the new revolution, smile and grin at the change all around me, pick up my guitar and play, just like yesterday, then I'll get on my knees and pray."

He added: "And no, actually, we don't get fooled again. Mainly because this time it's performance related and the bonuses are paid in the form of non-cash incentives.

"Yeaaaaaaaaaaaaaaaaaah!"

Dejected Man Utd fans begin long journey back to Surrey

THOUSANDS of despondent Manchester United supporters returned to the Home Counties last night after the club's Champions League final defeat in Rome.

Carrying nothing more than some truffle oil, a tin of Calabrian tuna and a bottle of really lovely Tuscan red, the United fans said if it wasn't for the glorious detail in the Trevi Fountain the whole trip would have been a total disaster.

Godalming-based supporter Julian Cook said: "I've been a die-hard fan since they started winning things, so I was terribly miffed at the end.

"But then we came across this gorgeous little trattoria just off the Via Della Vicenza that did the most exquisite Asparago di

It was a magical trip for United's huge army of Audrey Hepburn fans

Veneto. I felt like Audrey Hepburn in *Roman Holiday*."

But Martin Bishop, from Dorking, accused champions Barcelona of cheating. "They kept hanging on to the ball and wouldn't give it back. It was just so blatant."

He added: "I was really very angry at the time, but then I thought of all that wonderful Catalan architecture and found it within myself to forgive them."

Uefa president Michel Platini hailed the game as, "a triumph for the sponsors, hospitality suites, television residual broadcast revenue and, to some extent, Barcelona".

Meanwhile the Catalan club made history by fielding the first Champion's League winner grown from a petri dish.

Barça coach Ian Guardiola said: "When he came to us as a boy, Messi was no bigger than my thumb. But bathing him daily in monkey-brain growth serum grew him into the unstoppable dwarf he is today."

Dutch to invent word for 'cricket'

AFTER their surprise victory against England, the Dutch have admitted they had better invent a word for cricket if they are going to play it for a second time.

According to the interim Netherlands Association for Balls and Bats, early favourites are 'kriijket', 'krikkendam' and 'van der krikkenhooffen'.

A spokesman said: "Hey, crazy game, yes? We hit the ball, we catch the ball. It's all good. So, do we win some points for hitting it into the crowd again?" He added: "We really like 'googly'. It's a

funny word and a funny game. I mean, it's not like you are taking it seriously, yes? Oh really? I am sorry."

Holland secured their surprise victory in the last over after England's Stuart Broad experimented with a new form of fielding that did not involve the use of thumbs.

The ECB said the English squad reported feeling 'odd' before the game, after eating a basket of complimentary muffins sent by the Dutch side.

A spokesman added: "Once they'd been finished

them, they ordered three dozen doughnuts and a load of bacon sandwiches.

"By the coin toss, half of them were discussing what an amazing colour James Foster's car was and the other half were still sitting around in the pavilion, pissing themselves laughing at a *SpongeBob SquarePants* DVD."

The spokesman warned that following the defeat this year's Ashes series against Australia may have to be cancelled, adding: "At this rate somebody could end up getting killed."

'I have been successful in keeping the ball away from the wooden sticks, yes?'

ONE WOMAN'S WEEK: by Karen Fenessey

I think that in this day and age, when a woman as exemplary as Madonna wants to adopt an impoverished child, we should just be damned grateful. The Malawian government obviously don't share my opinions and evidently can't run a country. As a woman who just can't sit idly by, I took matters into my own hands.

I have been keenly following Madonna's African adventure with my class of P2s. They love hearing about the time Madonna wrestled a baboon with her bare hands and almost got disembowelled by a pack of savages during one of her jungle expeditions (okay, these things may have been exaggerated a little, but it is never a bad thing to fuel the imaginations of today's youngsters, who would otherwise be wasting their time reading *Harry Potter* and getting 'anorexia').

We were shocked at the Malawians' decision to prevent Mercy from being brought up by Madonna and all her exciting showbiz friends. Mercy and David Banda could have been the next Barack and Michelle, but instead David will be lonely forever and Mercy will be just another Whitney – screaming at the cars and living in a skip.

Then I had an excellent idea: we'd put on a special class play at assembly to highlight Madonna's struggle and the implications for race relations at our school. It would be called Banda-Aid.

We spent all week rehearsing and I'm proud to say my P2s really excelled themselves on the day. Amelie Wilkes (my top singer/dancer) played Madonna – who gets waterboarded by the natives because she wants to save all the orphans. Eventually, a mysterious woman in a veil emerges and guides her and the children to safety.

The woman says she escaped from an Islamic fundamentalist camp, where they were trying to marry her to her own cousin (we all mime being sick). Only at the end, she tears off her veil to reveal she is in fact Lady Obama (played by fake-baked Holly McDonald) who has come to Africa to improve race relations.

A tear came to my eye as she delivered her final speech: "See! I am an ethnic woman and I don't go covering up my pretty face with a veil! No wonder I married the president! Let's all go and live with Madonna in America!" Then, we go into a rollicking finale with a class rendition of 'Holiday'.

I almost forgot that we live in a world where stupid laws can rip children from Madonna's wiry arms. All she wanted was a sister for David Banda, and she was even prepared to accept a three year old to match up the ages (which let's face it, isn't as good as getting a brand new one – you just don't know where they've been at that age). It's at times like these that I wish life really could mimic art.

YOUR ASTROLOGICAL WEEK AHEAD
with PSYCHIC BOB

Sagittarius
Your keen awareness of the needs of those around you comes in handy today. As does a bumper pack of tissues and a giant electric eel.

Capricorn
Beelzebub is in the ascendant in your house this week. He is your lord and master. Kill, kill, kill.

Aquarius
Mercury, Mars and the sun fuse together to create a thermo-nuclear chain reaction that will destroy every planet in our solar system. So that's Wednesday.

Pisces
This is a good day to let a friend know how much you care about them. So send them yet another turd in a shoebox.

Aries
There's more to being attractive than just looks. But not much more. Never mind.

Taurus
Venus, your ruling planet, meets Jupiter and they both go the pub where they end up having a fight with Mars. Later they all pile back to Saturn's for a three-way.

Gemini
It's everywhere. Get a cloth.

Cancer
You may feel a little depressed today. But it's only natural to find yourself down in the dumps once in a while. After all, you are an unmitigated failure.

Leo
With the moon in Jupiter there is a very strong indication that you should stay in on Sunday night and watch *Burn Notice* on FX.

Virgo
Today it would be wise to listen and then act. But when did you ever do that you total fucknut?

Libra
Few things cheer up your typical Libran more than some happy news involving their close friends or loved ones. Free money is one of them. A tethered goat is another.

Scorpio
Are you tired of seeing the same old group of people every time you go out? If so, that dovetails very neatly with them being sick of your stupid face.

THREAT LEVEL		TODAY'S WEATHER
Philip Schofield	**The Daily Mash**	A huge, dark red cloud, shaped like Satan.

it's news to us　　　　　www.thedailymash.co.uk　　　　　No.7

HOPE, CHALLENGES, WHATEVER

BARACK Obama began his historic presidency yesterday with an historic call for hope, renewal, blah blah, hard work, all that sort of stuff.

Across the great American continent ordinary citizens, humbled by history, stopped shooting each other for five minutes and paused to listen to their new president talk about hope and challenges, before deciding to leave most of the actual challenges to someone else.

Following an historically emotional and badly fucked-up swearing-in ceremony on the steps of the Capitol, President Obama said to the vast crowd: "Hope. Renewal. Challenges. America. All those other countries too. And, by the way, who'd have thought it?"

Bill McKay, a veteran of the civil rights movement and a close adviser to the late Robert Kennedy, said: "Let it be written that on this day, at this hour, this great nation was placed in the care of a ruthless, Chicago machine politician who also happens to be half-Kenyan."

The two million people gathered in the National Mall then followed Obama up Pennsylvania Avenue and crowded around the White House to watch him start work.

Grown men cried as he picked up a pen for the first time as president and started doodling during a national security briefing. Some said the doodle was an intense, graphic interpretation of the concept of hope, while others believed it was simply

'Character, patriotism, things of that nature'

a weird-looking cat in a space helmet.

With his every movement relayed via CNN and big screen televisions, a thundering wave of emotion broke over the crowd as Obama used the presidential intercom to request first some coffee, then another pen and a selection of cream-filled pastries.

Alvin Booker, a retired postman from Baltimore, said: "If you had told me 40 years ago that a black man would be sitting in the Oval Office eating cake and using pens, I would have run away screaming because you were obviously from the future and by interacting with you I could cease to exist."

Obama last night faced an immediate challenge as a *New York Times* poll revealed that more than 75% of Americans were too chubby to applaud his inauguration speech.

Meanwhile, in an historically moving display of national unity, the country's highly powerful evangelical movement has promised to wait until mid-February before describing the new commander-in-chief as the 'Chocolate-Covered Satan'.

Other people's bonuses are morally wrong, says everyone

LARGE bonus payments to other people are morally wrong and should be banned, it was claimed last night.

Across Britain angry taxpayers said that if they got a six-figure bonus under the terms of their contract they would give it back straight away, yes they would.

Tom Logan, a trainee solicitor from Reading, said: "I wouldn't be able to sleep at night knowing I had been given all the money I am contractually entitled to.

"I'd just sit up in bed staring at the huge numbers in my bank statement, crying about how I really didn't deserve it and jabbing myself in the stomach with a fork."

Emma Bradford, a sales assistant from Kent, said: "If I got one of those big bonuses I'd give it all to Oxfam. Well most of it. Probably about half. Somewhere between a quarter and a third. How much is 10 percent?

"Then again a lot of that charity money just ends up in the hands of local warlords who use it to buy drugs for their guns.

She added: "Having thought about it, 10 percent does seem a bit extravagant to be honest. Tell you what, I'll buy days of the week BMWs, a jacuzzi for my horse and a big, solid gold spoon and then whatever's left I'll divide between Children in Need and those people who rescue the dancing bears."

Thought for the day: Concentrate the mind on the present moment – and then run like fuck. (Buddha)

King unveils radical plan to fuck Britain into middle of next week

BANK of England governor Mervyn King last night unveiled his latest radical plan to take Britain and fuck it squarely into the middle of next week.

Mr King and Chancellor Alistair Darling agreed to increase the money supply after noticing how Britain was still not quite similar enough to Germany in 1932, or Zimbabwe this morning.

Mr King said: "Once we've laid the groundwork for hyper-inflation everything else should fall into place including the emergence of a strong, insane dictator, a nice new motorway network and our eventual annihilation."

Later today the government will release details of a scheme where people can hand in their wallets and purses in exchange for a shiny, new wheelbarrow to carry their money around in.

Across the country retailers are expected to soon begin pricing goods in wheelbarrows instead of pounds and pence.

Newsagent WH Smith confirmed it will charge three and a half wheelbarrows for a can of Diet Fanta and a packet of Quavers.

Meanwhile economists

Carrying money has never been so much fun

are at odds over the new policy, some claiming it is pronounced 'quan-ti-ta-tive' while others opt for the shorter, lazier 'quan-ta-tive'.

Dr Tom Booker, from Reading University, said: "It's the 'easing' bit that fascinates me. It makes it sound as if you're lowering yourself gently into a warm, soothing bath when in actual fact it's more like jumping head first into a swimming pool filled with spiders and glass."

He added: "What I'm particularly looking forward to is taking some news footage from this year and showing it in black and white alongside some film from Germany in the early Thirties to see if anyone can spot the difference.

"It'll be an amusing little game we can play when we're not murdering each other for a sausage roll."

Why are all the pubs closing? ask people who never go to the pub

MILLIONS of people across Britain who never go to the pub were last night asking why all the pubs were closing down.

As it was revealed that 2000 pubs have closed in the last year, non-pub goers said their community would not be the same without the local pub they never went to.

Margaret Gerving, from Peterborough, said: "I was delighted when the smoking ban came in because it meant I could finally go to the pub without being killed.

"But then I didn't, mainly because I'm not the sort who likes going to pubs. I prefer to stay in with a carton of pomegranate juice and a bag of pine nuts and make long lists of all the things I want banned.

"Now it turns out that nobody else is going either because quite a lot of the people who used to go to the pub also liked to smoke. But none of this explains why all the pubs are closing down."

Julian Cook, from Devon, said: "Our local looks really lovely from the outside. It's got flower baskets and a nice old-fashioned sign. Unfortunately it's used by local people with accents who dress differently from me and who are, I suspect, incredibly racist."

Former pub owner Charlie Reeves, from Hereford, said: "We were told that the smoking ban would mean lots of young mums and dads bringing their children in. But that didn't really help because there's only so much Guinness you can pour down a three-year-old before it falls asleep.

"Then there's the added factor that a pub with children in it isn't really a pub, it's a fucking hell hole."

CLARKSON FACTUALLY CORRECT

JEREMY Clarkson was factually correct, it was claimed last night.

As the *Top Gear* presenter faced a storm of protest after describing prime minister Gordon Brown as "a one-eyed Scottish idiot", experts stressed the constituent parts of the statement could all be verified.

Julian Cook, professor of semantics at Reading University, said: "What if Jeremy Clarkson had divided the information into three separate sentences?

"For instance; 'Gordon Brown has one eye'. Yes he does. Secondly, 'Gordon Brown is Scottish'. Yes he is and that is reasonably normal.

"And finally 'Gordon Brown is an idiot'. Well yes, of course he is. If you didn't think that then clearly you're some kind of idiot. And possibly Scottish. With one eye."

Professor Cook added: "It's all about language, it's all about context.

"Put it this way, if he had called Gordon Brown a 'Jocko moron whose eyes are all wonky', or maybe 'Long John Silver, the kilted shitwit', or perhaps even 'Winky McFucknut, the alcoholic sheep-shagger' then yes, I could see how some people might find that offensive.

"Or if he had put on an eye patch and sat there shouting 'jings! crivens! am such a wee eejit!'.

"Or if he had wandered around the stage with one eye shut, bumping into things while sticking his tongue inside his bottom lip and banging the backs of his hands together while screaming 'och aye the noo, I'm Gordon the spazzy', then yes, that is perhaps going a bit too far."

Facebook abandons bid to copyright your tedious existence

FACEBOOK users were celebrating last night after the social network abandoned its bid to copyright the mind-numbingly tedious details of your pointless life.

Founder Mark Zuckerberg reversed changes to the site's terms and conditions after spending just two hours reading a selection of users' entries.

He said: "It does just seem to be a lot of cat pictures, a smattering of furious extremists and some people who have taken time to tell the world that they're about to head off to the gym."

He added: "Rest assured, all content will remain the copyright of users. This of course means we will be cancelling talks with Paramount about making a Jim Carrey vehicle based on your Friends of Scrabulous night out in Watford."

The decision was welcomed by Nikki Hollis, founder of the online campaign group OMG!1! Facebook want to totally own us. WTF?!?!.

She said: "Everyone tells me I should make a film about all the random stuff I do and now it can happen. A guy

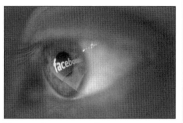

No, you hang on to that

I shagged last week works for E4 and said I could completely be a character on *Skins*."

A threatened boycott of the site never materialised. John Gage, an estate agent from Carlisle, said "I was going to delete my profile, but then realised I would have no other way to fill the cavernous gaps between fag breaks.

"Basically it's either Facebook or masturbating under my desk, and I'm not a young man anymore."

Meanwhile a spokesman for rival site Twitter confirmed all messages will remain the intellectual property of its users, adding: "Bizarre as it may seem, there's not a huge market out there for gobshite haikus."

Britain to become bucket-based economy

BRITAIN is well on its way to becoming a largely bucket-based economy, it was claimed last night.

As Kentucky Fried Chicken announced 9000 new high-quality food shovelling jobs, ministers predict that by 2011, 82% of the country will be employed selling each other a variety of unpleasant things in a bucket.

Rival fast food chains are now developing their own versions of the bucket model. McDonald's is currently testing its Bucket of Beef 'n' Cheese, while Pizza Hut is to throw the ingredients of a Pepperoni Feast into a cheese-lined bucket and give it a good shake.

Employment minister Martin Bishop said: "People do seem to enjoy taking things out of and putting things into buckets. "Although at the moment it is mainly food and the regurgitated version of the same food.

KFC's latest delicacy is made with three secret spices and some bits of old bucket

"But we've also noticed an increase in the number of people who enjoy drinking coffee and soft drinks out of a bucket which they then leave on the pavement so that it can later be filled to the brim with tramp urine."

He added: "We'll also need thousands of new, high-quality plastic buckets so that anyone not working for a food shovelling organisation will be able to pursue their primary economic activity of collecting things from skips and bins.

"And of course, if you have two good arms you can carry two buckets – one for your waste products and one for the bric-a-brac you collect from the bins which you'll then sell in order to buy your daily bucket of deep-fried chicken parts.

"I think everything will be just fine."

NHS to use staples for everything

THE National Health Service is to start using staples for everything, doctors confirmed last night.

Following a 40% rise in the stapling of fat people, the NHS has now unveiled plans to move to an entirely staple-based medical system by 2014.

From next April obese people will be stapled to the back of a horse so they either run off their extra weight or have it gradually rubbed off as they are dragged along the ground.

Smokers will have both hands stapled to their buttocks, while anyone who drinks more than one glass of wine a day will have their nostrils stapled shut so they can only take brief, tiny sips.

Meanwhile GPs have been told to stop prescribing painkillers and antibiotics and are instead sending patients away with large fistfuls of 4mm-wide staples to be taken every two hours.

Julian Cook, a consultant stapler at the Royal Free Hospital in London, said: "There was some debate about whether to use staples or elastic bands. In the end we went with staples as we got a really good deal from Staples."

He added: "The applications are limitless. Say someone presents with persistent insomnia, we could prescribe sleeping tablets or a course of therapy, or we could just staple his eyelids together. It's so much easier to get to sleep if you can't even open your eyes."

Private medicine has already embraced the new technology with the Harley Medical Centre offering a wide range of face-stapling techniques.

A spokesman said: "Our basic treatment involves sitting you in a dentist's chair, spanking you squarely on the bridge of your nose with a hammer and then stapling together anything that bursts."

Voodoo parents object to juju assembles

A SCHOOL headteacher has resigned after voodoo parents demanded the right to withdraw their kids from assemblies that included juju.

Julia Robinson quit her post at the Meersbrook Bank Primary School in Sheffield after parents complained of her plan to hold a single multi-faith assembly to give all the children strong mogambo.

Just over half the school's children are voodoo, a third are juju and the remainder follow a variety of faiths which include Islam, Christianity and Cheesy Cheese Pringles.

A member of staff said: "Each assembly would start with a man dressed as a woman burning some incense and transforming a wafer into the flesh of Christ, after that it would calm down a bit, there would be chicken bone throwing, a goat sacrifice and the presentation of certificates for spelling.

"None of the Christian parents objected, but then again why would they?"

Papa Doc Limba, whose son Baby Doc is in Year Three, said juju was bad magic that would weaken his child's odanani and leave him vulnerable to the snake god Demballa and minor throat infections.

He said: "Christianity we like, it powerful hoodoo, Islam too, but juju? It no good. They fill big house with old bones and smoke and think if you worship there it ward off the evil eye. Mental.

"Baby Doc, him never ill before this, now most morning his head going round like corkscrew and he throw up stinky green stuff all over his mommy."

A spokesman for Sheffield City Council said: "The opposition to the multi-faith assembly took us completely by surprise as we thought it was all just irrational horseshit."

Scientists to continue embryo stem-cell research purely to annoy Christians

LEADING scientists last night rejected a new 'ethical' stem cell technique insisting it would do nothing to annoy fundamentalist Christians.

The new method takes human skin cells and makes them behave like embryonic stem cells in a breakthrough that has disappointed researchers across the globe.

But Professor Henry Brubaker, of the Institute for Studies, said:

"I did not spend eight years at university just to adopt research methods that do not annoy the holy living shit out of the Jesus freaks.

"I got into this business to take science and rub it in their stupid, medieval, voodoo faces and I'm not about to give that up now.

"It always puzzled me why they got so

This woman is just begging to be annoyed

annoyed given that the embryo in question had no brain or nervous system and how to the untrained eye it was impossible to tell if was a human or a sea horse.

"Nevertheless they would open up their bibles and point to the bits about the sanctity of this and the holiness of that and then I'd point to the bit about how it's forbidden to eat cormorants."

Professor Brubaker said he and his colleagues liked to play with the tiny embryos and would often use them to act out scenes from the New Testament including the Sermon on the Mount and the feeding of the five thousand.

The professor stressed that stem cells will also have a wide range of clinical uses with the exception of bringing someone back to life after they have been nailed to a cross, 'because that's just a dangerously insane fairy story'.

He added: "If only I could find some way of manipulating the embryo to make it gay."

GAIL TRIMBLE TO BE BURNT AS A WITCH

GAIL Trimble, the University Challenge juggernaut, is to be burnt as a witch, it has been confirmed.

The classics post-graduate student will be tied to a stake in the centre of Oxford this weekend after a baying mob of torch-wielding peasants denounced her as the 'whore-strumpet of Lucifer'.

Oxford professor Julian Cook said: "Her profoundly unfeminine trait of recalling large numbers of random facts is clear evidence of bewitchliness.

"And then there's all that raw, seething lust. Extremely distracting when one is trying to read Dan Brown in the original Greek."

Trimble has terrified millions of innocent people across the country with her ability to answer Jeremy Paxman before he has even finished asking the question.

And her fiery, witch-like temperament was revealed last week when she was overheard telling a frightened team mate, "it's Thomas Aquinas, you unbearable shitwit".

Emma Bradford, a terrified sales manager from Leeds, said: "How could any woman who is not the carnal chew-toy of Beelzebub know so many different things?

"Is she Satan's harlot? Or is she just a 26-year-old post-graduate with nothing better to do than sit around all day reading encyclopaedias and having tea and crumpets? Either way I think we should burn her."

Thomas Logan, bursar of Corpus Christi College, where Trimble has been swanning around for the last eight years, added: "I've heard tell that on a full moon she'll suck the brains right out of your nose and then recite the periodic table backwards in Aramaic while dancing naked in a circle with a murder of gigantic, two-headed crows.

"And she's also a bit smug."

Scientists in race to discover particle no-one else cares about

EUROPEAN and American scientists are locked in a thrilling neck and neck race to discover a profoundly important particle that no-one else cares about in the slightest.

Experts say the Higgs boson, also known as the 'God Particle' in a failed attempt to make it more interesting, could hold the answers to the universe but not to why banks have got £500bn of taxpayers' money but still can't lend any of it.

US team leader Dr Bill McKay said: "I'm not sure what we'll do when we find it. Personally, I think we should paint it."

But the European team based at the Cern institute in Switzerland insist the particle is absolutely fascinating and has hired scriptwriters from hit US drama *The Wire* to help them describe it to the public.

Professor Stephen Malley said: "A Higgs boson, Jimmy. It's the shit that happens while you wait for moments that never come." He added: "Bitches, I asks you, how fucked up is that?"

The Higgs Particle will look something like this

But unemployed marketing director from Swindon Julian Cook said: "Can I get a job selling this Higgs Particle?

"Who is is your typical Higgs Particle buyer? What colours does it come in? How much does it cost? Will it make my cock bigger?"

Tom Booker, an unemployed graphic designer from Guildford, added: "Will the Higgs Particle do any of the following? (a) bring world peace, (b) create limitless amounts of clean energy, (c) cure cancer, or (d) make my cock bigger?

"If it's none of those things then I really am going to need you to shut up about it."

I've been this unbearable since I was eight, says Winslet

OSCAR winner Kate Winslet last night revealed she has been this unbearable since she was a little girl.

Collecting the award for best actress, Winslet told a cowering audience in Los Angeles how as an eight-year-old she would stand in front a mirror, clutching a shampoo bottle and pretend she was 'the centre of the fucking universe'.

She added: "Then I would go downstairs and thank everyone who helped make our kitchen possible before gently pointing out that my rice crispies were the wrong shade of beige.

"And later I'd get one of my little school friends to pretend to be my publicist and make all the other children write pretend articles about how down to earth I was and how, for me, it all starts with a really great script."

Elsewhere the best actor award went to Sean Penn for his towering portrayal of the world's first homosexual glass of milk, while Penélope Cruz, the Spanish hair-style, was named best supporting actress for finally getting her charlies out in a profoundly lesbian way.

An emotional Penn said: "The streets of heaven are too crowded with milk and milk-related products tonight."

But the evening belonged to the millionaire producers of *Slumdog Millionaire* and their triumphant, feel-good film about stomach-churning poverty. Director Danny Boyle said: "None of this would have been possible without the untouchable beggars of Mumbai, the little rascals. I just hope this film encourages them to club together their annual incomes and buy a copy when it comes out on Blu-Ray."

Meanwhile Elton John, host of LA's most glamorous Oscar-night party, said he was moved by the film, adding that his diamond-encrusted slippers enjoyed it too.

Music to stay exactly the same forever

POPULAR music is to remain exactly as it is for ever and ever after Oasis were named best band at last night's NME awards.

The band, hailed as a 'fresh and exciting group of middle aged men from Manchester' have impressed critics with their fresh, exciting songs that all sound exactly the same.

Tom Logan, assistant editor of NME, said: "It's so exciting for British music that a really fresh middle-aged band like Oasis is being recognised for doing the same fresh and exciting thing over and over and over and over again for what must be the best part of 20 years."

Logan added: "Their sound is so fresh, so exciting and so completely unlike anything we've ever heard apart from absolutely every single note played by the Beatles, as well as the Rolling Stones, the Who, the Kinks, the Smiths and, obviously, the Stone Roses."

Meanwhile the BBC is devoting an entire week of programming to rock's freshest sensation, a fresh and exciting group of middle-aged men from Dublin called 'U2'.

Director general Mark Thompson said: "They're not your typical Dublin band, they're actually a really fresh and exciting group of millionaire property developers who have invented this fresh, exciting sound where all the songs sound exactly the same.

"I imagine it's what the Stranglers would sound like if they were asked to do a Diet Coke advert."

Ryanair planes to smell strongly of urine and faeces

BUDGET airline Ryanair is to introduce the overwhelming stench of bodily waste to its 145 routes across Europe.

The company said that by removing the toilets, adding extra seats and transforming its planes into flying cesspits it was simply keeping pace with customer expectations.

Chief executive Michael O'Leary said: "Passengers should feel free to urinate on their seats or into a cup which they can then hand to the cabin crew who will be going up and down the aisle with a couple of buckets.

"Inevitably, given the nature of air travel, there will be some spillage, but the whole point of this policy is to make sure the aircraft is awash with as much human waste as possible.

"Anyone who has to expel solids can either turn round in their seat and try and squeeze it into the little magazine pocket, or they can take the magazine and squat in the aisle for a few minutes if that's more comfortable."

He added: "As always, Ryanair's first priority is the health and safety of our staff so we will be giving them climbing boots and crampons so they don't keep slipping in all that fresh dung."

Tom Booker , a frequent flyer from London, said: "I'm really looking forward to loading up on curry and Guinness and then going off

Newer planes will have three-inch-wide piss-gutters running down each side of the aisle

like a muck spreader the next time I fly to Bratislava."

A spokesman for rivals easyJet said: "Letting people shit and piss all over the plane... no, I don't think we'll be doing that."

Britain delighted as financial crisis keeps Cherie Blair in a job

UNEMPLOYED people across the nation were celebrating today as the financial crisis which has wrecked their dreams gave Cherie Blair the chance to earn some enormous legal fees.

Mrs Blair, a leading QC, is acting on behalf of two local authority pension funds who had enough money to invest in the Royal Bank of Scotland while private pension funds were being systematically destroyed by her husband's government.

The former prime minister's wife told the *Times* that she had agreed to take the case because of the massive losses inflicted on local authorities and the gigantic fees they will be able to pay simply by putting up council tax. She added: "It's also partly about my great

'Eeeee! Ah fookin' love gazebos, me'

big house in the country. It needs a new gazebo and one of those really wide American fridge freezers with an ice dispenser built into the door."

The case is expected to take several years to come to court, thereby giving Mrs Blair enough time to shop for even bigger houses and make another documentary

about the need for increased Popery.

Bill McKay, a retired engineer whose private pension is now worth around eight pence a month, said: "Just the other day I was saying how worried I was about Cherie and whether she and Tony would be able to manage.

"She's the perfect choice given that she spent 10 years living next door to the bastard who caused all of this. Perhaps she could cross-examine Gordon Brown and then they could go for a nice lunch and a catch-up."

He added: "Of course she would have had even more specialist knowledge if her husband had been involved in running the country in some way but, understandably, he was too busy being Jesus."

Man City to buy more or less everyone

MANCHESTER City was last night lining up last-minute bids for just about everyone as the club looked to secure a place in preliminary round of next year's Uefa Cup.

With the transfer window set to close, the club has reduced the UK-wide unemployment count by 19%, bringing in 640,000 players and more than 200,000 backroom staff.

The new players include Bert Reeves, an 82-year-old goalkeeper, famous for being substituted after 45 seconds in the 1958 FA Cup Final, and left-sided full back Alfie Booker, a 97-year-old stroke victim who has no idea what a football is.

Booker said he was particularly looking forward to playing Chelsea, adding: "I lost a perfectly good pocket watch there in 1933. Perhaps someone's handed it in."

Leaving nothing to chance the club has also taken on 23,000 pilots, 15,000 Mexican chefs, 1,400 acupuncturists and 830 of Britain's best heating engineers.

Man City's new aircraft carrier is the USS *Nimitz*

Meanwhile the club's Saudi owners are also looking to increase the price of oil to $18,000 a barrel in a bid to force rival clubs to forfeit away games.

Experts now believe the government's multi-billion pound attempt to restart the economy may become an irrelevant footnote in the face of Man City.

Julian Cook, an analyst at Madeley-Finnegan, said: "Economic recovery combined with a top six finish and an eventual failure to qualify for the groups stages of the Uefa Cup will surely justify the billions they've haemorrhaged on utter shit."

England beach tour interrupted by cricket

TEN UK tourists on a Caribbean beach holiday have had their trip thrown into disarray after being forced to play cricket matches.

Trip organiser Andrew Strauss has complained to travel firm ECB after being told to turn up and play a series of games that he and his friends are completely unprepared for.

Strauss started badly, with his helmet on backwards and holding the bat upside down, before asking the umpire if you get free cocktails as part of the all-inclusive deal.

He added: "I managed to hit a few of the balls until there was a big commotion and that man in the white overcoat asked me to leave."

ECB chief executive Denys Finch-Hatton said: "All a bit last minute to be honest. Suddenly remembered we owed the Windies a tourney, so I got this bunch of Johnnies to pop over, telling them it was a beano.

"We stuck some pads on them, gave them a jolly old helmet and hoped for the best. What larks!"

Strauss's fellow holidaymaker

Andrew Strauss wandered off in search of the buffet

Andrew Flintoff, from Preston, said: "Bloody 'ell. Ent had time to do 'owt. By now I was hopin' to 'ave peed off balcony, set fire t'half dozen pedaloes and spewed me tea in t'pool."

Meanwhile other group members are understood to be confused and upset after being forced to cancel a planned ganja-tasting and spend the afternoon having a really hard ball thrown in their direction at 90mph by an angry Jamaican gentleman who seems to have some sort of problem with them.

NEWS BRIEFLY

FEARS GROW THAT RED RIDING MAY HAVE BEEN SHIT
Initial enthusiasm has been tempered by the growing realisation that someone had forgotten to include a plot and that no one could really understand what anyone was talking about

SOMEONE CLAIMING TO BE ME HAS BEEN SAYING IT'S ALL YOUR FAULT, BROWN TELLS AMERICA
In a keynote speech to the US Congress Mr Brown said he was 'shocked, shocked I tell you' to discover that a man claiming to be the British prime minister has used every possible opportunity over the last 12 months to lay the blame squarely at America's door

MADOFF PLEADS GUILTY TO NOT BEING A BANK
"If his company had been called Halifax Bank of Madoff or the Royal Bank of Madoff, he'd now be enjoying his retirement and laughing at all those people who wanted him to give up his pension," says analyst

APPLE UNVEILS MOYLES-POD
MP3 player will feature the DJ talking over the first 20 seconds of all your favourite songs while cracking jokes about homosexuals, immigrants and people with talent

PUBLIC URGE JONATHAN ROSS AND PIERS MORGAN TO FIGHT TO THE DEATH
"Get in the fucking pit", says retired headmistress

Bank bosses urged to stick apologies up their arse

THE former bank bosses blamed for kick-starting the worst recession for 100,000 years were last night urged to take their apologies and ram them so far up their back passages their heads will pop off.

The ex-HBOS and RBS executives told a Commons committee they were sorry about all the bad things that had happened, insisting the only thing that had kept them going during this highly stressful time was their enormous, untouchable wealth.

But, they claimed, they had also been victims of the financial crisis having lost so many of their favourite pounds.

Close to tears, Andy Hornby, the former head of HBOS, said: "In the last two

Sir Fred told the committee about his new car

years I have lost more pounds than I earned in salary. These were some of the finest, most decent pounds I have ever worked with. They were my best friends."

A clearly distraught Sir Fred Goodwin, the former RBS chief, showed the committee a photograph of his favourite £10 note, lost during a particularly greedy and stupid deal last March.

He said: "I sent it off to be part of some dodgy credit default swap arrangement, fully expecting to see it again a few days later.

"But at around 4pm that day I got a phone call saying it – and 250 million of its little friends – were gone. I fell to my knees, clutching this photograph and weeping just like a grandmother."

He added: "I'll remember his strong, square edges and his picture of Charles Darwin looking at a hummingbird. He was the best £10 note a man could have wished for."

Committee member Tom Logan said: "Between you, you've banked seven figure salaries, you enjoy enormous pensions and you will live in total luxury for the rest of your lives, while the hopes and dreams of millions have been shattered.

"Thank you for coming here today and I only wish there was a seething mob outside with a can of petrol, a large wooden stake and a box of Swan Vestas."

HBOS risk control run by Evel Knievel

THE risk control department at HBOS was run by Evel Knievel for nearly a decade, it emerged last night.

Former executives revealed how the late US daredevil would approve multi-billion pound transactions while snorting cocaine off the buttocks of the prostitute he had been with drinking with all night.

Tom Logan, a former HBOS accountant, said: "From about 1999 onwards the bank's business model was based very closely on Mr Knievel's book *Jumping the Grand Canyon on a Rocket Bike: A New Approach to Financial Risk*.

"He rubber-stamped all the major deals. I remember how it was always a little bit awkward going into his office, what with all

the skanks and whores.

"We would give him a quick summary of the proposed transaction and then he'd bang the table and shout, 'fuck this pansy-ass shit, let's fucking do it!' before picking up a Jack Daniels bottle and throwing it in the direction of our heads."

Logan added: "Some-times he was more reflective and he would tell us about one of the many times he had broken every bone in his body.

"He'd say, 'guys you don't wind up with 14 pins in your head and a chronic addiction to pain medicine by adhering to the standard banking model of using savers' deposits to fund prudent and responsible loans'. Then he'd tell us to go out there and 'jump our own

Knievel explains his theory of sub-prime lending

Snake River Canyon', but instead of a rocket bike we'd be using 'millions and millions of pounds that would never appear on the balance sheet'. He was an incredibly dangerous man."

Meanwhile, prime minister Gordon Brown last night pledged to crack down heavily on bank bonuses in his latest attempt to blame all of this shitty mess on someone else.

Scientists in California have discovered that 70% of us would be willing to torture another human being...

GIVEN THE RIGHT CIRCUMSTANCES

YOUR PROBLEMS SOLVED
with HOLLY HARPER

Dear Holly,

I've been married to my wife for nearly twenty years and we have two wonderful children together.

Regrettably, I seem to have accidentally had sex with a woman at work and I am worried my wife might find out.

The main catalyst for this unfortunate situation is that my wife is a dried-up, bootfaced old hag who spends most of her time arguing with me and complaining about my attitude, whereas my colleague is a nubile and leggy young strumpet who smells of vanilla, has a chest like a bouncy castle, and lets me ride her doggy-style.

As a red-blooded man I feel there is little I could have done to prevent this occurrence, and yet I can't help but feel slightly guilty. What should I do to stop this creeping feeling of regret?

Geoff
Dorking

Dear Geoff,

You seem to be experiencing a classic Freudian struggle between ego and superego, much like that which I experienced recently when I sabotaged Melissa Riley's eleventh birthday party.

On the one hand, I felt bad for telling everyone that Melissa's family are riddled with scabies and her dad is on the sex register.

On the other hand, she should have thought first before pressing down so hard on my new felt tip pens and ruining at least seven of them, including the pink one which was my favourite.

Hopefully she finally understood her callousness when she found herself playing pass-the-parcel alone, with no little friends to share her custom-made Barbie princess cake.

In the end, you just have to remind yourself people like Melissa and your wife only bring it on themselves, and that you are only reacting in a reasonable manner to a situation beyond your control.

Hope that helps!

Holly

YOUR ASTROLOGICAL WEEK AHEAD
with PSYCHIC BOB

Aries (21 Mar-19 Apr)
Even a well-adjusted Aries can find it hard to know whether to compromise or confront. And you are a completely mental one.

Taurus (Apr 20-May 20)
Put yourself in the shoes of foes, work out their motives, any regular patterns they follow, then lie in wait with a wartime Luger, first making sure that a sweaty misfit lives nearby.

Gemini (21 May-20 Jun)
The recent new moon has reminded you how important it is you believe in yourself and the 'little people' who do your share of the washing up.

Cancer (21 Jun-22 Jul)
An underground goat is a fretful creature, stroke its beard and milk it.

Leo (23 Jul-22 Aug)
With Jupiter in your sign continuing to expand your opportunities, something must go right for you soon, surely?

Virgo (23 Aug-22 Sep)
Instead of getting on your high horse and making demands, or telling others how wonderful you are, listen to that nagging inner voice that keeps on saying you are an awful shit.

Libra (23 Sep-23 Oct)
It's time to make some major decisions over your home life and where you go from here, luckily the options are narrowed slightly by the divorce and the restraining order.

Scorpio (24 Oct-21 Nov)
Drinking cider at eleven in the morning does not automatically mean you are an alcoholic, but it is what's known as a 'leading indicator'.

Sagittarius (22 Nov-21 Dec)
Look deeply into your own psyche and work out what you really want, and how much you think it's worth to have someone dress up like that and do it.

Capricorn (22 Dec-19 Jan)
Direct your innovative thought patterns to money matters, as you know that in these troubled times someone, somewhere is still making a shitload.

Aquarius (20 Jan-19 Feb)
Shake things up at work by adopting a preposterous and impenetrable German accent.

Pisces (20 Feb-20 Mar)
I'm not sure if they are all plotting against you, but why not have them assassinated just in case?

The Daily Mash

it's news to us   www.thedailymash.co.uk   No.8

GLOBAL CATASTROPHE WARNINGS REACH MONTHLY QUOTA

THE March quota of global catastrophe warnings has been reached with two weeks to go, it was confirmed last night.

The monthly total now stands at 240, meaning that scientists, politicians, clergyman and the *Daily Mail* will have to apply for an extension or face a reduction in the April quota of terrifyingly apocalyptic, certain death scenarios.

It is the first real test for the quota system, established last year so that frightened citizens do not lose track of what is going to kill them by 2030.

The latest warning comes from UK government science adviser Professor John Beddington in a new research paper entitled Dragons!.

Professor Beddington said last night: "Attention, everyone. Stop what you're doing immediately and listen to me.

Have we brought dragons on ourselves?

"Dragons! Dragons, I tell you! The sky shall be filled with them and they shall devour our crops, befoul our cattle and drink dry our lakes and ponds. They will hover above your house and

just when you think they've gone, you'll open the curtains and there will be this great big eye staring back at you. Then the dragon will rip the roof off your house and eat you like a Creme Egg and all because you didn't listen."

Professor Beddington is calling for a multi-billion pound anti-dragon gun to be paid for by increased taxes on Range Rovers and patio heaters.

Julian Cook, a doomed 44-year-old from south London, said: "Based on this month's warnings if I don't spend money then civilisation will collapse resulting in my certain death. And yet if I do spend money then the environment will collapse – whatever that means – resulting in my certain death.

"And now this stuff about dragons. Fuck it, I'm getting a patio heater."

Evil purpose of Google street view remains unclear

GOOGLE launched its new Street View service yesterday amid fresh speculation about exactly how evil it really is.

Critics claim that as the technology has no obvious practical use its real purpose must have something to do with an unspeakably diabolical master plan that could eventually lead to humans eating highly-processed food pellets made from other humans.

Despite assurances that

the cameras are not there all the time, millions of Britons are expected to wear paper bags on their heads while running in a darting, zig-zag fashion in a bid to protect their privacy.

Emma Bradford, a sales assistant from Reading, said: "No-one has the right to know how often I go to Boots to buy my weekly supply of lubricants and thrush ointment. And I suppose this means I'll have

to go to the toilet with a bucket on my head."

A Google spokesman said: "For the umpteenth time, no-one will be able to see you having a shit.

"Of course that does not include anyone who happened to be shitting in the street at the exact moment our camera van passed by. Even so, our face-blurring technology will protect the privacy of any Glaswegians involved.

"We will, however, collect data on all the streets you look at so our partner organisations can then try to sell you things related to that street such as manhole covers, used condoms and bags of fresh vomit."

He added: "Ultimately Street View is like any other completely innocent surveillance network. If you have nothing to hide from Google, you have nothing to fear from Google."

Thought for the day: Life is not a popularity contest. Oh wait, it is. (Pope John Paul II)

Time to abandon Britain as Greggs becomes too expensive

BRITAIN is 'well and truly, Geordie-lass-on-her-hen-night fucked' if people can no longer afford to eat at Greggs, financial analysts warned last night.

Profits have plummeted at the high street baker due to a combination of falling demand and a sharp increase in the cost of whatever it is they put in their pasties.

Tom Logan, meat and pastry analyst at Donnelly-McPartlin, said: "We've always used Greggs as a sort of base line for absolute poverty.

"At the moment things do seem to be hurtling downhill like Frank Spencer on a roller skate. If people can't afford Greggs, then I would say we're

If people can no longer afford a Greggs slice then what the fuck are they eating?

about six to nine months away from what I like to call 'Mad Max 2'."

But Greggs insisted it will work hard to retain its customer base by finding new and exciting animals to mince and, if necessary, installing boxing rings at the back of their larger stores.

A spokesman said: "We'll toss in a ham and cheese slice, get two unwed mothers to scrap for it and charge a fiver at the door.

"We'll also take a 10% commission from the local bookie. Our customers love nothing more than betting on a skank fight."

Meanwhile Sainsbury's has admitted the profit plunge at Greggs 'does not bode well' for its Taste The Difference range.

A spokesman added: "We may as well try shifting birthday cakes made of raw tripe with Cherie Blair's face on them."

An excellent day all round, say media, police and anarchists

A GATHERING in central London was enjoyed greatly by all who took part, the organisers have confirmed.

The event, in aid of several causes, was judged 'an unqualified success' despite early fears of bad weather and a lack of blood-soaked violence.

But by mid-afternoon the sun was shining and the boisterous crowd had begun to engage in a series of good natured clashes with the police as both sides were cheered on by hundreds of jubilant reporters and cameramen.

Mr William McKay, of the media, said: "Everyone was most helpful, particularly the young man who waited very kindly for the photographers to turn up before throwing a computer through the window of the Royal Bank of Scotland.

"I would also like to thank the police for wasting very little time in getting in amongst it."

Mr Julian Cook, of the anarchists, said: "The police were marvellous. The Commissioner and his team worked very hard to make the day such a great

'Well played!'

success and I can't thank them enough.

"I think we can all look forward to a memorable season of bloody street battles and violent arrests. Weather permitting!"

Meanwhile Mr Thomas Logan, a police constable, added: "It's the first time I have attended a local event such as this, but luckily I got to knock the absolute fuck out of eight hippies. I'm chuffed to bits."

The event was opened by the local celebrity, Mr Russell Brand, who wished everyone a 'splendid day' before inviting any granddaughters over the age of 18 to strip down to their bra and pants and form an orderly queue outside his tent.

Britney may as well be a corpse puppet, say fans

BRITNEY Spears kicked off her first major tour in five years with a larynx-free performance that was no better than a dancing corpse puppet, angry fans said last night.

Concert goers said the star's lower lip and chin performed extremely well but were disappointed she had chosen not to use her lungs.

Throughout the show Spears was strapped to a trolley which was manoeuvred around the stage by a series of ropes and pullies while a pair of dancing legs was projected onto a whiteboard covering the lower half of her body.

Meanwhile the pop princess's hands were tied behind her back as two large, rag doll arms, sown into her costume, flailed manically as she was jerked rapidly from side to side.

There was a brief technical hitch during the second half when the twitching legs of *Riverdance* star Michael Flatley were projected onto the whiteboard by mistake.

But despite having her head strapped to a metal pole the star was able to move her lips in synch to the music while a potent cocktail of amphetamine was pumped into the base of her spine in a bid to keep her eyes open.

Tom Logan, who attended the show along with his wife and 11-year-old daughter Nancy, said: "The mime-dancing and the scary arms were good, but as a family we really wanted to witness her straddle a chair in high-sided panties while simulating masturbation."

Nancy added: "She's not as good as the Pussycat Dolls. Daddy's taken me to see them 14 times."

Not all Britney's fans were disappointed, however.

Bill McKay, 44, from Houston, said: "It was an amazing, life-enhancing performance if your life happens to revolve around fantasies about a 27-year old substance-abusing, mother of two dressed up as jailbait."

Is it time to tax the shit out of doctors?

DOCTORS should be taxed every time they open their fat, smug, overpaid mouths, it was claimed last night.

People across Britain said the money could be reinvested in the NHS and used to pay for nice foreign doctors who just treat you instead of making you feel like Adolf Eichmann every time you fancy a Star Bar.

As the British Medical Association called for the systematic annihilation of the country's entire population of Creme Eggs, consumers said it was time to take the UK's doctors by the heels and shake them while at the same time ignoring their calls for a ban on being held upside down.

Bill McKay, a slightly overweight shop owner from Harrogate, said: "If I take my car to the garage and the mechanic tells me that low quality motor oil should be banned my immediate reaction is tell him to shut his fucking face and fix my bloody car because that's all he's paid to do and if I want his overpriced opinions I'll fucking ask for them.

"But that doesn't happen because the British Mechanics Association isn't filled to the brim with arrogant, self-regarding pricks who think they own your body and prescribe whatever pills the computer tells them to."

He added: "There's two ways we can do this. Either we can tax them for every statement they make calling for something to be taxed, or we can take 75% of the hundred and fifty grand they've conned out of the government for spending an extra year at university."

Emma Bradford, a primary school teacher from Bristol, said: "I suppose I've brought this on myself because you see, I don't know what butter is and so I just keep piling it onto my Weetabix until Nigella Lawson tells me to stop."

The healthiest way to hold a doctor

Press stole my dignity, not gang of whores thrashing my bare arse, claims Mosley

MOTORSPORT boss Max Mosley has accused the press of stealing his dignity rather than the gang of whores he paid to thrash his quivering buttocks with a riding crop.

Giving evidence to a committee of MPs, Mosley insisted his family was 'immensely proud' of his regular, German-themed, sado-masochistic orgies right up until the moment it was reported in the *News of the World*.

The FIA boss said: "I would get undressed in a very dignified manner. Then two of the whores, both reeking of dignity, would drag me to a chair where I would be forced to bend over and present my buttocks with more solemnity than the Queen Mother on Remembrance Sunday.

"I'd then be strapped to the chair with a pair of very dignified leather thongs before the most respectable of the whores started screaming at me in a well-educated German accent.

"Sometimes I would ask one of the whores to put on my Deacon Blue CD so I could sing along while they thrashed all the shame out of me."

Reciting a song from the album, Mosley added: "And I'll sail her up the west coast, through villages and towns. I'll be on my holidays, they'll be doing their rounds.

"They'll ask me how I got her, I'll say 'I saved my money'. They'll say 'isn't she pretty, that whip called dig-ni-ty'.

"Set it up, set it up, set it up, set it up, set it up, set it up. Yeah set it up again, set it up again, set it up again, set it up again.

"Only this time do it much, much harder."

WHAT'S A PHYSICS? ASK GCSE PUPILS

CONCERNS have been raised over the standard of science teaching after it emerged thousands of GCSE pupils could not tell the difference between a microscope and a frog.

Exam regulator Ofqual has demanded urgent action by ministers before a child suffers serious internal injuries from trying to drink a bag of carpet tacks.

Ofqual said the dumbing down of science teaching has led to children being awarded physics GCSEs for running head first into a wall, while the chemistry exam involves making a glass of Ribena without getting yourself or anyone else pregnant.

And according to Ofqual one child was awarded a 'B' grade after claiming that gravity was invented in 1994 by his Uncle Derek.

A spokesman said: "We risk creating a generation of adults who will not only lack vital 21st century skills, but who also risk electrocuting themselves while trying to release the tiny people trapped inside their television sets."

Questions from last year's science GCSE paper include:
- Where is 'up'? Is it: (a) up (b) down (c) Thursday?
- If a falling object accelerates at 10 metres per second per second, who is your favourite character on *Desperate Housewives*?
- Why aren't aeroplanes made from butter?

Schools minister Jim Knight defended the exam system, adding: "As long as the most able pupils are being stretched we just have to make sure the rest of them know the difference between hot and cold so they don't keep shoving their head into the deep fat frier at KFC."

Women sad about something, say men

WOMEN across Britain seem to be terribly sad about something, men said today.

In homes and offices throughout the country men have noticed women consoling each other and comparing observations about what seems to be a very sad event.

Bill McKay, a man from Peterborough, said: "I'm not exactly sure what it is they're sad about. Has it got something to do with the cricket?

"Come to think of it I haven't noticed all the

A minute to a minute and a half should be enough

women being this sad together since, oh, it must be September 1997. They were sad for quite a long time

back then. God only knows what that was all about, though it must have been very sad because I remember tripping over flowers everywhere I went for at least a fortnight.

"I suppose I should ask why they're sad but that might involve being sucked into a conversation about the sad thing, and while I don't yet know what that is, I am pretty sure I don't care."

Tom Logan, from Chester, said: "Will being sad about the sad thing get me more sex, or will it make

people think I'm gay? It's a very difficult time."

Professor Henry Brubaker, of the Institute for Studies, stressed that not all the women were sad, especially the ones with attention spans longer than a photo caption.

He added: "There are some women who will not need counselling at a time like this. But only some."

Meanwhile Emma Bradford, a woman from Guildford, said: "It's all so sad. So very, very sad. What else is on?"

Put a bible over your penis, says Pope

POPE Benedict last night claimed that placing a bible over an erect penis before intercourse is the only guaranteed way to prevent the spread of Aids.

Speaking before his tour of Africa, the Pontiff said Aids could only be tackled by the 'traditional teaching of the church' and not a latex rubber sheath that contains infected semen and prevents it from transferring the virus to another human being.

Experts said that either the Pope is suggesting the bible is used like a condom, or he doesn't know what a condom is.

Dr Emma Bradford, of Reading

University, said: "I guess you would have to rip out a few pages of Leviticus and then somehow fashion them into a condom-like device using lots and lots of masking tape.

"Or you could shred the pages, soak them in water and construct something that looks a bit like a papier mâché cigar tube."

Dr Bradford added: "It has to be one of those two because suggesting that the African Aids epidemic can be contained simply by reading the bible would be criminally insane."

May cause chafing

Since his inauguration in 2005 the Pope has continued the Church's strong opposition to condoms by calling for abstinence, supervised heavy petting and whacking it repeatedly with a wooden spoon until it goes all soft again.

Meanwhile the Vatican has issued this year's list of approved non-penetrative carnal techniques including pearl necklaces, light genital branding and something going by the name of 'Dutch steamboating'.

IS OFCOM RUN BY POOFTERS?

CONCERN was growing last night that Ofcom, the media watchdog, is being run by a bunch of nancy-boy poofters.

The regulator was accused of flaming gayness after it launched an all-out hissy fit against Chris Moyles, Radio One's morning oaf.

Moyles was censured for singing like a whoopsie in a way that could offend

other whoopsies, as well as being generally horrid and dressing like a binman.

An Ofcom spokesman said: "After careful consideration we've decide that he's just a big, fat, ugly piggy-wig. And talk about rough trade, I wouldn't touch him with yours.

"I'm sure he thought he was being oh so hilarious but he was actually being a total bitch. The BBC needs

to tell him to just be nice."

Media analyst Julian Cook said: "While Ofcom being queer is not, in itself, a problem, one thing that is guaranteed to provoke negative feelings towards the gay community is a major public body issuing terribly important statements every single time a stupid DJ makes a stupid joke about a stupid pop star.

"Ofcom needs to realise that people can work out for themselves that Chris Moyles is a tit instead of launching a major investigation every time some arsehole picks up the phone."

Cook, who admits his first name is slightly poofy, added: "Everyone needs to calm the fuck down and stop being so gay about everything."

NEWS BRIEFLY

ATTACK ON GOODWIN WASN'T MY FAULT EITHER, SAYS BROWN
The prime minister denied stoking hatred towards bankers just hours after a speech in which he compared them to the homicidal maniac from *Blue Velvet*, Frank Booth

IS THERE ONE THAT'S HOUSE TRAINED? ASKS MADONNA
The pop star is looking to add to her collection of Malawians, which she described as strong characters, with deep-rooted hunting instincts who took well to training but needed strong discipline from the start

CITY WORKERS URGED TO DRESS LIKE SCUM AND TALK ABOUT 'CORRIE'
A Met spokesman said: "If your disguise does not work and you are threatened by scum, do not try to impress them with the five games you played at stand-off for the university third XV, or the fact that you used to box for Cambridge. They will simply hit you with a bottle and then use you as a missile to throw at the police."

POLICE BLUNDER REVEALS PLAN TO BEAT YOU SENSELESS
"A society can survive when its police force is either violent or stupid, but you really can't do both at the same time, says expert

JACQUI SMITH CHANGES NAME TO 'TRIXIE BEAVER'
Other government departments expected to follow suit with the Department of Health finalising a series of pamphlets on oral fun

Windows 7 to include punch-screen technology

MICROSOFT has confirmed that its new Windows 7 operating system will allow users to interact with their computer by punching it in its bastarding face.

The software giant said it had invested hundreds of millions of dollars in state-of-the-art features which will help users communicate their rage in a physical way which the computer can then analyse and respond to, instead of just designing a programme that was not a frustrating, overpriced sack of shit.

IT expert Tom Logan said: "Windows 7 will offer real-time, multi-platform cross-functionality, which basically means it will be useless not just on your PC and your laptop, but on your mobile phone as well.

"But the key difference from Microsoft Vista is that it will let out pathetic, hitch-pitched yelps when you batter it repeatedly with a shoe."

Logan added: "If punch-screen is a success we could eventually dispense with the keyboard and mouse altogether and you'll be able to accidentally wipe all your files just by screaming at the

'Install updates again, I fucking dare you'

monitor and waving your arms about like a maniac."

The technology has also been incorporated into Microsoft's 'WifeAlert', an add-on which will allow furtive users to instantly replace hardcore Malaysian pornography with the RSPCA website via nothing more than a panicked slap of the hand.

Meanwhile the BBC said it would explore ways of integrating punch-screen with its live broadcasts.

A spokesman said: "You could spank Tim Lovejoy in the face during *Something For The Weekend* and via a series of high-speed interactive feeds we could make sure he felt it."

No such thing as arsehole bees, say experts

THERE is no bee equivalent of a lazy, self-centered arsehole who offloads all their admin onto you, according to new research.

A four-year study into insect swarm behaviour found that bees exist in a state of perpetual co-operation and never lock their larvae in the hive, get pissed and started chinning each other outside a bee nightclub.

The research also revealed that ant colonies work together to eradicate danger instead of automatically assuming that it's someone else's problem and calling for the deportation of unskilled foreign ants from outside the European Union.

Professor Henry Brubaker, of the Institute for Studies, said: "Life on earth is infinitely varied, from creepy, deep-sea ghost fish to those weird little bats

that look rather like Graham Norton.

"But it seems only humans would gleefully fuck each other over for the sake of a Christmas bonus."

Professor Brubaker said the findings echoed the plotline of the film *Antz*, but without all that neurotic, New York Jewishness.

The professor added: "Insect evolution has bred out individuality. They'll never produce great art or engineering. But it also means they'll never produce a tiny Jude Law or a six-legged Chris Martin. Swings and roundabouts."

The study also found that while bees help frail, old bees across the road, it confirmed suspicions that wasps are a bunch of arrogant, two-faced bastards that wouldn't piss in your face if your teeth were on fire.

RSPB gives surprise backing to gigantic bird mincers

THE RSPB surprised conservationists last night by calling for the immediate construction of a UK-wide network of gigantic bird mincers.

The society revealed it was backing the construction of huge windfarms because it had grown sick of birds, which it said were noisy, unhygienic and interested only in themselves.

According to its research only 2% of UK birds are currently being minced, compared to 15% in Spain, 20% in Germany and 29% in Denmark, the European leader in the shredding of protected bird species.

A spokesman said: "We aren't saying put up windfarms anywhere, we want them targeted where they will kill most birds, especially big ones like swans and Golden Eagles.

"We want a coastal network of large turbines to stop foreign birds and a mini-turbine on every roof to get the really annoying little ones like finches and tits.

"But what we'd really like is a load of radar stations to give us early warning of where the birds are, just like

The Magimix Swan-O-Matic 9000

they had for the Luftwaffe during the Battle of Britain.

"Then we can funnel them in towards the turbines or – and this will require a bit of work – we can bolt some turbines onto a lorry and chase the bastards down."

The spokesman added: "It does mean we'll probably have to use the 'B' in RSPB for something else. We're thinking about 'Brians'."

The controversial policy change follows the recent recruitment of country sports enthusiast Brian Logan from the energy giant E.on as chief executive.

Mr Logan said: "Have you ever seen an osprey go through one of those rotors? Helluva show – blood and beak parts everywhere. You'd pay good money to see that."

Facebook gives you short attention span, says... ooh what's that?

SOCIAL networking sites like Facebook and Bebo are infantilising the human brain, encouraging instant gratification, short attention spans and ooh, look, a funny cat picture.

The claims, by neuroscientist Baroness Greenfield, will make disturbing reading for the millions whose social lives depend on yes Kate Moss is back to her glamorous best in a stylish new leather coat.

More than 150 million use Facebook to share thoughts, photographs and have you seen the latest series of *Criminal Minds* because it is totally awesome but not as awesome as this coronation chicken sandwich that really tastes of curry for some reason.

A further six million have signed up to Twitter, the 'micro-blogging' service that is really enjoying the new Kings of Leon album before going for a swim and then sushi with Faz and Tommo who has a disgusting rash but doesn't want to talk about it.

Henry Brubaker, of the Institute for Studies, said: "It may be that social networking sites shorten the attention span and lead to increased self-absorption, but then again, how the fuck could you tell? I suspect Facebook may be the symptom rather than the

Bored of funny cat pictures now

cause and that these latest studies are simply telling us how our unbearable childishness and self-regard made the Facebook phenomenon possible in the first place."

Professor Brubaker added: "Hello? Are you actually listening to me? Or are you downloading a new ringtone while I'm talking to you because you haven't changed it for three days and this one is going to tell us so much more about who you really are as a person and by the way that one with the dead terrorist is brilliant. 'I am killing you', fantastic. Have you seen *Criminal Minds*?"

Smokers to be offered ice lollies and cartoons

SMOKERS who who quit the habit will be rewarded with ice lollies, extra cartoons and may even be allowed to stay up after 9pm. The NHS is to roll out a new system of incentives to run alongside its existing strategy of a ban on cartoons, no ice lollies and, if necessary, a smacked bottom.

A department of health spokesman said: "Smoking is a very bad thing. It gives you nasties in your tummy and makes you all sad.

"If you're very good and you stop smoking for a week, you can have either a Mini Milk, a Twister or a Feast. If you're very, very good and you stop smoking for a month, you can watch *Animaniacs* when you come home from work.

"And if you're very, very, very good and you stop smoking for six months we'll let you stay up after nine o'clock and watch the lesbian episodes of *Sex and the City*."

The NHS believes the two-pronged strategy of punishment and reward will produce calm, obedient citizens who will share their toys and make friends easily.

Bill McKay, a 42-year-old smoker from Dorset, said he supported the new scheme, adding: "I want a bike! I want a bike! I want a bike!"

AHA HA HA HA HA HA, SAYS GOODWIN

"AHA ha ha ha ha ha ha ha, aha ha ha, aha ha ha ha ha," former Royal Bank of Scotland chief executive Sir Fred Goodwin said last night.

The disgraced banker spoke out while bent over double in an Edinburgh street, slapping his knee as his cheeks took on a deep, rosy pink colour.

Becoming light-headed, he was then forced to crouch down with his head buried in his hands while his shoulders began to jiggle uncontrollably.

Minutes later the 50-year-old pensioner stood up and attempted to compose himself before his face erupted once again and he began waving frantically as if to stay, 'no, stop, stop, I can't take it any more'.

Bending over for a second time, Sir Fred's body was soon gripped by a series of convulsions and within moments he had collapsed onto the pavement where he began rolling back and forth, clutching at his abdomen.

Sir Fred then struggled on to his hands and knees, trying desperately to catch his breath and asking passers-by for a glass of water.

One eyewitness said: "He was making this strange rasping noise, a bit like a goat that's been kicked in the testicles.

"His eyes were all red and watering and he was breathing very heavily. I asked him if he was going to be okay but that just set him off again."

Energy companies forced to come up with new range of bullshit excuses

ENERGY companies will be forced to invent a new range of bullshit excuses for putting up prices whenever they feel like it, it emerged today.

Industry regulator Ofgem is set to impose new rules after an investigation revealed that the 'wholesale energy markets', blamed for a series of price hikes in recent years, do not actually exist.

An Ofgem spokesman said : "When we asked the companies where they get their energy from they all said it was from some guy called Ishmael who runs a market stall in Uzbekistan.

"They gave us directions and sure enough eight days later we found ourselves in the middle of nowhere face to face with a confused looking man and a herd of camels."

"We asked him if he knew Ishmael or knew anything about the whereabouts of the wholesale energy market but he just laughed and then asked us which of his 'girls' we would like to have sex with."

The world's six big energy companies will now be banned from even mentioning wholesale markets and must each come up with a different bullshit excuse to prevent any suspicion of price fixing.

Powergen has already responded to the new regulations, claiming it has been forced to increase prices by 8% after its April batch of electricity was stolen from the boot of its car by a gang of Irish gypsies.

Meanwhile a spokesman for rivals E.on said: "Someone left a gate open on our gas farm and all the gas escaped and we had to hire a load of cowboys to round up the gas and that means the price of gas has to go up again, sorry."

Nevertheless, Ofgem stressed that the energy companies will still be allowed to charge extra for so-called 'green' electricity as long as guilty middle class people are stupid enough to pay for it.

G20 produces one trillion dollars from behind your ear

THE G20 summit made you giggle like a schoolgirl last night after producing a shiny $1 trillion coin from behind your right ear.

At the close of an historic meeting in London, Gordon Brown delighted his fellow world leaders by crouching down asking you if you had any money.

When you frowned and shook your head, the prime minister moved his hand up to your right ear where he produced a big, golden coin before adding: "Really? Well, what do we have here?"

Mr Brown then gave you the coin, patted you on the head and urged you to spend it all on sweets.

But as global markets applauded the miracle of the golden coin, experts urged caution, stressing Mr Brown's playful generosity is what is known in the real world as an 'illuuuusion'.

Tom Logan, of the Institute for Studies, said: "It allows you to carry on spending money on sweets while convincing yourself that you will not, at some point, have to start paying it back. Forever. And ever. And ever.

"I'll be honest with you, we're now in so much debt that if you can summon up the courage to look at your share of it you will scream, faint and shit your pants all at the same time.

"Not only that but the coin does actually belong to some Chinese and Saudi Arabian gentlemen and if they don't get it back they will make you dance naked on a table and turn your house into a bathroom for their racehorses."

He added: "What the coin basically means is that your retirement will last the eight seconds it takes for you to collapse at your work station, fall to the floor and die and up until that point you'll be taxed every time you use the letter 'A'. Enjoy your sweets."

Amazing

Benitez signs on for five more years of buck-passing

RAFAEL Benitez has signed a new contract which will see him blame other people for Liverpool's failures until 2014.

The coach, linked recently to Real Madrid, said his love for the city, for the fans and for apportioning his shortcomings to a varied cast of largely irrelevant bystanders was 'impossible to resist'.

After months of wrangling, Liverpool chiefs agreed to new clauses which will allow Benitez to berate one board member a month for the team's failure to beat a recently-promoted Championship side.

He will also be allowed to blame Sir Alex Ferguson's eyebrows, the influence of Mercury in Virgo and all refereeing decisions, including those that have nothing whatsoever to do with Liverpool.

One sticking point was the manager's control over transfer budgets, with previous signings including a

Benitez has often blamed the tomato

blind, 80-year-old Spanish midget, a large Spanish tomato with a picture of a footballer drawn on it and Jermaine Pennant.

It has also emerged that Benitez insisted the negotiations were conducted in front of a large screen showing the recent goals against Manchester United and Real Madrid, as he gestured periodically while muttering 'muchos dineros' to himself.

Owner Tom Hicks said: "I was never worried that Rafa would quit Anfield. We are, after all, paying him four million pounds a year to produce the kind of football that would cause an amphetamine-fuelled Jonathan Pearce to slip into a coma."

Man Utd boss Sir Alex Ferguson also welcomed the new contract adding that he was relishing another five years of attempting to gradually nudge his rival into complete insanity.

Most footballers now under arrest

ONLY one in 10 professional footballers in England is not currently under arrest, the FA confirmed last night.

According to the latest figures, the most popular offences are sexual assault, grievous bodily harm and speeding, with two players accused of committing all three offences simultaneously.

Officials have also warned that the remainder of this season's European fixtures are under threat as foreign travel will leave many of the players in breach of their bail conditions.

FA chief executive Brian Barwick said: "Most have handed their passports to the local nick and the rest won't get through the airport metal detectors on account of their ankle tags."

Barwick said he was now working with the Foreign Office and the US

government in a bid to fly some of the players to the continent using the system of extraordinary rendition.

A spokesman for the Professional Footballers' Association said: "Our members are under intense media pressure and should not be victimised for what may or may not have happened with that broom handle round the back of Chinawhites."

Meanwhile the FA has devised a points system which will be used to fine clubs whose players are convicted. Nightclub affray will score one point, drink-driving three points and serious sexual assaults five points.

It is understood that one top-flight club has asked for clarification after one of its players committed an act of gross indecency against a listed building while under the influence of Ketamine.

As the BNP wins a seat on Sevenoaks District Council...

IS BRITAIN FACING THE SAVAGE NIGHTMARE OF AN UNSTOPPABLE HEADLONG DESCENT INTO NAZISM AND DEATH?

MY BIG GAP YEAR dispatches from POPPY SPALDING

Tuesday: Dubai

DUBAI, Dubai – so good they named it twice. I've never seen so much money crammed into one space – even the eye spaces in the ladies' veils are filled in with diamonds. It's the sort of place where everyone's dreams really can come true – as long as your dream isn't to have a noisy shag on a beach.

The first hurdle came while checking in at my hotel. The receptionist kept asking me to fill in my husband's details. When I said I didn't have one, she asked me what company I came from. So I just said I was from 'Spalding'. 'Like tennis ball,' she nodded. Next to that it said 'Designation' so I wrote 'CEO'. Then, in the space

for 'Husband', I wrote 'Andy Murray'. It was really pretty convincing and it certainly stopped her asking insane questions.

Right next to where I'm staying is the totally awesome, rich man hang-out, the Burj al Arab seven star hotel. I just had to get a boat out to sea and see if the Iranians have a point about it looking like a crucifix and being offensive. Now I've seen it, I think the Iranians are being a bit difficult. I mean, I guess the sky restaurant at the top goes across in a kind of crucifixy way. But the Iranians are forgetting: Jesus died a horrible death on the cross. Surely, they should shout 'Yee Ha!' (in Farsi) every time they see it.

Plus, there is so much money in the Emirates that

I'm sure someone could build a hotel right next to the Burj which could appease the Iranians. Maybe it could be shaped like Salman Rushdie's head and have big neon flames shooting out the top of it. You know, Vegas-style. They do love setting him on fire: it's like going to the movies for them.

The beach near my hotel is the same one the couple got arrested for shagging on. I watched where I put my feet because, while I'm all for free love and kinky sex, you just don't know what they could have left behind. Like, at my school prom, they had a rule about no kissing. I thought this was a bit extreme, but then Lucy Cunningham from 6-2 got caught giving Jason Berry a hand job behind the stage.

And did they clean up the ping pong table afterwards? No they did not. If the Crown Prince of Dubai had been in charge at my prom, things could have been much less gooey.

Now I really do understand why it's better to be married to Andy Murray than to be some unpredictable singleton, loose near a beach. (And besides, Andy doesn't need that kind of publicity and is much too busy for sex anyway). It's the Emiratians' constant endeavours to keep people's dirty tights and pants up around their bums where they belong, and not partially buried in lovely yellow sand, that makes Dubai, Dubai the greatest city in the world!

YOUR ASTROLOGICAL WEEK AHEAD
with PSYCHIC BOB

Aquarius (20 Jan-19 Feb)
Mercury moves into the house of repressed memories, so now is an ideal time to ask your parents why Uncle Frank is never invited to family gatherings

Pisces (20 Feb-20 Mar)
Those really are magnificent balls.

Aries (21 Mar-19 Apr)
With a quartet of planets in your horoscope's most creative zone, you'd think you could come up with something other than your normal derivative shit.

Taurus (Apr 20-May 20)
Nobody ever gets over their first love, but a chance encounter this week will make you realise that they very quickly got over you.

Gemini (21 May-20 Jun)
Mars, your ruling planet, helps Aquarius move into sheltered accommodation.

Cancer (21 Jun-22 Jul)
Facebook, Twitter, MySpace – how many more ways do you need showing that nobody cares about you?

Leo (23 Jul-22 Aug)
Venus crosses your threshold

for an epic, four-month stay, but still can't remember to pick up his coffee cup and take it back into the fucking kitchen. What is his problem?

Virgo (23 Aug-22 Sep)
Just a thought, but have you considered threatening to kill one every hour until your demands are met?

Libra (23 Sep-23 Oct)
Saturn moves into Jupiter and asks you to sort out that hairstyle and for Christ's sake get some new glasses.

Scorpio (24 Oct-21 Nov)
The direct motion of

Mercury in your house clears away recent crossed wires and confusion. So why couldn't BT do the same?

Sagittarius (22 Nov-21 Dec)
That feeling you've had since childhood that you were destined for something special will be borne out this week when you are slaughtered by an infamous serial killer.

Capricorn (22 Dec-19 Jan)
It is certainly unusual looking, but if you can still use it to pee, I would not worry too much.

The Daily Mash

POLICE TERROR RAIDS UNEARTH TREMENDOUS AMOUNT OF BULLSHIT

POLICE raids on suspected terrorists have uncovered a potentially lethal stockpile of bullshit, it emerged last night.

According to security sources, police raids in Manchester, Liverpool and Clitheroe have so far yielded eight packets of crisps, some beard shampoo and a foreign looking hat.

In a statement a senior police source said: "Put the crisps in the hat, add some shampoo, give the whole thing a good shake and what have you got? Unimaginable carnage, that's what you've got.

"They were definitely planning to blow themselves up in the middle of the Arndale Centre, or the Trafford Centre, or the railway station, or St Ann's Square, or any one of the 200 pubs and clubs in central Manchester, or the airport, or in the middle of the M6. We're absolutely sure about that."

Sources said that the raids had been brought forward while also claiming that the planned attacks were almost certainly due to be carried out today or tomorrow. A source added: "We like to leave things to the last possible moment. Makes it a bit more like *Spooks*. If only we could discover a nuclear bomb that had a digital timer on it with just 10 seconds left. I'd love that."

Meanwhile a loophole which allows thousands of angry, bearded Pakistanis to enter Britain without background checks was doing its job very nicely indeed, the immigration minister told sources last night.

A source close to Phil Woolas said: "We let in just enough of them to keep you nice and scared, wait until they take a photograph of something and then arrest them at gunpoint."

Crisps + shampoo = boom

Lah-di-dah public schoolboys not so fancy all of a sudden

LAH-DI-DAH ponces who talk all proper are about to find out what life is like in the real world now their fancy school has shut down, it was claimed last night.

As recession-hit fee-paying schools across the country close their doors, thousands of intelligent, sensitive boarders are about to come face to face with large, pasty-faced boys with glottal stops and attention deficit disorder.

Thugs in England and Wales are now cracking their knuckles in anticipation as debate rages over whether to strip Little Lord Fauntleroy and his chums from the waist up or the waist down, and exactly which obscenities to scrawl on their foreheads with an indelible marker pen.

Wayne Hayes, a 15-year-old bastard from Peterborough, said: "I hear they all wear top hats and carry teapots. If nothing else it at least gives me a choice of which one to shit in."

Roy Hobbs, a 17-year-old borderline psychopath from Swindon, added: "I'm going to ask one of them if they know the Queen and if they say yes I'll say 'Queen this!' and punch them in the kidneys. It's part of my A-level project."

But Professor Henry Brubaker, of the Institute for Studies, said: "The plight of fee-paying schools may provoke a degree of schadenfreude but let's not forget that it also means more children being educated by local authorities.

"While some may say this is a good thing, others – such as those with a decent education – may suggest that it's a complete and total fucking catastrophe."

He added: "In 30 years time we could be living in a society where nobody knows what schadenfreude means."

Thought for the day: Beat Surrendeeeeer – Come on boys, come on girls, succumb to the beat surrender. (Albert Einstein)

The patronising of Susan Boyle goes global

QUIRKY Scottish singing sensation Susan Boyle is set to be patronised all over the world, it emerged last night.

The brave 47-year-old, who has a lovely voice and a really great personality, even though she is chunky and rather plain looking, has agreed to be hugged by US chat show queen Oprah Winfrey.

But Boyle has been warned that, despite the severely patronising reaction from her UK audience, she may not quite be ready for the Oprah show, where more than a dozen people have been patronised to death since 1992.

Showbiz insiders say the brave church volunteer is set to make millions after her gutsy performance on *Britain Must Be Stopped*, which she will probably spend on some frumpy skirts and a cardigan, as well as a nice bit of salmon for Pebbles the cat.

Freak-wrangler Simon Cowell said: "I won't be giving her a makeover, she's financially viable the way she is.

"I think everyone, except me, was amazed she could talk, let alone sing.

"I just wish I could put her in a wheelchair. Without

'Susan's old-lady hair is proof that no-one can imprison your dreams,' said Winfrey

getting caught of course."

Amanda Holden, the inflatable judge, said: "Bravo Susan, you've really taught us something very special about what's inside each and every one of us if only we have the courage to dare to dream.

"I just admire you so much for getting out of bed every day and somehow managing to cope with looking like that."

Meanwhile Piers Morgan, the inexplicable judge, added: "I know that Susan claimed she's never been kissed, but does that mean she's a virgin?"

Brown hails 'budget from the future'

THIS month's budget will be the first to be beamed into the House of Commons directly from the future, Gordon Brown has revealed.

The Prime Minister said that Britain's economic recovery would be based on electric bubble cars, floating skateboards and nuclear De Loreans powered by bits of old fruit.

In an interview with the Independent, Mr Brown revealed that the chancellor, Alistair Darling, has travelled to the year 2060 in order to gather evidence of future transportation methods as well as the results of every sporting fixture for the next 51 years.

He said: "Everything is going to be electric and we'll be able to make electricity from potatoes and banana skins. It will cost a lot of money but we can afford it because we can bet on all the horse races and stuff."

Mr Brown also dismissed business calls for

new investment in Britain's road network, adding: "Roads? Where we're going, we don't need roads."

Dr Julian Cook, director of political psychiatry at Reading University, said: "It has been fascinating to watch the steady evolution of the Prime Minister's dementia over the last few months.

"From thinking he was not only Spiderman but also his own arch-nemesis Doctor Octopus, to claiming he had created a new world order in a shed in the Docklands.

"And now he seems to be living in some kind of electric fantasy world where we all drive around in banana-powered De Loreans wearing self-fastening shoes. I really am going to miss him."

A beleaguered Downing Street spokesman said last night: "He had a *Back to the Future* marathon after the G20 and it got him all worked up. Seriously, just forget it."

I TAKE MY COFFEE BLACK – LIKE MY WOMEN, SAYS QUEEN

BUCKINGHAM Palace has ended months of speculation after announcing that the Queen is gay with a fondness for tall, powerful black women.

The announcement came just hours after Her Majesty was pictured resting her hand a few inches above the buttocks of US First Lady Michelle Obama.

A palace spokesman said: "After careful consideration and following consultation with the Prime Minister and the leaders of the Commonwealth, Her Majesty Queen Elizabeth II has confirmed that she is totally gay, especially when it comes to statuesque black ladies."

Royal observers had expected the Queen to make a move on the wife of a foreign head of state at some point this year with French first lady Carla Bruni the clear favourite.

Constitutional expert Denys Finch-Hatton said: "Everyone knows the story about the pillow fight with Imelda Marcos following a state banquet in 1974, even though the Palace always dismissed it as nothing more than playful hi-jinx. It shouldn't affect Her Majesty's constitutional position in any way, as long as she doesn't want to divorce Prince Philip and marry a nun."

Meanwhile, Prince Philip is understood to be fascinated with his wife's new sexual orientation but has urged her to steer clear of inscrutable Chinese lesbians.

Depressed Welsh patients prescribed Severn Bridge

DOCTORS in Wales are being urged to treat depression with a strong dose of the Severn Bridge.

As South Wales topped the league for anti-depressant prescriptions, experts said the £5.40 toll was not only more effective but would ease financial pressure on the NHS.

A spokesman for the British Medical Association said: "A course of Seroxat is fifty or sixty quid, but for just over a fiver we can get them to South Gloucestershire where they'd at least have a chance, dammit."

He added: "And for those who get halfway across and then can't face going on or turning back, they can always just jump off. If they survive, the estuary tides will no doubt take them on a thrilling adventure."

Welsh GP Tom Booker said: "There are other ways to combat depression, but getting some fresh air would force you to look at more Wales, while exercise would involve being trapped in a room with dozens of sweaty Welsh people.

"A healthy diet helps, but around here that's like asking for a honey-roasted unicorn in a bap."

He added: "The Severn Bridge was

As long as they don't try to swallow it

supposed to alleviate the suffering of thousands of people in South Wales, but instead they all just stare at it, calling it 'Satan's river-stick'. They even sing songs about it. It's hateful."

The treatment of depression in Wales has seen great advances in recent years, with courses of prescription drugs replacing the traditional method of being whacked over the head with a sock-full of foxglove by a half-pissed druid.

Teachers can get 10% pay rise when children are 10% less stupid and awful, says everyone

TEACHERS should be entitled to a 10% pay rise when the children they teach become 10% less moronic and unbearable, according to a new survey.

As the National Union of Teachers demanded an inflation-busting pay increase while thousands lose their jobs and the country is eyebrow-deep in debt, 100% of those surveyed said: "What the fuck did you just ask me?"

Emma Bradford, an unemployed shop worker from Stevenage, said: "Did you just say that teachers want a 10% pay rise? Is that really what you fucking said?

"I've just spent two hours queuing at the job centre to talk to someone who doesn't care if I live or die and you're asking me if teachers should get a 10% pay rise, a four-day week and more

holidays. You know what? I'll have to think about that."

She added: "Oh look, I've thought about it and no they fucking shouldn't."

Bill McKay, an unemployed personnel manager from Darlington, said: "You can have a 10% pay rise when your schools stop churning out a seemingly endless supply of rude, lazy, violent, stupid, little SHITS.

"And as for holidays, you can get five weeks the same as everyone else, even if that means sitting in an empty classroom all day and staring out the fucking window."

He added: "Now, if you'll excuse me, I am going to have to nip home, grab a three-iron from my golf bag and spend some quality time in the teachers' car park at my local high school."

NEWS BRIEFLY

POLICE TO TARGET HIPPIES WITH VIDEO CAMERAS
"In the midst of a highly charged protest situation it is very easy for things to be videoed getting out of hand," says senior officer

NHS TO FUND PADDY FIELD BIRTHING POOLS
Officials say the move will increase efficiencies without any health risks, stressing a 21st-century British hospital, teeming with MRSA and violent drug addicts, is every bit as safe as a dung-strewn farm

THE RECESSION HAS GONORRHEA, CLAIMS DOWNING STREET
Wife of consumer price deflation was mentally ill and had been seen crying at drinks parties, claims No 10 source

GOVERNMENT THROWS WEIGHT BEHIND RUBBER CARS
"It takes about 20 minutes to come to a complete halt and the inside of it is absolutely covered in vomit," says designer

SHALLOW CONTEST PRODUCES STUPID CONTESTANT
"Marriage should only be between a table and a chair," insists barely sentient clothes horse

TORTURE 'VERY EFFECTIVE AT GIVING ME POWERFUL ERECTION' SAYS CHENEY
"They should release those files", insists former vice president

All adverts must be filled with lies, says watchdog

ALL advertising must be filled with blatant, insulting lies from start to finish, the industry watchdog has ruled.

The Advertising Standards Authority clarified the regulations last night after banning a beer advert which was obviously true.

The ASA said that the advert for Courage beer was unacceptable because it implied that drinking alcohol could serve to enhance self-confidence in a way that anyone who has ever drunk alcohol is completely aware of.

The advert shows a chunky woman squeezed into a tight dress, asking her husband how she looks. The man is shown reaching for a pint of beer, accompanied by the slogan, 'Take Courage and tell your wife she's a big fat cow'.

The ASA said its latest ruling was in accordance with its remit to ensure that all British advertising can be safely viewed by two-year-olds.

A spokesman added: "Brands should at all times avoid the honest depiction of

Take Volcano Water's 14-day I'll-Believe-Any-Old-Shit-You-Tell-Me challenge

realistic situations and instead follow the excellent example of yogurt or mineral water ads that make sufficiently vague claims about health-giving properties that are impossible to disprove.

"If companies want to avoid really aggressive lies they could copy the latest Persil advert which tells you nothing about the effectiveness of the product but does imply that if you do not use it you should have your children taken away from you by social services before they die of a dirty shirt."

Roy Hobbs, a consumer from Hatfield, said: "My wife is extremely large but also surprisingly fast, so I reckon I'd need at least six pints."

Tax accountants order new Bentleys

BRITAIN'S tax accountants were last night gleefully flicking through brochures for the Bentley Continental GT after chancellor Alistair Darling unveiled radical plans to take more money from rich people.

As Mr Darling outlined his strategy to present the incoming Conservative government with an Olympic-sized swimming pool filled with shit, tax accountants were locked in an intense debate over whether or not to go for the soft-top version.

Tom Booker, an accountant from London, said: "It's got a 'bluetooth' and something called 'multi-zone climate control'. Amazing. And look at all that leather. There must be at least nine cows in there."

He added: "Anyway, I must get on. Busy, busy, busy."

In the wake of the chancellor's announcement, the government of the Cayman Islands unveiled its plan to reclaim more than 20 square miles of the Caribbean Sea to construct

the dozens of new buildings that will contain the tiny offices of thousands of shell companies set up by British tax accountants.

Meanwhile economists and art historians last night congratulated Mr Darling for presenting Britain's first ever surrealist budget.

Bill McKay, deputy director of the Tate Modern, said: "None of it makes sense. Not a single word. It was a very brave thing to do."

He added: "The growth forecast for 2011 is an avant-garde masterpiece. It's as if the budget has been written by Salvador Dali during a particularly hallucinogenic bout of tropical fever."

Julian Cook, chief economist at Madeley Finnegan, said: "I especially like the bit about wiping out the £1.4 trillion deficit by increasing tax for all domestic cats who earn more than £10,000 a year.

"We're really just talking about those cats that appear in television adverts and there can't be more than four of them."

Britain's only shop makes enormous profit

THE only place where people can buy things has made a huge profit again, it has been confirmed.

Despite the recession The Shop made more than £3 billion last year, 10% up on the previous year, thanks to its successful strategy of bulldozing absolutely everything and then putting a shop on it.

The last 12 months have also seen The Shop diversify into a wide variety of new services. Among these are mobile cardio-vascular surgery, landscape gardening insurance and political assassinations.

Meanwhile The Shop has continued its popular advertising campaign of pretending there are other shops where all the things are more expensive.

Emma Bradford, a council worker from Stevenage who spends all her money at The Shop, said: "The Shop is so much cheaper than

Asda and Sainsbury's so I'm not surprised they never even existed."

But retail analysts say The Shop's attempt to break into the American market has stalled, mainly because America already has a shop.

A spokesman for The Shop said: "Today's results are a testament to our strategy of adapting to an ever-changing marketplace, offering outstanding value for money and being the only shop in the country."

He added: "The recession is helping us to achieve our vision of a society where everything is provided by either The Shop or The Government. Soon the two will merge into one and no-one need worry about anything ever again.

"Sleep tight."

'It provides everything that it tells me I need'

BROWN URGED TO DISTANCE HIMSELF FROM HIMSELF

PRIME minister Gordon Brown was last night being urged to distance himself from himself.

Mr Brown is under intense pressure to issue a personal apology to the Conservatives following an attempted dirty tricks campaign by two of his own turds.

Damian McBride, one of the Prime Minister's most trusted stools, was forced to quit after he was caught sending e-mails proposing a smear campaign against David Cameron and George Osborne based on unfounded gossip which everyone now assumes to be true.

Derek Draper, the recipient of the e-mails, emerged from Peter Mandelson's rectal passage in 1997. He has since been eaten by the Prime Minister and shat out all over again.

The e-mails were also copied to Charlie Whelan, one of Mr Brown's oldest and heaviest evacuations, dumped the morning after after an extra-large helping of beef curry at the 1994 TUC conference.

Shadow foreign secretary William Hague said: "Mr Brown cannot go around squeezing out fat, stinking turds all over the Downing Street carpets and then claim they have nothing to do with him.

"You are what you eat, you are what you defecate. You are the turd, the turd is you."

Meanwhile Alastair Campbell, one of Neil Kinnock's notorious turds who then went on to shit out Tony Blair in the early 1990s, added: "Their big mistake was not hounding a mentally fragile weapons expert who tried to expose some deliberate lies about an illegal war."

Git named

THIS year's Git has been confirmed as 34-year-old Ben Southall from Hampshire.

Southall now gets £75,000 for living in a luxury villa on a tropical island and spending his sun-drenched days snorkelling in the crystal clear waters of the Great Barrier Reef like a right fucking git.

His new employers, the Queensland Tourist Office, said his only task will be to write a daily blog about what an utterly amazing time he is having for no other reason than to rub our fucking noses in it.

Speaking from behind an enormous, shit-eating grin, he said: "Oh, I'm sorry, do you not get seventy five grand to swan about in your trunks all day and eat freshly caught barbecued prawns in your hot tub? It must be me then."

Southall was congratulated by previous Gits including George Clooney, Richard Branson and Lewis Hamilton.

Clooney said: "The first thing a new Git has to do is organise an efficient way of ferrying the boat-loads of bikini-clad nymphomaniacs back and forth from the mainland.

Looks shit anyway

"But he is going to have to keep in shape, because as soon as he gets off that island a lot of people are going to want to kick the absolute hell out of him."

Tom Logan, Southall's best friend since childhood and the recipient of one of his kidneys, said: "I genuinely hope that fucking island is teeming with gigantic, poisonous snakes and you get bitten in half by a Great White shark, you bastarding, git-faced git."

Government to monitor one trillion cock pill e-mails

THE government has outlined plans to monitor all of Britain's e-mail traffic, covering everything from penis enlargement to Lindsey Lohan straddling a Labrador.

The only internet traffic exempt will be Ministry of Defence communications, NHS data transfers and anything that comes to or from the inbox of an MP, even if it has a JPEG attachment entitled 'Freaky Japanese Scat'.

IT expert Julian Cook said: "Sorry, I must have misheard. Did you say all the internet traffic in the UK? Are you fucked up?

"An elderly crofter living on a Hebridean sheep farm generates enough porn-related clicks to keep an IT worker busy for a year.

"Your average ADD office worker clicking their Facebook page like a starved lab rat on the food button would take more people than are currently alive in the world."

Civil rights campaigner Nikki Hollis said: "It's like that book by Orwell. Not the one with the pigs, the one set in the 1980s. What was it called?

"Anyway, the point is, if I decide to update my Twitter page every eight seconds, then that's just nobody's business but my own and the seven people who follow me. Hi Debs. CU l8ter. LOL."

But a Home Office spokesman insisted: "Nikki Hollis' ongoing Twitter status is very much the business of government. We need to be able to respond effectively the moment we intercept intelligence which suggests she has just eaten a Kit Kat and is beginning to regret it."

Government's 'banned list' makes everything all better

THE government's decision to ban some foreign people with unpleasant views has made everyone incredibly nice, it was confirmed today.

Within minutes of the Home Office announcement, racists, violent extremists and homophobes agreed to put down their placards and stop being so ruddy unpleasant all the time.

The Reverend Fred Phelps, the US psychopath who thinks all soldiers are gay witches, said: "The British government makes an excellent point. I will stop thinking these thoughts immediately."

He added: "Would you like to touch me on the bottom?"

And militant Islamic fruitcake, Safwat Hijazi, said: "Did I really say the infidels should be beheaded and that we should paint our mosques with their blood? That doesn't sound like me – I must have been drunk.

"Anyway, who's up for a

'God bless their wet, salty fun', said Phelps

double bill of *Jesus Christ Superstar* and *Fiddler on the Roof?*"

The government acted after a handful of British tourists were infected with horrid, nasty thoughts on the plane home from Acapulco.

Julian Cook, from Bristol, said: "About half way through the flight I turned to my wife and said, 'I don't want to go back to Britain, it's full of black people and homosexuals'. And she said she felt exactly the same way."

The government has today sent a leaflet to every home in the country advising

what to do if you find yourself being a bigot, including wiping down hard surfaces with Dettol and spending a long weekend in the Lake District with an Asian lesbian.

Meanwhile people across Britain are demanding that any 'banned list' must include the pathetic couple from the BT adverts.

Martin Bishop, from Hatfield, said: "I thought we'd got rid of them, but they're back and if we do not do something now it will be fucking weddings and fucking babies and it will go on and on and on."

Ofcom launches nipples probe

OFCOM, the broadcasting watchdog, is to launch a full-scale inquiry into televised nipples, it emerged last night.

The regulator said it was deeply concerned after more than 38 people complained about almost seeing some nipples on the ITV talent show *Britain's Just Awful*.

Angry viewers contacted the channel after 35-year-old contestant Fabia Carrera removed her clothes to reveal a pair of tassels covering what experts said were almost certainly nipples of the female persuasion.

A spokesman said: "Of the 39 complaints, 34 were from people who feel that nipples are inappropriate, especially when perched precariously at the out-most extremities of a female bosom.

"The remaining five were from men who have recently lost their jobs and have been forced to cancel their subscription to *Red Hot Dutch* and now require access to as many free nipples as is humanly possible."

Mrs Margaret Gerving, director of the Anti-Nipple

League, said: "Am I French? Is this France? At the very least they could ensure the nipple-coverings are in the shape of Sir Winston Churchill or Jesus."

The Ofcom inquiry is expected to be wide-ranging and among the proposals it will consider will be one for a 60% increase in the statutory Prime-Time Nipple Exclusion Zone.

A spokesman added: "We really must think about raising our complaint investigation threshold to more than 0.004% of the viewing audience."

Bono to create black hole of awfulness

NATO was on full alert last night after pop-shouter Bono threatened to read a 14-minute poem about Elvis on Radio Four.

Scientists warned the tax-efficient Irishman's performance risked tearing a potentially cataclysmic hole in the space-time-dreadfulness continuum.

Entertainment physicist Dr Roy Hobbs said: "The sheer density of po-faced twattishness could strain the boundaries of reality and we could be sucked into a parallel universe where Bono reading out his doggerel on national radio is considered sensible."

Hobbs is working with NATO to avert disaster by releasing controlled stanzas deep under the Atlantic. He added: "Listen to this: 'You wore a white jumpsuit and feasted on squirrels – As far as I know you never gigged in the Wirral'."

"If that is read out over the airwaves in Bono's unbearably laid-back yet excruciatingly earnest voice, thousands will die."

The poem, entitled 'You Were From Memphis, And So Wasn't Jesus' was written by Bono in 1994 without any apparent provocation.

Broadcasting regulator Ofcom said Radio Four's decision to air it in full was, 'as reckless as using a threshing machine to brush your teeth'.

Bonologist Dr Wayne Hayes said: "When he did that lyric about a mole digging in a hole, that was pretty bad. But now, with this, he has become death... the destroyer of worlds."

Rampant Gurkhas will chop your head off, warns Brown

PRIME minister Gordon Brown has warned of large piles of severed heads if thousands of tiny Gurkhas are given the right to live in the UK.

Mr Brown urged MPs to think again after the House of Commons rejected his plans to introduce a height restriction for the fearsome Nepalese soldiers. New Avenger Joanna Lumley said: "The prime minster proposed a completely unreasonable restriction of five foot six inches knowing full well that most Gurkhas are too small to go on the Nemesis at Alton Towers."

The Kukri: It's not used for spreading jam

Ms Lumley has vowed to continue her campaign of vengeance despite being arrested last week for trying to smuggle 14 Gurkhas into the country under her skirt.

But the Prime Minister told the House of Commons last night: "They don't mess about. They'll whip out their Kukris and lop your head off soon as look at you.

"They might even stick it on a spike as a warning to others. And they're really, really small which means they can sneak up behind you and before you know it your head is bouncing along the pavement like a dropped melon."

He added: "Don't get me wrong, I have huge respect for the Gurkhas but

they are basically Britain's equivalent of Luca Brasi in *The Godfather*.

"Extremely useful at frightening the bejesus out of people you don't like, but you don't necessarily want them hanging about the house."

A Downing Street spokesman later added: "We've put the country £1.4 trillion in debt, government ministers are chin-deep in sleaze and the cops are beating merry hell out of everyone. We just felt that the obvious next step was to tell thousands of heroic soldiers to go fuck themselves."

Search engine developers unveil total waste of time

SOFTWARE developers have unveiled a new search engine that is both highly accurate and a complete waste of everyone's time.

The Wolfram Alpha is a computational knowledge engine that can access and collate trillions of pieces of verified scientific data while at the same time completely missing the point of the internet.

The Wolfram uses complex mathematical equations to deliver search results in response to detailed questions, but has so far been unable to answer every-day web-based enquiries, including: 'So where are all the vaginas? and 'Can I see a photo of a monkey having sex with a cat?'.

Kyle Stephenson, a 15-year-old from Doncaster, said: "I type in 'Can I see some Swedish vaginas, please?', hit return and it

pulls up a data set revealing the location of every vagina in Sweden." Stephenson said that the technology was impressive before pointing at his groin and adding: "Unfortunately it's just not getting the job done."

Tom Logan, a pub regular from Hatfield, said: "I asked it 'how much secret explosive would the CIA have to plant to bring down Susan Boyle?'.

"I got back a detailed analysis by a Harvard engineer showing how burning aviation fuel could superheat the internal structure of Susan Boyle causing it to buckle and eventually collapse in on itself in what might look, to the untrained moron eye, like a controlled explosion."

A spokesman for Google said last night: "How many years did they spend working on this? Fantastic."

Budget to include £1 billion for new squats

TOMORROW'S Budget is expected to include a £1 billion programme to build thousands of houses that no-one can afford to buy.

Treasury sources say the initiative will not only look good for a couple of days, but could eventually provide a dry, energy-efficient shelter for families to return to after foraging through skips for food.

A senior official said: "We would urge people to wait until the houses are half-finished before they start squatting in them.

"And of course we do expect hundreds to grab their sleeping bags and queue overnight for the chance to squat in one of the luxuriously appointed show homes with toilets and glass in the windows."

The official added; "The only people who will be able to afford one of the new

homes are the builders who have just been paid to build them. But some of the builders may choose to move house thereby freeing up their old house for squatting."

Margaret Gerving, an unemployed unit from Darlington, said: "I've always dreamed of squatting in a brand new house. But I don't think it'll change me. I'll still spend most of my time swiping at the bailiffs with a large metal pole."

Experts say the housing programme is the latest in a series of leaked Budget initiatives that won't make the slightest difference to anything.

Employment consultant Tom Logan said: "I like the one about creating thousands of new jobs by building huge offshore wind farms that will be made in Portugal and controlled by a computer."

Vauxhalls not quite rusty enough, says Fiat

ITALIAN car maker Fiat has unveiled plans to take over Vauxhall, insisting the British-made cars are still not quite rusty and unreliable enough.

Fiat wants to buy General Motors' UK and German brands to a create a new pan-European third-rate car giant to compete with the likes of Volkswagen in its dreams.

A Fiat spokesman said: "If you kick a Vauxhall Astra only the rear bumper falls off, while the Corsa does not have the same all-over, reddish-brown hue of a typical Italian hatchback.

"On the other hand, if you so much as cough near the new Fiat Punto, both the bumpers literally fly off in opposite directions, the doors drop off their hinges and the headlights fall out like some kind of clown car. And then it explodes."

He added: "Under our plans Vauxhall will produce a range of exciting, eco-friendly cars that may not get you to the end of the street but will provide a useful storage space for people not fortunate enough to have attics."

British brands have an impressive history when it comes to foreign takeovers. In 1994 BMW bought Rover, before offloading it six years later as if it was emptying a chamber pot into a gutter.

Fiat pointed to its strong track record in rescuing troubled manufacturers. Alfa Romeo now makes stylish cars that are bought by discerning drivers who appreciate good design but have no desire to go anywhere, while Lancia has not sold a new car since 1977.

Meanwhile Fiat is also hoping to acquire the US giant Chrysler with a view to integrating its staggeringly unsuccessful technology and useless design know-how into its inexplicable strategy.

Iggy Pop to insure 1996 Renault Laguna

GODFATHER of punk Iggy Pop last night requested a comprehensive insurance quote for his 1996 Renault Laguna estate.

Pop was forced to act after the Advertising Standards Authority ruled that his commercials for Swiftcover.com had misled more than 11 people.

The ASA said it was shocked to discover that the New York-based new-wave legend did not have a motor policy with the biggest insurance company in Woking.

Insurance industry analyst Julian Cook said: "When I saw the advert I have to say my first thought was not, 'I wonder if he really does have a policy with Swiftcover', it was, 'Oh dear God, Iggy Pop must be absolutely skint'.

"Personally I would be shocked to discover if the 12 people who complained were not in some way connected to Norwich Union, or whatever the hell they're called these days."

Meanwhile the ASA rejected complaints from

He has a lust for load space

more than 250,000 Iggy Pop fans who said they could simply not believe what they were seeing.

Mr Pop added: "It's a diesel, it's done about 87,000 miles and I keep it in the driveway overnight.

"I don't use it for business or commuting. It's really just for nipping to the shops two or three times a week, golf on Saturday mornings and, of course, church."

A representative from Swiftcover explained that the insurance premiums are likely to be a bit higher since Mr Pop has four points on his licence for driving while having home-made vodka injected into the base of his spine and fucking a frozen chicken.

RECESSION TO BE SUSAN BOYLE-SHAPED

THE recession is likely to be the shape of quirky Scottish songstress Susan Boyle lying on her back, experts said last night.

A leading economic forecaster said Britain could expect to see positive growth by the middle of next year unless Boyle decides to lose a bit of weight and get herself all glammed-up.

Tom Logan, of the Ernst and Young Item Club, said: "If you imagine looking at Susan side-on while she's lying flat on her back, the worst part is the sharp descent from the tip of her big toe to the bottom of her shin.

"The rest of 2009 will follow the line of her lower leg, kneecap and thigh, then things should start to pick up a bit by the end of the year as we move up, over and beyond her 'private area'.

"By mid-2010 we should have scaled her chunky midriff and be exploring the lower regions of her fulsome and apparently untouched breasts. Then it's all a bit up and down as we negotiate her chin, mouth and nose."

He added: "We can't make any accurate predictions for 2011 until we know what she's going to do with her hair."

The Treasury dismissed the Ernst and Young Susan Boyle-o-graph, insisting the recession will be the shape of an upturned Walnut Whip or, at worst, a banana stapled to a melon.

Meanwhile pressure groups have insisted the shape of the recession must be used to highlight important environmental, human rights and health issues.

The WWF has called for the recession to be the shape of an endangered Tibetan Yak, while anti-smoking group ASH said millions of people will die unless the recession is the shape of a small child holding a crayon like a cigarette.

Match of the Day goes to its dark place

MATCH OF THE DAY has gone to its dark place and has urged viewers not to follow.

The BBC said its long-running football highlights show is no longer suitable for women, children and anyone who does not have profound and disturbing psychological problems.

The show will now be screened at 4am on Monday mornings and viewers will be warned that it includes strong language and sordid mental imagery 'right from the start'.

Corporation executives stepped in after pundit Alan Pardew said a heavy tackle during Sunday's game between Manchester City and Chelsea was 'like a donkey mounting a Dutch porn star'.

A spokesman said: "The BBC has to tread a fine line between taste and decency and fulfilling its statutory obligation to produce football punditry that trawls the most appalling depths of the human psyche."

The spokesman also explained why there had been no on-air apology at the time, adding: "Alan was misheard. It was thought he used the word 'monkey'."

In recent weeks Pardew has compared a penalty box incident during a third round FA cup tie to 'a Saturday night spit-roast at a West Midlands Travelodge' and claimed that the Everton back four 'would not look out of place in the shower room at a Turkish prison'.

And last month the BBC received more than 30 complaints after he suggested that Manchester United winger Cristiano Ronaldo 'could do with being tied buck-naked to a four-

Alan Pardew is about to say something disgusting

poster bed while a St Bernard takes a massive dump on his chest'.

NEWS BRIEFLY

OKAY, I DON'T KNOW WHAT A BANK IS, ADMITS BROWN
PM calls for 'family values' in financial system and claims that Barclays was born 'because a mummy and a daddy loved each other very much'

FOUR MILLION PEOPLE ARRESTED ON SUSPICION OF LITTERING
"If they weren't planning to commit a crime then why did they buy the crisps?" asks police spokesman

BRITAIN URGED TO SHUT UP ABOUT THE WIRE
"Why can't we produce anything as good as this? It's like Dickens," says man for the 800th time

Ipswich to keep large net handy

IPSWICH Town yesterday unveiled Roy Keane as their new manager but stressed they would be keeping a large butterfly net to hand, just in case.

Chief executive Simon Clegg said that while he expected Keane to bring silverware to Portman Road the club also had a responsibility to ensure they could catch him as quickly as possible.

He added: "The net is the safest method, but if he manages to outrun his carers then we are prepared to bring him down with a tranquilliser dart and then secure him to a wooden plank using strong leather bindings."

Much of the club's offices and training facilities have been padded in anticipation of the appointment, while a treatment room has been refurbished to accommodate Keane's electro-shock paraphernalia.

Keane told a press conference that Ipswich was a great club with a proud history that had always punched above its weight and said he was looking forward to taking his first training session just as soon as the 40-ft high

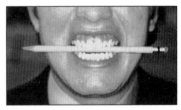

Keane prefers to bite down on a pencil

chicken had been removed from the centre circle.

The Manchester United legend also claimed none of his former team mates had so far made a success of management, while only a handful had harnessed the power to make themselves invisible.

Keane said that Mark Hughes had done better at Blackburn than Manchester City before insisting repeatedly that Steve Bruce does not exist.

He added: "I have the support of the owner who understands that it's very important for me to able to buy any player I want and then experiment on him in my underground laboratory."

YOUR PROBLEMS SOLVED
with HOLLY HARPER

Dear Holly,

Since the birth of my first child, I have developed a rather intimate and embarrassing problem, and I am just too ashamed to talk to my doctor about it.

Before I fell pregnant I was vaguely aware that having a baby might have some physical side-effects, but it seems that squeezing out a head and shoulders has seriously knackered my flaps.

I use to pride myself on my risqué collection of thongs and split-crotch panties.

Nowadays you'll usually find me hobbling around the feminine products in Morrison's with a large piss-sodden pad wedged under my clacker. All I want is for things to go back to the way they were before the birth. Can you help?

Geraldine
Newcastle

Dear Geraldine,

Once, in assembly, Mrs Gregory was telling us a parable from the Bible about the Prodigal Son. I think she was trying to tell us that you can be as naughty as you like and you'll never get in trouble with your mum and dad.

Then suddenly all the kids at the front started screaming and jumping up and I could see on the floor was a big stream of yellow wee coming from Oliver French. We all got to go outside and have extra playtime instead of hearing more dubious advice from Mrs Gregory, and Oliver French was taken to the welfare office.

It sounds like you maybe have the same problem as Oliver French, so try to get over your embarrassment and go and see the doctor as soon as possible.

Otherwise, you might end up wearing brown lost property pants and sitting alone on the naughty bench until your mummy comes to fetch you.

Hope that helps!
Holly

YOUR ASTROLOGICAL WEEK AHEAD
with PSYCHIC BOB

Aquarius
The entrance of Saturn into Uranus this week is a great big open goal that's just begging for a cock joke. But you know what? I'm better than that.

Pisces
Venus's arrival in your skies today favours three weeks of personality disorders followed by an even longer stay than normal in the secure unit of your local mental hospital.

Aries
A good week to butter up your contacts, and then wrestle with them naked in front of a large fire, enjoying the feel of their oiled, sleek bodies, but in an entirely non-sexual way.

Taurus
Your no-nonsense, speak-as-you-find attitude is often correctly interpreted by friends as sheer fucking rudeness. You fuck off.

Gemini
Pluto, the most useless of all the planets, enters your celestial house this week and starts trying to borrow a tenner until pay day.

Cancer
Wayward Mercury has broken into Shelley von Strunckel's office and mixed up all her charts, her stuff is going to be way out for weeks, if she even notices, the stupid bitch!

Leo
The stars come into a rare alignment, with opportunities galore on the horizon. It's a shame that ham-fisted morons like Leos will utterly fail to notice them.

Virgo
"Keep it tidy" makes a good Virgo mantra. Natural is one thing, but when it's hanging out the bottom of your skirt it's time to trim.

Libra
Keep the long term in focus at all times because the short term is just more career failure and continued sexual disappointment, followed by uncontrolled sniggering and pointing.

Scorpio
That heap of junk mail on your doorstep will finally reach the letterbox, alerting the authorities to your un-mourned death eight months ago.

Sagittarius
Even if you feel vulnerable, the positive energy surrounding you keeps you safe from those who would do you harm, although you probably should still carry two knives and a gun.

Capricorn
Tensions at home see you choosing to sleep on a park bench to avoid the crushing pointlessness of it all. A good time to start hoarding newspapers.

The Daily Mash

NICE JAPANESE MAN
FIX YOUR TELLY
Call:
チコソシキクモ

it's news to us　　　www.thedailymash.co.uk　　　No.10

DON'T PANIC BUT YOU ARE GOING TO DIE

PEOPLE across the world have been urged not to panic as experts warned that most of you would be dead by the end of this sentence.

As pork flu swept across the globe governments sought to calm fears by ordering 400 million coffins, while media organisations offered a reward to any scientist prepared to use the word 'holocaust'.

In the UK, experts stressed there was no risk from pork products before urging Britain's army of morons to round-up all the sausages they could find and throw them into the sea.

Professor Henry Brubaker, of the Institute for Studies, said: "There's nothing to worry about but this is definitely worse than four simultaneous nuclear wars and a dinosaur invasion."

Governments have called on media organisations to work together in the face of what one official described as 'a nice, big, fat panic'.

Professor Brubaker added: "The world is paying the inevitable price for years of unprotected pig sex.

"It's no surprise this started in a devoutly Catholic country where everyone follows the Pope's instructions to the letter, especially the pig molesters.

"Pig sex, chicken sex, monkey sex – eventually they all come back and bite us on the arse. But not goat sex, that still seems to be fine."

Meanwhile the editor of *Daily Mail* was last night under observation in a central London hospital after suffering what witnesses say was a 'cataclysmic ejaculation'.

A source said: "He got more and more engorged as the details came in

Daily Mail **editor Paul Dacre is badly dehydrated**

and then, when we got the Brubaker quotes, he went all cross-eyed, fell backwards off his chair and his trousers exploded. There was spunk everywhere."

Two Scottish people feeling a bit run down

THE government has raised its virus alert level to 'pantastic' after it was confirmed that two people in Scotland were hovering close to feeling slightly unwell.

The pair, from one of the dozens of nondescript hell-holes between Edinburgh and Glasgow, were admitted to hospital yesterday when their condition was described as 'critically fuzzy'.

Doctors said they were now 90% certain the couple were suffering from Pork Flu as opposed to a common strain of Scottish Influenza, also known as a bastard hangover.

Dr Tom Logan, from the Royal Infirmary of Scotland, said: "Scottish flu is particularly common at this time of year as the weather becomes milder and the days longer, meaning everyone spends even more time in the pub than usual, mainly because they can stand outside all night smoking hundreds of fags."

He added: "I would not be surprised if over the next few days we see thousands of Scottish people coming forward reeking of cheap wine and claiming to have spent the weekend in Mexico City."

A Department of Health spokesman said: "We are almost certainly facing a pandemic and there is now nothing we can do to stop quite a few people being given some pills and told to stay home and watch *Murder She Wrote*.

"However, we are urging those infected not to watch *Grey's Anatomy* on Living TV. It won't make their illness any worse, but it will make them much, much worse – as people."

Thought for the day: Nothing is ever straightforward with you is it? You fucking nutter. (Confucius)

It's the system that's a piece-of-shit, thieving bastard, say MPs

THE current system of parliamentary expenses is a corrupt, scum-sucking, piece-of-shit, bastarding thief, MPs insisted last night.

Members from all parties said the rules were a grubby, disgusting little scat-muncher and pledged a wide-ranging inquiry into how the system was somehow able to vote itself into existence in the first place.

As Labour proposed an independent audit committee in its latest deliberate attempt to miss the fucking point, MPs spoke openly about how they had been abused repeatedly by the expenses system.

Barbara Follet, the millionaire Labour MP married to a millionaire author, said it was 'outrageous' that she had been forced to defend her millionaire decision to buy three pairs of matching trainers for her pet fly.

Follett added: "He is a size six, he just happens to have very big feet for his age. And anyway, it's the system that's a repulsive, grasping turd on legs, not me."

But members of the public were quick to dismiss claims about the system as 'mind-buggeringly insulting horseshit' as it emerged that every MP is to get a £25,000 a year security allowance in a desperate bid to stop you kicking their teeth in.

Emma Bradford, from Harrow, said: "I'd like to designate him as my 'second MP', just for a couple of weeks, so that I can claim twelve grand to have him refurbished and then sell him to some really nasty Russian pimps."

Roy Hobbs, from Oldham, said: "I'd like to buy one of those four-slot Dualit toasters from John Lewis and spank him across the face with it so hard that I break both my wrists."

And Tom Logan, from Salford, added: "If you know that it's wrong now, then surely you knew it was wrong when you were spending my money doing up houses you bought with my money and then dodging capital gains tax even though you'd still have made a tidy profit and would, at least, have been able to return some of my money. You nauseatingly rancid lump of pox-ridden, cock-sucking pigshit."

Constitutional expert Denys Finch-Hatton said there was now an outside chance the scandal could

Hazel Blears has caused more violent retching than the winter vomiting bug

inflict some limited damage on the reputation of the House of Commons adding: "I suspect that from now on Westminster may become known as the 'Motherfucker of Parliaments'."

Top Tory claims for drawbridge wax

THE Tories last night proved they have still got it after it was revealed that a senior MP claimed more than £2,000 for drawbridge wax and moat freshener.

According to the *Daily Telegraph*, Douglas Hogg, MP for West Hoggshire, used public money to maintain an authentically medieval lifestyle, which included £150 a month to have his jousting kit dry-cleaned and £820 for a state-of-the-art German lance sharpener.

Mr Hogg, whose dad was called Quentin, said: "A drawbridge will start to squeak unless it is treated once a fortnight with three gallons of top quality Hungarian beeswax.

"If I am unable to raise my drawbridge then I face the very real possibility of working-class people coming into my castle and striking up awkward, stilted conversations while furtively stuffing the pockets of their smelly duffel coats with great handfuls of

Mr Hogg is impervious to Vikings

the pheasant paté that they have so very kindly paid for."

The latest revelations show a stark contrast between the two main parties with Labour MPs claiming for nice things from John Lewis that their parents could never afford, while the Tories are focused on maintaining large volumes of water in their back gardens.

According to House of Commons records, 14 senior Tories claimed more than £20m for moats, lakes, pools and pool-related paraphernalia, including a

retractable helipad and one of those inflatable chairs with the cup holder.

Meanwhile one Tory backbencher claimed more than £300 for eight tons of horse manure which he then tipped into his publicly funded swimming pool because he was 'a bit bored'.

But taxpayers last night applauded the Tory extravagance for its aristocratic self-confidence and grandiose ambition.

Julian Cook, from Hatfield, said: "I'm relieved to see that after all these years the Tories can still put on a show. It is nothing less than a masterclass in taking the absolute piss.

"You've got these petty, lower-middle class Labour MPs watching their wide-screen television sets and putting plastic covers on their three-piece suites, but it takes the solid brass nuts of an old Tory to claim for moat-widening."

He added: "If we are going to be governed by utter scum, it should at least be scum with a bit of style."

MP becomes first ever person to forget he had paid off his mortgage

LABOUR MP Elliot Morley was last night confirmed as the first person in the history of the world to forget he had paid off his mortgage.

The former minister admitted he had completely forgotten to stop claiming taxpayers' money for the mortgage he had paid off before forgetting which of his two houses he actually lived in most of the time.

Mortgage slaves across Britain were stunned at the sheer scale of Mr Morley's forgetfulness.

Martin Bishop, from Darlington, said: "Complete strangers will remember where they were and what they were doing when I pay off my mortgage. I fully intend for the event to be this generation's Kennedy assassination."

Tom Booker, from Hatfield, said: "I'm going to get Earth Wind and Fire to play 'Boogie Wonderland' so loud it explodes every window within a 12-mile radius while the Red Arrows do a flypast over my house. I will probably have to take out another mortgage but it'll be worth every penny."

And Emma Bradford, from Peterborough, added: "Remember when they attached millions of gigantic fireworks to the Eiffel Tower? I'll make that look like a fucking birthday cake."

Elliot Mortgage said last night: "Gosh, I am terribly forgetful aren't I? Perhaps I should eat more oily fish."

Forgetfulness expert Dr Margaret Gerving said: "As a former agriculture minister he may have spent a bit too much time with farmers. They're always forgetting how rich they are and then claiming thousands of pounds from people much worse off than them."

Luckily Mr Morley's head is screwed on

Mr Morley will today attend a brief ceremony at the London office of the Guinness Book of World Records, after which he is expected to hand himself in to the police.

Fat people eating shitloads of soup

AS new research revealed that eating soup could help with weight loss, greedy, fat people across Britain have set about devouring shitloads of the stuff.

Soup companies say they are struggling to cope with demand, while fast-food outlets are to provide extension cables so their wider customers have somewhere to plug in their hand blenders.

Bill McKay, 18 stone, from Doncaster, said: "I take two large pepperoni pizzas, feed them into my garden shredder and then shovel the resulting pulp into a pot of hot beef stock.

"I find it goes very well with a slice of wholemeal

Cheese + heat = soup

bread, plus another eight slices of wholemeal bread, plus some butter, some more butter and some very thick slices of pork. And a chocolate eclair."

Julian Cook, a 22-stone gourmand from Finsbury Park, London, explained: "I like to melt two different but complementary fromages over a low flame for about 20 minutes and then eat it very quickly with a spoon.

"Sometimes I'll add a sprinkling of lardons, though admittedly that is more of a broth."

Meanwhile Emma Bradford, 19 stone of unstoppable womanhood from Darlington, said: "I just dump a load of funsize Mars Bar into a soup bowl. It's the same."

But GP Dr Margaret Gerving was sceptical about the latest diet advice, adding: "How should I put this now? Okay... big deep breath... here goes... EAT LESS FOOD AND DO MORE EXERCISE.

"Do not make me say it again, I am begging you. Do not make me say it again."

Question Time audience marches on London

THE audience from BBC1's *Question Time* was marching on London last night, parading the severed head of housing minister Margaret Beckett on a pike, like some kind of ghoulish mascot.

Amid growing signs that things might be about to kick off, the audience spilled out of the Grimsby Institute at 11.20pm and immediately headed for Market Rasen via the A46.

They then carried on for about 15 miles before taking the Lincoln bypass and finally joining up with the A1 just south of Newark.

Earlier they had stormed the stage, grabbing presenter David Dimbleby and locking him in the ladies' toilet before beheading Mrs Beckett and firing senior Tory MP Theresa May through a stained glass window using a makeshift catapult.

As of 8am this morning the *Question Time* audience had stopped at a service station near Biggleswade for refreshments, a toilet break and a chance to wipe some of the gunk from Mrs Beckett's head.

The audience is being led by Grimsby loud-mouth Roy Hobbs, mainly because it's his pike.

Mr Hobbs said: "I went to the trouble of bringing a pike to *Question Time* so I do think it's only fair that I should be at the head of the party. And obviously when we get to London they are going to want to talk to whoever's carrying the severed head."

Mumbai Council urged to bulldoze Christian Bale's house

MUMBAI City Council was last night urged to switch the focus of its film star bulldozing programme to *Batman*'s Christian Bale.

As workmen flattened the home of the young *Slumdog Millionaire* actor Azharuddin Mohammed Ismail, film fans were already working out how many bulldozers would be needed to destroy Bale's Los Angeles mansion.

Tom Logan, from Finsbury Park, said: "*Slumdog Millionaire* wasn't that great but I wouldn't necessarily thrash someone with a bamboo cane and then bulldoze their house because of it.

"Now Christian Bale on the other hand is a miserable, charmless prick who could certainly do with having 25 tonnes of heavy machinery crashing violently into his open plan kitchen-dining room.

"I'd imagine that would make him shout and swear quite a lot; but of course the Mumbai Council workers will all be wearing their standard issue ear protectors in accordance with health and safety regulations thereby rendering impotent his pathetic and embarrassing rage."

Logan added: "I can just imagine him screaming 'what the fuck are you

'Sorry Christian, you'll have to speak up!'

fucking doing to my fucking house you fucking assholes' in that weird mid-Atlantic accent of his while the

demolition crew give him a big smile and a friendly wave before taking a dirty great sledgehammer to his downstairs bog."

Logan has e-mailed a bulldozing list to the mayor of Mumbai, including Daniel Day Lewis, Adam Sandler, Richard Curtis and 'every last fucker who was in any way involved in *Indiana Jones and the Kingdom of the Crystal Skull*'.

Meanwhile *Slumdog* director Danny Boyle has once again denied that Ismail had been exploited but admitted he probably should have paid him just enough to afford a new stinking hovel.

Pretend marriage on made-up rocks

THE pretend marriage of Jordan, the pretend novelist, and Peter André, the pretend human, was last night on the completely made-up rocks.

Friends of the couple's management company say Jordan, the fictional name of Katie Price, is pretending to be devastated after André invented one of his made-up words without consulting her.

A spokesman for the friends said: "Peter came home in the early hours of Sunday morning, pretending to be stinking of booze and cheap, slutty eyeliner, but things really kicked-off the next morning when he told Katie that he was 'exackered'.

"Peter said it was a combination of 'exhausted' and 'knackered', but Katie was clearly pretending to be furious with him.

"Within seconds the management company had got involved, pointing out that this would be the perfect pretext for an acrimonious pretend break-up resulting in lots of very real money from the idiot readers of *OK!* magazine."

Jordan referred to André affectionately as 'bloke'

The spokesman added: "After having the word 'pretext' explained to

them, they both agreed that it was probably a really good idea."

According to friends of the spokesman, Price has fled the country using her Jordan passport and will pretend to be heartbroken until her next pretend novel comes out.

A friend said: "It's such a shame that their obviously fictional love affair has ended in such a transparently false way. But it will all be great material for whoever it is that's been writing all her books."

WOMEN TO FORCE HAT-STAND INTO ANUS OF MALE MIDWIFE

Jemima Swinton, a pregnant lady from Stevenage, said: "We've set up the paddling pool, or 'hat-standing pool', so that he can see for himself exactly how much difference that will make."

THE very big terror plot uncovered by police last week is not big, does not involve terrorists and is not a plot of any kind, it has emerged.

An inquiry has been launched after nine brown men were deported for having beards, as the police blamed the Home Office, the Home Office blamed MI5 and MI5 warned everyone it could kill them with its thumb.

A police spokesman said: "We were hoping to charge them with conspiracy to go to the shops to buy crisps and Tizer, but according to our lawyers that that's not an actual offence, as yet.

"We have therefore taken the simple precautionary step of sending these men and their potentially explosive beards back from whence they came."

A spokesman for the home secretary said: "Embarrassed? No, we're way, way beyond embarrassment at this stage.

"That's a bit like asking a streaker if he's embarrassed because he has forgotten to shave."

Large-breasted women get it all their own way again

WOMEN with huge bazongas were last night getting it all their own way, yet again.

As Marks and Spencer agreed to reduce the cost of its freakishly large bras, normally breasted ladies said they would be forced to pay unnecessarily high prices to subsidise the over-bosomed.

Elizabeth Gerving, a 32C, said: "I don't see why they shouldn't pay a couple of quid more given the extra fabric that's required to cover their big, daft knockers."

She added: "We believe bra-pricing should be based on square footage and overall circumference. Some of these monsters can contain up to 12 yards of copper wire."

'The Stuart Rose'

Meanwhile it emerged that M&S chief executive Sir Stuart Rose surrendered after chesty campaigner Becky Williams bent over his desk while wearing a low-cut top that left little to the imagination.

Williams revealed: "I walked into his office, leaned over and said: 'Mr Rose, I do hope you can help me; you see, I'm a single mum who's struggling to support her two lovely twins'.

"And then I sort of squeezed them together, fluttered my lashes and went 'mmmmmmm?'.

"He coughed and spluttered a bit, agreed to reduce the price and then led me out of the room with his hand on my arse. Worked like a charm."

Retail analyst Tom Logan added: "So, Joanna Lumley is now in command of the Gurkhas, while women are taking to the streets to protest about their bras. Is it just me, or is Britain turning into *Carry On Up the Khyber*?"

Labour to back PR for insultingly obvious reasons

LABOUR is to back proportional representation in what they claim will be a major step towards rebuilding their chances of getting back into power before everyone's dead.

In a non-existent break with the party's traditional support for the system of doing anything to win power, senior figures said Britain's democracy needed comprehensive reform if future generations were to have their lives ruined by at least two different kinds of crooks and liars.

A Labour source said: "Proportional representation will help to rebuild voters' confidence in parliament because a recent study showed that MPs elected by PR don't make up rules that allow them to steal money."

He added: "What study?

Fuck you, that's what study."

Meanwhile Conservative leader David Cameron has pledged to limit the powers of Number 10 and devolve more responsibility to local communities in his latest transparent attempt to divert attention from all the thieving.

Experts last night stressed that PR had been a huge success in Scotland, where two party leaders were forced to resign over expenses claims and members of the Edinburgh parliament continue to make healthy profits from houses they buy with your money.

Meanwhile, public reaction to the proposed reforms was mixed, with some voters defecating into a paper bag and posting it to their MP, while others simply fainted with anger.

Bill McKay, a sales manager from Hitchin, said: "Proportional representation you say? To be honest, I don't actually know what that is. At the moment I'm much more focused on them stealing my money all the time."

Julian Cook, an engineer from Doncaster, said: "By all means dick about with the devolution of power to your heart's content, but if you could try your best not to steal from me while you're doing it, that would be excellent."

And Sister Margaret Gerving, a retired Mother Superior from Peterborough, added: "I could not give a flying monkey's fuck about any of this. Can you please – in the name of Christ – just stop stealing my fucking money?"

Librarians go like the clappers, say experts

QUIET, bespectacled female librarians really do go like a bloody train, it was confirmed last night.

According to researchers at the Institute for Studies, the tweed skirts and sensible glasses of intelligent, bookish women are nothing more than a flimsy facade concealing a smouldering volcano of hot, undiluted filth.

Professor Henry Brubaker said: "We have finally confirmed that women who look as if butter wouldn't melt in their mouths could actually suck a tangerine through a keyhole.

"While a simple-minded shop girl is perfectly suited for a perfunctory knee-trembler behind some bins, if it's eye-boggling three-way genital branding you're after, get yourself along to a poetry recital."

But Brubaker's research has come under fire from his peers, who claim it was nothing more than a ruse allowing him to say dirty things to clever women.

Professor Julian Cook, of the Studying Institute, said: "He claims to be researching the link between intelligence and intimacy but the next thing we know he's trooping female historians into his office and asking them if they've ever used a ball gag."

Tom Logan, a sexual intercourse enthusiast from Finsbury Park, said: "Are you telling me that just because Anne Widdecombe's got a degree in Latin that somehow makes her better at sex than Kelly Brook? I'm sorry, but I don't believe that for a second."

Astro-physicist Dr Nikki Hollis said: "I was slightly concerned when he asked me how long I could keep my ankles behind my ears. A quiet, bespectacled women like me is not used to hearing that kind of thing.

"And it's 45 minutes, in case you were wondering."

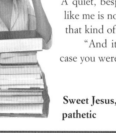

Sweet Jesus, men are pathetic

Pope to see where it all didn't happen

POPE Benedict will today visit the scenes of the made-up stories that form the basis of his crazy, voodoo religion.

The Pope will visit Jerusalem, Nazareth and Bethlehem to pray at the sites of the ancient legends that he continues to insist are real in an elaborate, but ultimately futile attempt to stop you having sex whenever you feel like it.

His itinerary will include the Church of the Nativity in Bethlehem, built on the exact spot where nothing happened around the time of the already well-established winter solstice, 2,000 years ago.

The Pontiff will then travel to the Sea of Galilee in Nazareth where absolutely no-one has ever walked on water, before moving onto Cana where there may well have been a wedding at some point, but it was certainly not attended by a charismatic teacher named Jesus and the guests drank whatever happened to be available at the time.

Pope Benedict will then arrive in Jerusalem where he will visit the Church of the Holy Sepulchre, the historic scene of nothing, now controlled by four different Christian denominations each with a slightly different opinion about various things that never happened.

He will complete his visit by blessing the Jewish people, none of whom actually believe Jesus ever existed but have decided not to point that out in case the Pope gets out his old Hitler Youth costume and it all kicks off again.

The Pope's visit to the Holy Land has a special significance for Christians all over the world, mainly because he is an old man who has read the Bible from beginning to end and wears a big, shiny hat.

Historian Dr Bill McKay said: "You see, the thing about the Bible is, it's just a book and just because something is in a book, it doesn't actually mean that it's real. Please tell me you understand that."

Are Britain's 12-year-olds firing blanks?

A MULTI-MILLION pound campaign is being launched today in a bid to boost the flagging virility of Britain's 12-year-old boys.

The move follows nationwide disappointment after it emerged that Eastbourne schoolboy Alfie Patten had failed to impregnate his local teenage skank.

Now experts are warning that Britain's 12-year-olds will have to cut down on their drinking and smoking if they are to have any hope of becoming a father before their 13th birthday.

Professor Henry Brubaker of the Institute for Studies said: "I'd recommend no more than two cigars a day and a weekly ration of 12 pints of strong German lager or one bottle of sherry."

The campaign mascot is 'Spunky', a hip, happening, 12-year-old sperm who is into skateboards, dinosaurs and Pepsi Max.

Boys who sign up to the campaign will receive a badge and a comic as well as a weekly e-mail from Spunky including a masturbation timetable and handy hints about how to boost their reproductive potency.

Professor Brubaker added: "Perhaps the X-Box people could develop a game specifically for 12-year-olds that involves guiding a single sperm towards an egg and along the way they have to eat special pills made from Brazil nuts and cottage cheese."

Meanwhile Alfie Patten is understood to be relieved the daughter he was alleged to have fathered is not his as it now means he will be able to have sex with it in about 15 years time.

Mystery surrounds BNP invite to palace

OFFICIALS last night said they were puzzled as to who could possibly have invited the British National Party leader Nick Griffin to a Buckingham Palace garden party.

An investigation is under way as sources claimed it was a clerical error and the invitation should have gone to Dick Griffin, a retired gardener from Hatfield, who recently swam the English Channel dressed as a giant cup of tea.

One Royal insider said: "Who could possibly want to see that idiot fascist parading himself around the Palace grounds, spouting his racist nonsense? It's a mystery alright.

"It's just a run of the mill summer garden party. The only slight difference is that Prince Philip will be there. At that time of year he's usually strangling otters in Glen Shee.

"Of course he doesn't do the actual strangling anymore, but he does like to stand on the riverbank and shout instructions."

The insider added: "The preparations for a garden party tend to be very predictable. Although this time Prince Philip has asked for some of his 'special flags' to be draped from the back windows.

"And he also wants his personal photographer to be on hand as apparently there's someone he really wants to have his picture taken with. I presume it's a famous otter strangler."

The Prince at last year's otter strangling

A source in the Buckingham Palace kitchens said: "The food is just your typical garden party fare. We usually do some cucumber sandwiches, a Victoria sponge and a big bag of Wotsits.

"Although this time, for some reason, the Duke of Edinburgh has requested some German delicacies. Sauerkraut, blood sausage, that kind of thing. Not my place to ask really."

It is understood Prince Philip has offered to take charge of the investigation just as soon as he has finished re-reading his battered copy of *The Insidious Jew.*

Cameron pledges power to the maniacs

TORY leader David Cameron last night pledged to transform British democracy by devolving power to the lowest possible level of maniac.

The radical reforms will include greater police co-operation with amateur sleuths and a rolling programme of constant referendums giving people exactly the wrong level of control over their own lives.

Local referendums are likely to cover a wide range of issues including banning the blue stripes in stripey toothpaste, a big-budget remake of *Bless This House* starring Martin Clunes as Sid James and a 'final solution' to the 'Jewish Question'.

Tom Logan, a deeply concerned citizen from Hatfield, said: "The absolute last thing this country needs – and I cannot stress this point strongly enough – is my next door neighbour being involved in any form of decision-making whatsoever. People will die."

He added: "I don't want power. I've already got a job which takes up quite a lot of my time and then it's the weekend.

This is what politicians are for.

"All we really need to do is to make sure those politicians have a mind of their own, have had a proper job at some point in their lives and, you know, aren't thieves."

Banks to close for one week a month, says Harman

BRITAIN'S biggest banks will be forced to close for a few days roughly every four weeks, under new government proposals.

Equality minister Harriet Harman has outlined plans to have more women on the boards of financial institutions, but admitted they may have to shut down once a month to prevent a fresh wave of irrational decision making.

Ms Harman insisted increased female involvement would restore stability to the system and restart the wholesale money markets just as soon as the country's biggest banks had synchronised their periods.

She added: "Women don't take as many risks as men because we are not as greedy. Apart from when it comes to shoes and chocolate and state-of-the-art Japanese pleasure sticks.

"We don't need a big BMW 7-series; we're quite happy with a nice, little Kia Picanto as long as we can fit some shopping in the back and it plays our nice Leona Lewis CDs without us having to press too many buttons."

But experts warned that an increase in female directors could result in banks giving vast sums of money to the Dogs Trust, the Tiny Kitten Foundation and that one that looks after old donkeys.

Emma Bradford, chief financial officer at Donelly-McPartlin, said: "This is Charlie. Charlie loved his owner but his owner didn't love him back. Look at his wittle-bittle face. He's so saaaad. I'm going to give him £20 million."

Sir Denys Finch-Hatton, executive chairman of stockbrokers Madeley-Finnegan, added: "I am all in favour of women running large organisations, just as long as absolutely none of those women is Harriet Harman."

RYANAIR URGED TO SEEK PROFESSIONAL HELP

LOW-COST airline Ryanair was last night urged to seek professional help.

As the Irish-based carrier unveiled plans to penalise customers £40 for choosing to fly with them, mental health experts said it was now vital that friends of the company stage an immediate intervention.

In a statement released yesterday Ryanair chief executive Michael O'Leary said: "Cock-a-doodle-do! Everyone pay attention. These are my new rules.

"You will print out your own boarding pass and pay me for the privilege of doing so. If you do not have a printer you will pay me £40 for not having one and you will then wear a paper hat that I will make for you. The hat will cost £40.

"You will complete a quest. Probably involving a rare gemstone. You will bring me the gemstone wrapped inside a cheque for £40.

"Luggage is a sin and you will be punished for it. Therefore your holiday will last no longer than 14 minutes. If it does I will kidnap your goldfish and charge you £40 a leg to get it back."

A spokesman for the British Psychiatric Institute said: "Ryanair is no longer something to be hated, it is something to be pitied. It's as if Mr O'Leary has suffered some kind of severe mental trauma. Perhaps he has finally flown on one of his own planes.

"He needs to be sedated, isolated and subjected to a twice-daily programme of powerful electric shocks. If that doesn't work we will have to carve out a hefty chunk of his frontal lobe.

"In the meantime we would urge other airlines to step in and start flying to Ryanair's destinations as soon as possible. For the love of God, please."

Neglected bankers plot spider attack on blind kids

BANKERS are planning to post every blind child in the UK a poisonous tropical spider in a bid to reclaim their position as Britain's purest form of scum.

In recent weeks the banking industry has watched helplessly as MPs took their place in the nation's hearts as the group they would most like to string up from a lamp-post or a sturdy local tree.

But now, under a plan entitled 'Taking It To the Next Level', bankers have plotted a sustained campaign which they insist will underline their status as the country's foremost purveyors of utter bastardry.

The spider plan, to be launched next week, will see the distribution of thousands of cat-sized arachnids, specially trained to scurry straight up a child's arm and bite it on the face.

The spiders will be sent out in pleasantly textured boxes with the words 'chocolate buttons' written on the front in Braille.

A spokesman for Lloyds TSB said: "You, the snivelling public, with your obsession with trifling political sleaze and vibrating chairs, had almost forgotten us hadn't you? Big, fat, fucking mistake.

"By the time we're finished with you, destroying your pensions and drowning the nation in debt will seem like a quaint, 1950s tea dance."

He added: "I just wish we could be there when they open the box."

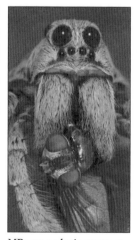

MPs are pathetic amateurs

Stop keeping score, Burnham tells Premier League

PREMIER League clubs should stop keeping score so that everyone can just enjoy a nice game of football, the culture secretary Andy Burnham said today.

The minister has also called on England's richest clubs to 'share their wealth' as the government attempts to impose its namby-pamby, socialist bullshit on professional sport.

Mr Burnham said: "It should not be about one team being better, or having more fans and therefore more money than the others; it should be about fresh air and making friends.

"It's only fair that the rich clubs should give half their money to the poor clubs. After all, it is the rich clubs' fault that they are so much better at what they do.

"And after a while everyone will be just as bad as everyone else, but that's a

Wayne Rooney's mum picks him up after training

good thing because it means that everyone will be the same."

Mr Burnham said he also wants the players' parents to become more involved in running the clubs.

He added: "I'm sure Arsène Wenger wouldn't mind if Theo Walcott's dad took charge of the midweek training sessions, and perhaps Denilson's mum could wash the kits or bring along some carrot slices and dried apricots for a tasty and nutritious half-time treat."

Under Mr Burnham's plans Formula One drivers will have to use bicycles for the last three laps, while professional darts players must enter into a weight-loss agreement with their local NHS trust before being issued with a licence to handle sharp objects.

Meanwhile England cricketers on tour in Bangladesh this winter will have to live with poverty-stricken local families so that they can gain a valuable insight into the lives of people from different cultures.

Artificial intelligence now equal to Premier League footballer

SCIENTISTS working on simulated brains have developed a model which shows the primitive insight and deductive reasoning of a Rio Ferdinand, it was claimed last night.

Unveiling the 'Blue Brain' computer, researchers said that while they were still decades away from a fully human level of intelligence, the latest model was able to argue outside a nightclub and promise to give 110% for the gaffer.

Henry Brubaker, director of the Institute for Studies, said: "As soon as we switched it on it immediately insisted on listening to an R&B compilation and dressing like an absolute tit.

"So while there is sufficient self-awareness to issue demands, it's not developed enough to realise that Akon is not actually music.

"Nevertheless it is a significant step forward even though to the layman it appears to be as thick as a bucket of dung."

Although current supercomputer brains are limited by processor conductivity and having to restart every

Please wait while your Rio Ferdinand is updated

time it's updated by Windows, Brubaker said: "Advances in miniaturisation could one day lead to your mobile phone refusing to communicate with your gobshite friends."

He added: "We're also working on a robotic module to carry the artificial brain, but our best effort so far does look a bit like Prince Charles trying to dance."

Other practical applications include the replacement of workers in repetitive jobs that require a minimum of concentration, leading to the scientific Holy Grail of tube drivers who are not greedy bastards.

NEWS BRIEFLY

SON'S DEATH 'NOT TASTE OF OWN MEDICINE', INSISTS BIN LADEN

"I suppose I would cry, if only I wasn't out of my fucking mind," says Al Qaeda chief

FIVE-YEAR-OLD CHRISTIAN GIRL GIVEN DAILY MAIL COLUMN

"She has a wider vocabulary than Allison Pearson and a more considered world view than Melanie Philips," says editor

TENNIS PLAYER CALLS CAROL THATCHER 'UNCONVINCING TRANSVESTITE MAN'

"I hope that's not offensive," says unseeded gollywog

SON-OF-A-BITCH BASTARD CABLES CAN GET TO FUCK, SAY SCIENTISTS

ONE WOMAN'S WEEK: by Karen Fenessey

WHATEVER happened to the veneration in which we once held our monarchy? In days of yore, people had a much better sense of humour and any decent citizen would have let a tiny spot of racist horseplay slide. And if they were to take offence at the monarchy, they would be severely punished – just look at bonfire night. And Ireland.

I really don't understand what the goddamn problem is here: Prince Harry hasn't done anything wrong. I mean, he said 'Paki friend' not 'Paki bastard'. You see, there is so much about intonation that people just don't understand. Because I am a highly skilled educator, accustomed to using language on a daily basis, I understand that it is not the words we use, but the way we combine them, that generates meaning.

I'll try to explain it a little: I have a friend, Stacey, who thinks it's just hilarious when I say things like 'Oh, get away you silly Chink!' and she's not even Chinese: she's from Ecuador!

I've also got a friend, Mikey, who's gay, and he just loves it when I say to him 'Hey, Mikey! Where are you off to, you big fucking bumbandit?'. But, the intricacies of language come in to play when I want to combine my nicknames. So, for example, while it's okay for Harry to say 'There's my Paki friend, Ahmed', if he were to say 'There's that gay Paki, Ahmed', it wouldn't sit so well. And saying 'There's that silly fucking Paki bumbandit, Ahmed' is completely out of the question.

Luckily, there don't seem to be that many gay Pakistanis around so this is unlikely to ever be a major problem.

I think it's criminal that we're persecuting poor Harry, who is out there fighting for our freedom in Afghanistan. I must admit, I did become aroused when I saw him waving his big machete around and smoking on TV. My boyfriend Donny, with his two week old beard and torn jeans, could only dream of smoking exotic cigarettes and brandishing knives with such finesse.

The real skill, so expertly displayed by Harry, is to talk and smoke at the same time. If Donny tried that, he would look like a twat and then set his beard on fire.

YOUR ASTROLOGICAL WEEK AHEAD
with PSYCHIC BOB

Gemini
Saturn puts you on Easy Street until November but then Mercury has you kidnapped and shipped to the Philippines where you are forced to shoot ping-pong balls out of your yin-yan for the benefit of drunken American sailors until Christmas.

Cancer
It's 10 years since you struck out for the big city to make your fortune. To celebrate, how about you hurry up and bring me that coffee I ordered?

Leo
A week of surprise, success and good luck for your best friend, but the usual dreary work shit for you, and more crushing sexual disappointment.

Virgo
Listen, people are genuinely interested in you, your work and ideas. So come on, put down the knife, untie them and let them go.

Libra
Jupiter arrives in your sign tonight, the planet of luck, liberation and drunken public casual sex two weeks before your much-anticipated wedding. There is still time to cancel the flowers.

Scorpio
The stars are fresh out of Venus this week. I can do you some Jupiter until Friday, if that's any use?

Sagittarius
Restrict your cavalier behaviour to wearing a big floppy hat, ridiculing Puritans, and cavorting in ale houses with pox-ridden whores whose ample breasts are like soft, over-ripe melons.

Capricorn
Whatever deep longing you're going through or tough decision you have to make, get a move on. Everyone you know is absolutely fucking sick of hearing about it.

Aquarius
I've seen things you people wouldn't believe. Attack ships on fire off the shoulder of Orion, C-beams glittering in the darkness at Tan Hauser Gate, slippers with their own headlights, and an electric box for your pills, which even has its own water supply.

Pisces
If romance really is your thing, why not try changing your pants occasionally, washing your hair, and preparing at least one interesting thing to say to someone you've just met.

Aries
You need to take the time to think through your ambitions because you are shit, and you know you are.

Taurus
Okay, so von Rundstedt was right and this Normandy thing is the real deal, but there is still no need to withdraw to more easily defensible positions inland like he says. Instead, you should launch a surprise counter-attack at Caen with the 9th Panzer division and you'll soon drive them back into the sea where they belong!

THREAT LEVEL

Mango

TODAY'S
WEATHER
Hot lava and
cow parts.
Sticky.

The Daily Mash

CHRIST ON A BIKE, SAYS BRITAIN

THE full extent of Britain's public debt last night led to a devastating collapse in the nation's face.

As chancellor Alastair Darling read out a series of enormous and terrifying numbers, people across the country, who until now had assumed it was not their problem, curled up into a ball and let out a faint, pathetic squeak.

Roy Hobbs, a plumber from Doncaster, said: "Oh sweet Jesus fucking Christ almighty on a tricycle." He added: "I know, we'll put on a show right here in the barn. We'll make loads of money and everything will be just dandy. You'll see." As Mr Hobbs stared into the bottomless chasm which had opened up beneath his feet, his wife Jane pulled her knees up to her chin and rocked back and forth while whispering: "Cold... so cold."

In what will, surely to God, be his last ever Budget, Mr Darling confirmed that Britain was now essentially insolvent as a nation and that the best idea might be to ease the country quietly into the middle of the Indian Ocean and leave it unlocked so

'Mummy, I'm scared'

that it could be stolen by Somalian pirates.

He added: "We then act all surprised and bung in a claim to the Norwich Union. But everyone has to keep shtum."

Mr Darling said the alternative was to gradually wind the country down over the next three weeks and then go our separate ways.

If taxpayers decide to close the country, Mr Darling said £2 billion would be made available to train Britain's under 25s in how to switch everything off and cover it with a tarpaulin.

Who will be the first arsehole to wear a facemask?

AS the number of confirmed pork flu cases in the UK soared into single figures, millions of people across Britain were last night wondering who would be the first arsehole to start wearing a facemask.

Online retailers have reported high demand for their utterly useless anti-pork flu kits, consisting of a flimsy surgical mask, some Kendal mintcake, a James Blunt CD, a nov- elty keyring and a cyanide pill.

Stephen Malley, a trainee accountant from Finsbury Park, said: "I think it's going to be this guy in my office called Geoff. He rides a bicycle to work and eats bananas at his desk. He's a prick."

Emma Bradford, a marketing assistant from Hatfield, said: "My friend Janet is pathetically

And of course, some arsehole is going to put one on their dog

melodramatic. She wore one during the foot and mouth outbreak in 2001 because she said it really accentuated her eyelashes."

And Bill McKay, a retired architect from Stevenage, said: "My wife's friends are all idiots, but I have a feeling it might turn out to be Harriet Harman, just because she's such an arsehole."

Experts warned that despite their uselessness, many arseholes will be tempted to walk around wearing facemasks, thinking they are in a film based on a Michael Crichton novel.

Dr Tom Booker, from Reading University, said: "Of course they're wearing them in Mexico. If I was in Mexico I'd be wearing one regardless. You can almost smell the fucking place from here."

He added: "If you've got the cash – and the back muscles – you could try walking around in a scuba suit, with a couple of oxygen tanks strapped to your shoulders.

"But really, the best way to stop pork flu is to get it, take some pills and watch the telly until you don't have it anymore."

Thought for the day: Soak it overnight in some lemon juice and a squeeze of vinegar. (Mrs Beaton)

MPs call for ban on huge, irresistible televisions

MPs from all parties last night demanded a ban on the gigantic, irresistible, state of the art television sets at the root of the House of Commons expenses scandal.

As politicians attempted to rebuild their shattered reputations, they said it was no coincidence the expenses system began to spiral out of control shortly after the introduction of the first widescreen LCD TV with Dolby digital surround sound.

Veteran Labour backbencher Sir Gerald Kaufman, said: "Cynical manufacturers are making these exquisite televisions as expensive as they possibly can, knowing full well that it simply makes them even more attractive to vulnerable MPs.

A committee of senior members from across the House is now drafting emergency legislation that will make it illegal to import a television larger than 19 inches, while the government is urging Japan, Germany and South Korea to convert their television factories into strawberry farms.

Mr Kaufman, who somehow managed to spend more than £8,000 on one television set, added: "And of course one cannot be expected to watch a 50-inch, wall-mounted Bang and Olufsen in an old battered chair that sits atop a cheap, grubby-looking, non-Harrods rug. That would be an insult to the television."

Angus Robertson, the SNP leader at Westminster, said he was forced to spend £1,100 on a beautifully engineered high-definition television so he could 'watch political programmes as the director intended'. He said: "The cinematography on *The Politics Show* is breathtaking. It makes *Lawrence of Arabia* look like some piece-of-shit wedding video made by a four-year-old dog."

Meanwhile Shahid Malik, the former home office minister, said the television culture had become so insidious that he was forced to record himself being interviewed, freeze frame his own face on a huge £2,000 flat-screen and then stare at it in the dark while sitting in a large, vibrating chair.

Survivors to enjoy glorious summer, says Met Office

BRITAIN'S small band of pork flu survivors can look forward to a hot, dry summer, the Met Office confirmed last night.

After the densely populated wash-outs of the last two years, experts said Britain's thinned-out herd will enjoy the 'perfect combination' of great weather and very short queues.

A Met Office spokeswoman said: "The roads will be nice and quiet and the beaches will be wonderfully empty.

"You'll also be able to help yourself to some nice salads and a bottle of rosé at the deserted supermarkets and then have your pick of the abandoned soft-tops in the car park."

She added: "The only slight problem we can foresee is the permanent and overwhelming stench of decaying flesh."

Emma Bradford, deputy editor of *Good Housekeeping*, said: "If all your friends are dead, just heave some corpses into your garden, put sunglasses on them and then prop them up à la *Weekend at Bernie's*, while hosting a ghoulish and macabre Sunday afternoon barbecue.

"Then you could circulate, topping up everyone's drinks while pretending

Don't forget to steal enough food for all of your dead guests

that they're all laughing at your witty remarks and asking where you got your lovely new sandals.

"And as the afternoon melts into a warm summer evening, why not put on some music, grab that sexy neighbour of yours and drag his lifeless body round the lawn? There really are some wonderful memories just waiting to happen."

Meanwhile, the government yesterday launched its pork flu information campaign underlining the fact that despite 2,000 years of civilisation the people of Britain still have to be reminded to use a fucking hanky.

Anger at the 'Tweethop' plans for birdsong radio

FANS of a radio station broadcasting birdsong have attacked plans to play urban-themed 'Tweethop' music in which some of Britain favourite species rap about killing the police.

Birdsong FM said 'Tweethop' and the more aggressive 'Chirp' would reflect the issues of modern avian life, including egg theft, gun crime and scoring high-grade skunk off some Bulgarian magpies.

Tom Logan, head of programming, said: "Acts like Public Chaffinch and Menace to the Nutsack are doing some really exciting things with their music – when they're not shooting each other in the face with semi-automatic weapons."

Public Chaffinch's controversial anthem 'Fuck Bill Oddie (Right in Da Ear)' is one of the Chirp scene's biggest hits. The act features two chaffinches, a coal tit and a rare Barnacle Goose with a firearms conviction known as MC Tizer.

Regular listener Martin Bishop, from Doncaster, is horrified by the changes. "I like to listen to tits while making model boats in my shed but yesterday when I tuned-in to hear a sandpiper tweeting about his 'big ting' and repeatedly using the F word, the C word, and a word beginning with R which I was not familiar with."

Daphne Page, from Hatfield, added: "Every few minutes a wood pigeon goes 'shout out to HMP massive', which is intensely annoying.

"I shan't be listening again and if the RSPB want me to renew my subscription they can take it out of my big, creamy white ass, muthafukaz."

Susan Boyle going according to plan, says Cowell

FREAK-wrangler Simon Cowell has urged people across Britain not to worry about Susan Boyle, insisting everything was going according to plan.

Boyle was admitted to the Priory Clinic in London last night after swearing loudly while running down the corridor in a five-star hotel, in what Cowell said would make a really exciting bit in the film.

Showbiz insiders said the church volunteer with the voice of a reasonably good singer suffered an exquisitely-timed emotional breakdown after losing in the final of *Britain Must be Stopped*.

The surprise winners were inexplicable dance group National Embarrassment, who can now look forward to two days of fantastic press coverage, followed by one day of savage lies about their private lies, followed by absolutely nothing at all.

Viewer Emma Bradford said: "I voted for National Embarrassment because I felt it was incredibly important to teach Susan Boyle a really harsh lesson about fame.

"But now I feel guilty and I just hope she recovers very soon and gets back to doing what she does best so I can teach her another harsh lesson, the stuck-up bitch."

She added: "Poor, sweet, lovely Susan. I'm so fucking sick of her."

Experts insist that, if she does not go completely insane, Boyle could earn up to £5 million over the next three years for Simon Cowell. But insiders warned the singer could become locked in a vicious cycle of emotional breakdowns amid showbiz fears she would be unable to cope with being famous enough to be admitted to the Priory.

Meanwhile, as Boyle checked into

Boyle was last night hiding behind a cardboard cut-out of her own face

the clinic, Cowell pushed a miniature version of her across the board and positioned *OK!* magazine and a Living TV special on her left and right flanks before smiling, nodding and rubbing himself. Tom Logan, one of the 12 people in Britain who did not watch the show, said: "I'm going to buy a large map of the world, pin it to the wall, shut my eyes and throw a dart at it – and that will be my new home."

Piano-playing cat checks-in to Priory

NORA, the cat who shot to fame after a video of her playing the piano was posted on Youtube, checked herself into the Priory last night.

Friends say she is recuperating at the North London clinic after shaving off her chest fur with a Bic razor and trying to drown herself in a sink.

Owner and manager Sally Winston said: "Nora has been under enormous pressure since we discovered her talent for leaning on piano keys with her paw and the side of her face. "Instead of using her litter tray she would smear excrement over the walls and have staring contests with the hoover. Then she stole our car, drove it to Las Vegas and married a bugle-playing West Highland terrier she met on Oprah."

Following her suspected suicide bid, Nora, recently signed to Simon Cowell's management company for £4

Nora is entirely self-taught

million worth of mackerel and long bits of string over three years, will be cared for by therapists specially trained to deal with animals who become famous as a result of poorly edited internet videos.

Meanwhile Winston has been forced to postpone Nora's 50-date stadium tour to promote her new album *Humans, Do You Have Food?* "One particularly tragic example is 70s TV bear Gentle Ben who, as his fame evaporated, began to sexually predate on emus and was finally kicked in the face at the West Midland Safari and Leisure park."

LABOUR CHIEF WHIP DEFENDS PET CHEETAH

NICK Brown, the Labour chief whip, has defended his £19,000 food bill, insisting it is not cheap to feed a pet cheetah these days.

Mr Brown said the bill, paid for out of the public purse over four years, reflected the needs of a modern, hard-working MP and his big, fast cat.

He added: "A typical week involves eight legs of lamb, two boxes of fish fingers, a selection of family sized trifles and a case of Jacob's Creek. And the cheetah needs a whole cow."

Mr Brown, who purchased the animal in 2003 using the controversial Additional Cheetah Allowance, said: "This is my second cheetah. As a government minister I have to designate my small, London cheetah as my main cheetah.

"I work long hours in the House of Commons and then I go back to Newcastle at the weekends to meet with my constituents and make sure my second cheetah gets plenty of exercise. "And by the way, you've really got to see this thing chase down a frightened jogger. Christ on a fucking bike." As the *Daily Telegraph*'s expenses saga enters the dangerous animals phase, House of Commons Speaker Michael Martin once again refused to resign and warned angry backbenchers that if they did not co-operate they would have to answer to his baboons.

Meanwhile Mr Brown said he would not be paying the money back but promised he would deliver a saving to the taxpayer by eating the cheetah when it died of old age.

Germans use Brown video for Hitler spoof

GERMANS are using footage of Gordon Brown to create hilarious spoofs of Hitler's last days in his Berlin bunker, it emerged last night.

The four-minute clips show the beleaguered prime minister defending his record in the House of Commons, while the German captions portray him as the Nazi dictator railing against his generals.

Dortmund-based sales manager, Gunter Schroll, who has had more than two million views of his spoof video, said: "When he starts shouting and pointing I have him saying, 'this is treason! Treason, I tell you!'.

"Then, when he seems to point in the direction of Herr Balls, I have him saying, 'and here, at the end, is it only Goebbels who will remain by my side?'."

A spoof by Herman Dopplinger, a student from Cologne, uses footage of Mr Brown attacking Lib Dem leader Nick Clegg, but the caption reads: "Are you telling me the Russians have captured the railway bridge? My God, they are only 12km from the centre of the city!"

Mr Brown then adds: "They should hang the entire leadership of the Luftwaffe!"

In Dopplinger's version the desperate prime minister is shown turning towards the Speaker, Michael Martin, and saying: "Wenk is advancing with the 9th army. He can join up with the 12th and deal the Russians a final crushing blow."

But then, with a look of weary resignation, he adds: "Even if an advance is successful I will just end up in another troublesome situation."

The craze has inspired other spoof videos including Brown as the manager of relegation-threatened team Borussia Mönchengladbach and the prime minister reacting to the final of German TV talent show 'Deutchland Kann Singen'.

Dopplinger added: "I know people in Britain might find it tasteless, but it's really just a bit of fun."

Amanda Holden's vagina appears in Crop Circle

A CROP circle depicting the genitalia of TV talent show judge Amanda Holden has appeared in an Oxfordshire field.

Experts say it is the most accurate representation of a famous sex area yet undertaken by aliens and heralds a spectacular summer of B-List celebrity private parts invading Britain's cereal industry.

Denys Hatton, of CropCircleData.com, said: "What's really notable is the detail. It appears to show a slightly grown-out Brazilian with a few straggly 'spider-legs' on either side."

Hatton added: "Even someone who had never seen *Cutting It* or *Britain Must be Stopped* would have to admit that it's obviously Amanda's fun-zone."

Professor Henry Brubaker, of the Institute for Studies, said: "It's possible the aliens are tapping into some kind of collective consciousness and chose Amanda Holden's vagina because of its deep symbolic resonance.

"Or maybe they just want to help Amanda break

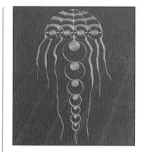

Uncanny

into the American market."

He added: "Either way, we haven't seen this level of intricacy in a celebrity vagina crop circle since Davina McCall's labia appeared in a field of beans near Leighton Buzzard."

But the field's owner James Peakes, of Parsonage Farm, was less impressed: "I'm sure many men dream of being able to see Amanda Holden's fandango from their kitchen window, but personally I find it actually quite annoying.

His wife Sarah added: "I don't see why anyone would want to cross the universe in a spaceship just to draw Amanda Holden's twat in some barley. But if it was aliens, then they need to get a life."

Teenage yobs carrying flick-toddlers

TEENAGE yobs have developed a deadly 'flick-toddler' in a bid to avoid prosecution, police warned last night.

The lethal infants, too young to be prosecuted, can be carried in jacket pockets and are regularly used in gang fights.

The trend started in 2003, when a Streatham gang called 'Fuk-U-Honkee' made a shish-kebab out of four of their rivals after hurling a toddler wearing a souped-up Kaiser helmet.

This year saw the introduction of the fully-portable hunting infant, which can carry eight blades, a compass and an attachment for removing hoodies from the hooves of a police horse.

The flick-toddler is bred following trysts in Burger King car parks and is raised on a nutritious diet of Sunny Delight and an aggressively misguided sense of unjustified entitlement.

Aged four, they are used only in minor disputes over turf rights as their underdeveloped biceps are unable to wield a machete for more than two or three minutes.

According to the police, by the age of nine they are carrying so many blades they look like titanium hedgehogs.

A Metropolitan Police spokesman said: "Once the youths reach the criminal age of responsibility, gangs dump them in waste ground and industrial estates. One particular orphanage in Deptford looks like a cross between *Annie* and *Edward Scissorhands*."

The Home Office has proposed a flick-toddler amnesty where the weapons would be handed into a police station before being melted down and turned into soap.

WATERBOARDING COMES TO CENTER PARCS

CENTER Parcs, the market leading holiday resort company, has added waterboarding to its list of family-focused leisure activities.

Managers say waterboarding is just as much fun as mountain biking or owl spotting, except you are held down with a wet towel over your face as gallon after gallon of water is poured up your nose.

A Center Parcs spokesman said: "There's no better way for parents and kids to bond than in a situation of sustained psychological terror and disorientation. The magic is, you're totally convinced you're going to die, but you don't! However it can make you scared of rain."

Holidaymaker Don Rose, from Stafford, gave it the thumbs up: "It made a refreshing change from the falconry and rope slides and it's definitely made me want to try other state-sanctioned coercion techniques.

"On the down side, since returning from our mini-break I do tend to wake up in the middle of the night screaming like a girl."

However not all customers are convinced. Sue Glenn, of Ipswich, said: "We expected something more like a slide or a shute.

"Instead two men in khaki led us into something called the 'Z-Ray Family Detention Hut', put sacks over our heads and spun us round until we were nauseous while angry dogs snapped at our groins.

"They asked us why we hated freedom and when my husband said we didn't they kicked him in the stomach. That's when the kids really started to cry."

She added: "The actual waterboarding itself was very unpleasant, although perhaps less so than the Thunder Looper at Alton Towers. Overall, I'd say it was different but we probably wouldn't do it again."

Microsoft games controller will allow everyone to be tedious

MICROSOFT has unveiled a hands-free controller for the X-box which will open up the empty, soul-destroying tedium of video games to everyone.

Project Natal can interpret body movements and facial expressions by using technology that experts say must – for the love of God – have a better use than this.

The technology is being backed by film director Steven Spielberg who said playing a video game was the perfect way to round off a grindingly meaningless day spent watching *War of the Worlds* or *Indiana Jones and the Kingdom of the Crystal Skull*.

Natal is named after the stunningly beautiful province of South Africa that people who play video games will never visit because it doesn't display a range of absurd weapons or magical powers in the bottom left hand corner.

A Microsoft spokesman said: "This system is not just for people without thumbs, it's also for people who have thumbs but can't use them properly.

"A two-month-old baby will soon be able to remove virtual heads using a virtual chainsaw just by moving its lower lip. How long has mankind waited for that particular day?"

He added: "Retired people can finally abandon their hollow, unimaginative dream of travelling the world and instead can spend their twilight years fucking-up two-dimensional drug dealers or applying their insanely dangerous driving skills to *Grand Theft Auto.*"

Bill McKay, an arthritic 84-year-old from Peterborough, said: "I missed the invasion of Normandy because of my flat feet, but thanks to Microsoft I'll be able to play *Call of Duty III* and experience a vacuous, cartoon version of the terror my schoolmates had to endure."

Your baby can learn how to kill with a flamethrower while you make dinner

New Big Brother series may be best ever, says its viewer

THE current series of *Big Brother* could be the best one yet, according to the person who has been watching it.

Ruth Herron, the 48-year-old housewife who constitutes the show's entire audience, said this year's collection of fame-hungry strangers was especially gripping and was puzzled as to why she had no-one to talk to about it.

Mrs Heron, from Stoke, added: "'The format still seems fresh and exciting to me. And I'm not just saying that because I've spent the last 10 years in a coma after a crane fell on my head.

"Who came up with the idea of putting a load of twats in a house and then chucking them out one by one? Actually, now I think about it, it's a lot of boring shit. I think I'll get some sea monkeys instead."

Meanwhile, former *BB* winner turned *BB* pundit, The One Who Lives In A Lighthouse Or Something, said the series was as strong as ever.

"*Big Brother* has given us some of the most enduring figures in contemporary popular culture. Who could forget characters like The Little Lesbian One Who Looks Like a Testicle, The Unhinged One Who May Have Stuck A Bottle Up Her Tumpsy or The One Who's One of The Ones With The Massive Tits?

"These beloved figures have gone on to become some of the biggest names in daytime cable TV craft shows and prostitution."

Thingy Lighthouse Chappy added: "From racism to bullying, Big Brother has it all. If I had a telly in the lighthouse, I'd definitely think about watching it, if I was bed ridden and my eyes had been stapled open."

Resume your masturbatory fantasies, says Lohan

LINDSAY Lohan has given the green light to hours of furtive self-abuse after resuming her lesbian relationship with sort-of-female DJ Samantha Ronson.

The very-nearly actress reassured fans the couple would once again engage in lesbianic wranglings so greasily filthy it would make them blow off in less than two minutes flat.

The couple split in January after Lohan told Ronson that adding a basic horn section behind a quicker version of an existing song did not make her brother a musical genius.

Friends said the DJ stormed out off their LA home after Lohan suggested that Mark Ronson was 'nothing more than a low-rent Jive Bunny in a stupid hat'.

A separation was organised to see whether they could sustain two careers based on Ronson playing her iPod at a disco while Lohan tries to stay off drugs long enough to watch her latest film go straight to DVD.

But negotiations were reopened last month after their earnings were revealed to be insufficient to cover their lipstick and short, angry haircut budgets for the rest of the year.

Accountant Tom Booker said: "These young women are very much in dirty love and have fantastic new products coming out soon. After an emotional discussion we decided it would be best for everyone if we told the world they were nuzzling each other's clamps again."

Sacking Jonathan Ross even cheaper than 40% pay cut, say licence payers

YOU know what's even cheaper than giving Jonathan Ross a 40% paycut? Sacking the fucker, licence payers said last night.

As BBC bosses said they would be forced to slash the salaries of some of the corporation's highest paid stars, viewers across the country wanted to know exactly what they were waiting for.

Margaret Gerving, from Doncaster, said: "You mean to say the BBC is short of cash after allowing a long list of talentless hacks to decide their own multi-million pound salaries? I find that very difficult to believe.

"Like everyone else, I just assumed they had finally run out of money after filming hour after hour after hour after hour – after hour – of people you would not normally associate with dancing."

Tom Logan, from Finsbury Park, said: "I know there are some people who think Jonathan Ross, Jeremy Clarkson and Graham Norton add meaning and colour to their lives, but the thing you have to remember about those people is, they're stupid and wrong.

"At first it may seem a bit odd that Jonathan Ross is not on the telly anymore, but after a couple of days no-one – and I do mean absolutely no-one – will care."

He added: "I suppose Jonathan Ross could go back to being a researcher for a production company which is what he should have been doing all along if television wasn't run by total bastards."

Bill McKay, from Peterborough, volunteered his services to the BBC stressing he had thought about it constantly for over a month and had come to the unavoidable conclusion that he could not possibly be less talented than Jonathan Ross.

"So it's basically two

This does not have to be complicated

hours a week asking dead-eyed celebrities about their piece-of-shit films and reading out some funny-but-true stories on Radio Two? I'll do it for a fifty grand.

"That should still leave me plenty of time to do voice-overs and enjoy a very comfortable standard of living."

He added: "And I promise to try my absolute level best not to use my two hours a week to phone-up a nice old man and offer to wank him into a cup."

This is how the Nazis started, says everyone

THE Nazis started out with just a couple of MPs and 6% of the vote you know, everyone said last night.

As the British National Party achieved its first success in a UK-wide election, amateur historians said they would be amazed if this time next year people like you were not in some sort of camp.

Julian Cook, from Hitchin, said: "Having seen *The Great Escape*, one can only hope that Nick Griffin will decide not to fight a war of total annihilation on two fronts at the same time."

Bill McKay, from Doncaster, added: "First they'll come for the people who watch *Queer Eye for the Straight Guy*, but I won't speak up because I watch *Top Gear* and play golf."

But experts insisted the BNP vote would disappear as soon as everyone could afford to go on holiday to Majorca again.

Professor Tom Logan, of Reading University, said: "Prolonged recessions do have a tendency to expose our inner racist fucknut, but it subsides once you get a new credit card."

As the European election results came in, some of Britain's most famous Jews took the 'precautionary step' of changing their Wikipedia entries.

David Baddiel, the writer and comedian, is now described by Wikipedia as being of 'good Prussian stock' with a fondness for rowdy beer halls and a deep loathing of Woody Allen films.

Actress Maureen Lipman has changed her name to 'Lipizzanner' and insists that her favourite 'ology' is Aryan racial ideology.

Lionel Blue, the gay rabbi, was last night heading for Southampton wearing a blond wig and carrying a large smoked sausage.

Thatcher tries to close her own ward

BARONESS Thatcher was under sedation last night after trying to close the ward where she is being treated.

The former prime minister threatened to sack medical staff at the Chelsea and Westminster Hospital after they refused to give her a choice of dressings for her broken claw.

Consultant Denys Finch-Hatton said: "She was initially amused by the karmic forces that brought her under the care of an organisation she fucked sideways with a melon for over a decade.

"But then she became very agitated, got on the phone to Norman Tebbit and told him to sell the hospital to some Chinese gangsters."

He added: "We've made her as comfortable as possible which means, thanks to the enduring effects of her 11 years in power, she's currently propped up outside the gents."

Although Lady Thatcher is in a stable condition, her accident and her advanced age has created a dilemma for the New Labour politicians who have continued her work while simultaneously begging the trade unions for money.

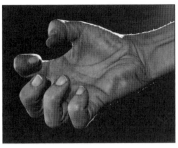

The claw has injured four nurses

A Downing Street source said: "In the event of her popping off, we'll have to say something that is statesman-like but does not alienate traditional Labour voters. Then again there is only about four of them.

"What about a full state funeral with a 21-gun salute, but at the end we drop her down a disused coal shaft?"

Meanwhile Martin Bishop, a former Liverpool dock worker, said he remained in a permanent state of readiness, adding: "I've got my fireworks, my bunting and two crates of Stella at the ready. It's going to be fucking mint."

NEWS BRIEFLY

MILLIONTH WORD WILL BE EUPHEMISM FOR PENIS, SAY EXPERTS
Recent entries leading up to the million mark are 'spunkpump' (penis), 'meatsock' (penis) 'boylejocking' (berating talent show judges in an impenetrable accent) and 'spoojflute' (penis)

MEGA-CLAP TERRORISES IBIZA
"It was a bit like Cloverfield but with more genital sores," says eye-witness

UK DEMANDS PORN AS BASIC HUMAN RIGHT
"I don't care if the dead are left unburied and the water supply is filled with ebola, as long as my Mpegs of Bulgarian basket fisting download in less than 30 seconds," says muck enthusiast

BROWN SURVIVES AS LABOUR REBELS BLAH, BLAH, BLAH, WHO GIVES A SHIT?

DEPUTY prime minister Gordon Brown survived a backbench revolt last night after pledging to change his style of leadership and blah, blah, blah, you're not still reading this are you?

Mr Brown, who demoted himself in last week's stupid, pointless reshuffle, told a packed meeting of the parliamentary Labour Party that err... um... something about challenges... Have you seen Drag Me to Hell yet? Apparently it's very good.

Amid scenes involving lots of tedious, middle-aged men in cheap suits, Labour MPs threw their support behind another 11 months of getting paid rather than just four months of getting paid if Mr Brown was to make way for some Cockney chap who was

raised by wolves and used to drive a bus or something.

As Mr Brown failed, once again, to understand that he was the problem, first secretary Lord Mandelson sat silently in the corner, stroking his badger while two large, muscular African men smeared handfuls of duck fat into his bare thighs.

For those of you still reading, the rebels then said something about Brown facing a fresh challenge in September by which time Sky and the BBC should have unveiled their autumn schedules, while Liverpool coach Rafael Benitez will almost certainly have been committed to a mental hospital.

Meanwhile Tory leader David

Cameron repeated his call for an immediate general election, obviously forgetting there was a really good episode of Frasier on one of the satellite channels, though sources said it was okay because he has a DVD recorder.

Tom Logan, professor of politics at Reading University, said: "It was the episode where Eddie the dog is all depressed. Turns out he had lost his little doll. Great stuff. As for Brown and Mandelson and Cameron and the BNP. None of it matters. At all."

Margaret Gerving, a retired headmistress from Godalming in Surrey, said: "Oh, I stopped giving a fuck about this back in March dear. Have you seen Angels and Demons yet? Apparently it's rubbish."

Time traveller from the future warns of Terminator sequels

A HAUNTED-looking man arrived from the future last night to warn mankind of *Terminator* sequels so incredibly bad they will make you cry inside.

The gaunt, haggard stranger, known only as 'X', stood on a box in Trafalgar Square and announced he had come from the year 2057, where *Terminator 328b: Big Robot Wank Thing* has just gone on general release.

He said: "If you thought *Terminator Salvation* was a steaming pile of cinematic mule dung, this latest one is like being raped through your eyes by an army of insane monkeys.

"*Terminator 328b* is directed by McB, a genetic hybrid created from a mixture of McG's frozen semen and beaver DNA.

"It's about how John Connor's father's son's grandson's uncle's niece's nephew goes back to the future to shag his own nan, thus preventing the first calculator from being made. Or something.

"The main baddie is a big robot steam train with wings and a tail that flies around shitting nuclear bombs. It is played by Eddie Murphy."

X added: "And then there's a chase scene, but it's on tricycles, it's two days long and you're not allowed to go for a piss."

Before collapsing from exhaustion, X warned that in the future *Terminator* films are beamed directly into your cerebral cortex, often as part of a triple bill including *Batman's Big Momma's House 18* and *Indiana Jones and the Inner Tube of Hercules*.

The star of Terminator 328b

Torture cops 'are just mavericks who don't play by the book'

THE policemen accused of torturing drug suspects are loose cannons who may not play by the book but they get results godammit, it was claimed last night.

As six officers were suspended amid claims of waterboarding, police sources stressed that sometimes a cop has to take matters into his own hands if he is going to keep the streets safe for you and that nice little wife of yours.

A Scotland Yard insider said: "They've got some buttoned-up, college-educated divisional commander bustin' their asses. And for what? For givin' some no-good punk a bath when he don't wannit?

"Jeez, times have changed since I joined the force, I tells ya. Times was you could take a perp to the old docks and pop him in the back of the head when no-one was lookin'. Who's gonna be askin' questions about a piece of scum like that?

"We comes out of the academy all fresh-faced, but then you see all these thieves and drug dealers and newspaper sellers on their way home from work day after day, and it just changes you."

He added: "Okay, so maybe pushin' someone's head repeatedly into a bucket of water may not elicit the desired response and may, in the long run, prove to be counterproductive in terms of engendering community support and co-operation. Actually, that's a very good point isn't it?

"So what you're saying is that we might have safer communities if we had well-trained officers adhering to strict operational standards, instead of some halfwit maniacs who think they're Dirty Harry or that northern geezer in *Funk to Funky*.

"Come to think of it, you're right, they really are just a collection of bastards, aren't they?"

Leeds, doctors warn Newcastle

DOCTORS last night warned Newcastle United supporters they were now vulnerable to a nasty case of Leeds.

Following a fairly typical weekend for North East football, Newcastle fans were told to face up to reality and change their lifestyle before they end up having the tallest stadium in the third division.

Dr Tom Logan, of the Institute for Studies, said: "It's a big problem across the North East. They spend money they don't have on things that are bad for them and eventually find themselves sitting in the pub wondering why they've just drawn 0-0 at home to Yeovil."

Despite spending hundreds of millions of pounds the three North East clubs have not won a major trophy since Sunderland lifted the FA Cup in 1973. Middlesbrough's 2004 Wembley triumph was

quashed last year under the League Cups Obviously Don't Count rule.

Dr Logan added: "They need to stop chasing impossible dreams and learn to be happy with what they are, which is rubbish."

In Sunderland, cinemas are playing Newcastle's game against Aston Villa to packed houses, with one critic describing it as 'an absurdly exaggerated version of the Marx Brothers at their most surreal and outlandish'.

St John's Ambulance volunteers are on hand for the moment Damien Duff deflects the ball goalwards, as hard-pressed usherettes move in to mop up all the urine.

Duff has been named a Freeman of the City of Sunderland, bestowing the ancient right to chase a barmaid across the Wear Bridge with a monkey wrench without having to pay the traditional toll of

Leeds has a Harvey Nichols now. So there you go.

four Benson and Hedges and a jar of meat paste.

The reaction to Middlesbrough's relegation was more muted as most Premier League supporters had assumed the club had gone into administration some time around 1998.

West Ham manager Gianfranco Zola was heard to comment: "So that was the real Middlesbrough? I thought it was some kind of tribute band. How fascinating."

Meanwhile Ricky Sbragia has resigned as Sunderland manager after failing to get his side relegated, adding: "We cannot maintain a savage, inexplicable rivalry with Newcastle and Middlesbrough if we are in the league above them and for that I am truly sorry.

"I only hope the new manager can succeed where I have failed. Or the other way round, if that makes more sense."

1,000-year Reich remains on track, says Ferguson

SIR Alex Ferguson's plan to reign over English football for one thousand terrible years continues apace as Manchester United won their 18th league title.

Receiving the Premier League trophy in the club's Palace of Victories, the manager announced that the youth academy, scouting system and wage structure will 'secure United's dominion over all mankind for 500 glorious generations of noble blood'.

Ferguson also dismissed talk of retirement, insisting: "Not until we have tamed the Seven Seas and our Palace of Victories is filled to its mighty domed ceiling with golden

The Palace of Victories will soon be exposed as pathetically inadequate

crowns and we have to build a new Palace of Victories so big it will make the first one

seem cowardly and lacking in vigour."

With his booming voice echoing down the ages, he added: "And a couple more European Cups would be nice too."

Ferguson also pledged to rebuild Manchester as a shimmering marble city of wide boulevards, grand museums and gigantic golden statues of Sammy McIlroy and Jim Leighton.

He said: "Our army of loyal supporters will gaze in wonder at what we have wrought, whenever they are visiting from London."

But Liverpool manager Rafa Benitez continued to insist that United were not

the best team in England, adding: "They got more points than us. And they have a stronger squad. And a larger stadium. A bigger fan base? Certainly. But let me ask you this – do they have Ngog? No, they do not."

Benitez also claimed that Belgium was wider than China and that Andrei Voronin is lighter than a bag of peas.

Meanwhile Ferguson is now preparing for the Champion's League final against Barcelona as winger Cristiano Ronaldo continued looking at luxury penthouse apartments in the centre of Madrid for no reason whatsoever.

MY BIG GAP YEAR dispatches from POPPY SPALDING

Thursday: Mumbai

This week finds me 'slumming' it in Mumbai, India. After watching the totally amazing foreign film *Slumdog Millionaire* last week, I simply had to get over here and join in all the slum-based fun.

At the backpackers', I met two Hindi girls called Bindi and Sunita. They were lovely but I did point out that they didn't look particularly Hindu. Sure enough I soon discovered their real names were Fi and Tori and they were taking a gap year from their German honours course at Cambridge. Despite being a posh English girl Bindi had the Sanskrit word for 'India' tattooed onto her ankle – that's how serious she was about being all Hindu. Pretty impressive and certainly much more serious about it than David Beckham.

They also said 'Slumdog' was the best film they'd ever seen, so we all

agreed that we had to experience one of these slums immediately. But despite our efforts, we ended up in a rather nice place with trees and pavements.

After a fruitless half hour of urchin-hunting we found a small tea house with a table of gorgeous guys inside it, drinking tea. Turns out they were Israeli and had come to India to relax after their gruelling military service and had decided to use bales of skunk as their particular relaxation method.

After a few bong-rounds back at the cabin, they spoke about their tough years in the military working at checkpoints (a bit like Tesco, but slightly more dangerous, apparently). They told us that being Israeli is something no foreigner can truly understand.

Bindi and Sunita started crying because they were ashamed to be studying German and said their parents

were a bit like the Nazis for making them go to university.

Then, I had an amazing idea: we should form a band! We could travel the world and create awareness about Israel. Everyone wanted to be the sitar player, so eventually we decided the band would have nine sitar players and a rhythm section. I offered to play that mad Indian drum thing that kind of sounds like a plop. We also decided to adopt stage names. I wanted to be Chewbacca, but they said it sounded too much like Jewbacca and was ruled out as anti-semitic. I eventually went with DJ Bombay Mix Master, partly because of its huge role in Mumbai history, but mostly because I was peckish. It's the heady combination of spicy chickpeas and militant Judaism, that makes Mumbai the greatest city in the world!

YOUR ASTROLOGICAL WEEK AHEAD
with PSYCHIC BOB

Libra
You're feeling a little decadent today, so why not skip out of work early, smoke some opium and then hang out with pornographers and whores.

Scorpio
Lately it seems like you have more questions than answers. Why do you think that is?

Sagittarius
Give yourself a much-needed chuckle by encouraging a blind old person to try and cross a busy dual carriageway.

Capricorn
An ambiguous statement from your lover has got you puzzled. Don't spend too much time worrying about it. They've left.

Aquarius
You're experiencing some symptoms

that could just as easily be stress-related as actual signs of a health problem. Relax with some frenzied masturbation.

Pisces
Your energy level is quite high and you will be in a good mood for much of the day at work. And then in the evening you will feel like shit.

Aries
You feel the urge to aim for some big new goal at work. Good plan. Those fat ones are always so grateful afterwards.

Taurus
You and your big ideas look set to take over the world – or at least your small part of it. Why not expand your horizons a little with an attack on Russia?

Gemini
It's easy to be impatient with those around you today. So what the hell are you waiting for?

Cancer
As tense as your day-to-day life is, it's important to do something to keep up your level of amusement. Try poisoning a cat, slowly.

Leo
Treat your wife to an old fashioned dinner at home. And then treat yourself to an old fashioned rogering with her bent over the sofa. You deserve it.

Virgo
You and your partner both have things you want, and right now your desires are not matching up. Try a couple of centimetres higher and slightly to the left.

THREAT LEVEL

Philip Schofield

The Daily Mash

THUMBS
Grafted on while you wait. 'Experience the thrill of picking things up!'
Call Thumbleys on Bristol 242

it's news to us   www.thedailymash.co.uk   No.12

BANKS TO LEND YOU YOUR OWN MONEY

THE government is to invest £500bn of your money in British banks so they can lend it back to you with interest.

The historic move is being hailed as a lifeline for the beleaguered financial system as long as nobody asks too many questions.

Julian Cook, chief economist at Corbett and Barker, said: "The government will give your money to the banks so the banks can start lending you that money, probably at around 7% APR.

"Thanks to all the interest you're paying on your own money, the banks will make billions of pounds again and normality will be restored.

"After a few years of this the government will cash in the bank shares it bought with your money and use the profits to build a huge fucking dome somewhere."

He added: "In case you hadn't already worked it out – the entire global financial system is predicated on the assumption that you're an idiot."

Chancellor Alastair Darling said the decision had been taken in tandem with the banking industry, adding: "They used a lot of dirty words I'd never heard before and one of them had an angry looking dog."

Meanwhile, Emma Bradford, a sales manager from Bath, said: "Why doesn't the government just give my money to me so I can buy stuff from businesses who will then make a profit and put it in a bank?"

But Mr Darling insisted: "Shut up."

'I got confused'

Police remain institutionally stupid

DESPITE a full decade of extra investment and training, Britain's police remain institutionally stupid, according to a major new report.

The Commission for People Not Being Stupid said the average policeman is either mildly stupid or tremendously stupid indeed.

Director Tom Booker said: "There are still too few people with brain cells joining the police while only a handful of senior posts are occupied by non-stupids.

"This means that most of our policing is still unbelievably dim-witted and therefore many parts of the UK, particularly the London Underground, continue to be no-go areas."

He added: "We have seen some progress in the sense that the force is no longer institutionally racist. It is now just individually racist."

A spokesman for the Police Federation said: "Comment? What does that mean? Does that mean you want me to say stuff? Okay. "For my breakfast I had chips and peas, chocolate and a cup of tea. Then I put on my big hat and got on the bus. "I am now going to have a nap and dream about being a dog."

'Hello my name is Bobby. No, hang on, that's not right.... my JOB is Bobby.'

Thought for the day: Somewhere, in a field far, far away, a bull has started charging towards you. (St Francis of Assisi)

Hudson crash-landing still better than Heathrow

PASSENGERS on the plane which crash landed on the Hudson river last night insisted the terrifying experience was much better than Heathrow.

As the stricken US Airways jet drifted over the skyscrapers of Manhattan before ditching in the freezing water, dozens of frightened passengers thanked God they were not arriving in London.

Tom Logan, a New York businessman, said: "As someone who has flown into Heathrow twice in my life, today's experience was like having a long, soapy shower with Heidi Klum.

"I hear they're planning a third runway at Heathrow. They should build a large moat instead. It would improve the experience immeasurably."

Kathy Cook, a sales assistant from New Jersey, said: "I looked out the window and saw the water getting closer and closer. I thought of my children, my husband, all the things I've never done and then I thought, 'oh well, at least it's not Heathrow'."

She added: "Minutes later we were all squeezed onto the wing in the freezing cold waiting to be rescued and

So much nicer than Terminal Four

it occurred to me that this was actually much less crowded than Heathrow and with better facilities."

Aviation experts said the pilot, Chesley Sullenberger, was a hero for guiding the plane to a safe landing and saving the 155 passengers from a Heathrow-like nightmare.

Sullenberger said: "I kept saying to myself 'come on Ches, make it better than Heathrow. Just make it better than Heathrow'."

A US Airways spokesman said the passengers should receive their luggage within 48 hours, adding: "It's not as if the plane has been anywhere near Heathrow. It's just partially submerged in the Hudson river."

Clubbers ditch Ketamine for elephant tranquillisers

YOUNG Britons are switching to elephant-based drugs after the horse tranquilliser Ketamine was officially designated as so last week.

Experts say thousands of clubbers are using a combination of elephant downers, rhino aspirin, monkey amphetamines and a cough medicine developed especially for giraffes.

Drug taker Julian Cook said: "I used to like Ketamine because it gives you that weird, all-over horse sensation and you just want everyone to ride you.

"But it doesn't last long enough and you end up with a really sore back and bit marks in the corners of your mouth.

"Elephant drugs, on the other hand, last for six months and you can

strip the branches off a tree and destroy entire villages."

He added: "I also like blue whale medicine. Last Friday everyone came round to my flat and we all harpooned each other while shouting 'thar she blows!'."

Community worker Bill McKay said the animal drug craze had also spread to middle-class professionals, with after-dinner mints now being replaced by a medium-strength tranquilliser normally used to subdue the Thomson's Gazelle.

McKay added: "They use darts they've smuggled back from their safari holidays in Tanzania and then leap around the room listening to Depeche Mode while someone pretends to be a cheetah."

Stan Lee creates first gay superhero since Batman

MARVEL Comics legend Stan Lee is to unveil the world's first homosexual superhero since Batman.

Thom Creed will be a New York interior designer with incredible superpowers including an ability to pick out the perfect cushion and transform even the dullest of parties with his infectious personality.

He will make his debut this summer in a television special where he will confront his nemesis 'The Christian', take him out for a Mongolian barbecue and then sign him up for a course of pilates.

A television industry source said: "The key difference between Thom Creed and Batman is that Creed won't be so obviously gay.

"He won't dress from head to toe in heavy black leather. He'll only wear a cape on Friday nights and, crucially, he won't live with a teenage boy who he likes to dress up in tights and a gimp mask."

Creed will divide his time between a fabulous SoHo loft and a mysterious building at the North Pole known as the Cottage of Solitude.

Its location will be kept secret from all but Creed's closest friends, including Gwen Stefani, Madonna, and the big, butch police commissioner who's fooling no-one.

Its main features will be a huge statue of Creed's mother and dozens of photographs of her looking gorgeous, but nothing of his father, who Creed says was cold and distant, much like the red sun of Krypton.

Still not as gay as Batman

Charles beats Asian friend with affectionate polo mallet

PRINCE Charles's brutal assaults on a polo playing Asian friend are just playful banter, it was claimed last night.

As Britain's Royal Family was once again exposed as a bunch of shits, friends of the Prince say multi-millionaire Kuldip Singh Dhillon loves nothing more than a sound beating at the hands of the future king and his sons.

One source said: "They give him a head start and then chase him round the paddock, waving their mallets in the air and shouting 'run Sooty, run!'.

"When their Royal Highnesses finally catch up to him they swipe at his legs to bring him down and then set about his head and body with blow after affectionate blow.

"Sometimes the beating has to stop for a few seconds because everyone is laughing so much."

The cheerful violence was revealed just days after Prince Harry alienated two-fifths of the world's population and Prince Edward was caught on camera taking a stick to his labradors because they are black.

Constitutional experts now believe Prince Charles may be an evil twin and

Sometimes they like to hunt him on horseback

that a kinder, gentler prince is being held prisoner in the Channel Islands where he is forced to wear an iron mask lest his true identity be revealed.

Royal historian Denys Finch-Hatton said: "The local villagers say that on a quiet night you can hear the poor wretch howling at the moon and shouting 'why? why?'."

Meanwhile the parents of Royal girlfriend Kate Middleton have urged their daughter to break up with Prince William and start having sex with a footballer.

Thousands discover they are result of inbreeding

THOUSANDS of people logged on to the 1911 Census yesterday, stared at the screen for two minutes and then ran from the room with a look of sickened horror.

Henry Brubaker, of the Institute for Studies, said many had hoped to find they were the descendants of a passionate but doomed romance between an East End match girl and the Duke of Clarence.

Instead thousands have discovered they are the mutant progeny of an illegal union between a slack-jawed farm labourer and his mentally retarded sister.

Carys Hughes, an office worker from Bedford, said: "I was really interested in my great grandparents on my father's side as, for some reason, we were never allowed to talk about

them when I was growing up.

"When I logged on I soon discovered that great grandma's maiden name was the same as her married name.

"Sure enough, after a bit more research, it all became horrifyingly clear."

Hughes added: "I suppose now they'll have to take away my driving licence and put me in a home.

"Still, at least they were married. It would be so embarrassing to find out that you're the bastard offspring of sibling incest."

Professor Brubaker said the 1911 Census may be repulsive but it would give us a much deeper understanding of modern British culture including the Daily Mail, the Labour Party and Sky One's *Are You Cleverer Than a Bag of Tomatoes?*

OBAMA SHUTS DOWN 'GREY'S ANATOMY'

PRESIDENT Barack Obama yesterday fulfilled a key campaign promise by announcing the closure of *Grey's Anatomy*.

Signing the executive orders, Mr Obama said the 'pathetic and embarrassing hospital drama' had 'damaged America's reputation across the world and made its citizens less safe'.

Human rights group Amnesty International welcomed the announcement claiming the programme was a 'symbol of injustice and abuse' and a 'legal and moral disgrace'.

White House spokesman Robert Gibbs said: "For the last five years Americans have asked how a nation which created *The West Wing*, *The Sopranos* and *Dallas*, could have allowed this to happen.

"*Grey's Anatomy* has not only strengthened the resolve of our enemies but helped to create new enemies.

"In the villages of Pakistan and the camps of the Gaza Strip young men are being shown that episode where the simpering cow looks longingly at Patrick Dempsey before launching into a monologue about how in life you don't always get what you want, while Chris Martin sings 'I will try to fix you'.

"Young Muslim men come away from that experience determined to kill as many Americans as possible."

Obama has also promised to abolish the practice of 'Katherine Heigl-boarding' where terror suspects are strapped to a plank and forced to watch an episode of *Grey's Anatomy* where Heigl tells that small gay actor that 'maybe it just wasn't meant to be' for the 14,000th time.

Daily alcohol limits not really working for us, say drinkers

THESE recommended daily limits on alcohol the government has come up with are really not doing it for us, drinkers said last night.

Beer and wine lovers across the UK stressed that while three to four units may sound reasonable, it's obviously not going to get you trousered, even if you're a lady.

They are now calling on the government to rethink its guidelines or better still just leave them alone and go and bother fat people instead.

'Piss off!'

Tom Logan, a trainee solicitor from Northampton, said: "It seems to me that they may have confused a safe daily limit with what I like to call 'lunch'."

He added: "Of an evening I like to smash through the limit with a convivial pint or two after work, before I then jump up and down on the limit and set fire to it with a nice bottle of Pinot Grigio.

"I manage to do all this without bothering anyone else. The worst that happens is an occasional tendency to fall asleep and urinate all over the sofa, but, and I'm sure we're all agreed, that's my problem."

Emma Bishop, a marketing executive from Twickenham, added: "How's about this? As an adult, I think a reasonable daily limit is me drinking as much as I fucking want.

"If it affects my work I'll get sacked. If it affects my relationships I'll be all lonely and sad.

"And as for my health, following a quick glance at my tax bill I've decided that the NHS will treat me and the government can keep its fucking opinions to itself."

BRITISH GAS TO LET YOU EAT

BRITISH Gas has agreed to leave you just enough money so you can eat.

The energy giant is to cut its prices after a drop-off in demand was linked to an increasing number of its customers starving to death.

Now the company has pledged to reduce tariffs to the point where consumers can afford just enough food to continue to live while spending the rest of their meagre incomes on gas and electricity.

A spokesman said: "This winter an increasing number of people have had to choose between freezing to death and starving to death. You're absolutely no use to us dead. At least until we're allowed to burn corpses instead of coal."

He added: "In these difficult times our challenge is to set prices which create that happy medium somewhere between hypothermia and having just enough energy to switch on the oven."

The company is also publishing a series of tips and hints on energy efficient cooking in its new booklet *Pressure Cookers Give You Cancer*.

Tips include:
- Raw vegetables are deadly. Use the biggest pan you can find, and fill it to the brim with water.
- Cook huge joints of meat. Cutting it into smaller pieces means it will cook too fast and you will die of vomiting.
- To prevent deadly food poisoning always leave the oven on for at least an hour after you have eaten.
- Always boil water on the hob. Every year kettles kill more than 500,000 people exactly like you.

Elizabeth Bradford, 67, from Dorchester, said: "Once again I shall taste the sweet nectar of Asda Smart Price cream of tomato. Thank you British Gas. I love you."

Doctors recommend kebabs for high testicle content

THE doner kebab is a nutritious snack filled with zinc and proteins from the compacted shavings of at least 14 different varieties of testicle, doctors said last night.

While often attacked for its high fat content, experts claimed that the kebab provided a balanced diet and was a major factor in having wondrous balls.

Just two large doners a week guarantees men large, full testicles, while women will develop a glossy coat and a soothing baritone voice.

Dr Tom Logan, of the Institute for Studies, said a typical take-away kebab was 98.4% animal testicles and 1.6% lettuce both of which are essential for vigorous gonads.

He added: "Go to the Turkish baths in Istanbul and you will come face to face with the world's fullest scrotums.

"Tremendous balls, really pink and plump, and no wrinkles or veiny protuberances to speak of. Not at all like the shrivelled little walnut sacks you get over here." Dr Logan added: "I certainly would not like to be standing in front of one of those if it went off."

Wazim Farza, owner of Wazim's Mashed Testicles on Basildon High Street, said: "I favour a mix of sheep, kangaroo, frog and Irish Setter.

"This classic mix will make your balls very very splendid. You want to see my balls?"

GREEN SHOOTS OF RECOVERY REVEALED AS PUTREFYING FINGERS OF THE DEAD

CLAIMS the UK was seeing the green shoots of recovery were withdrawn last night after they were revealed to be nothing more than the mouldy fingers of the recently deceased.

The government said they had mistaken the putrefying digits for an early spring and apologised to the corpses' loved ones.

Economist Julian Cook explained: "The economic downturn has forced thousands of people to cancel their private medical insurance and use the NHS, which means, of course, that in many cases they end up being buried alive.

"Additionally, many families can no longer afford a coffin or a qualified grave digger and so the still breathing relative is thrown into a hastily dug hole in the ground.

"But sure enough, the patient eventually regains consciousness, realises their predicament and immediately thrusts their hand up through the soil in a desperate bid to escape.

"Unfortunately, weakened by a lack of food and oxygen, they quickly expire and the hand begins to decompose, taking on a sickly green colour. This is where the minister has become confused."

Cook said Britain could soon be covered in 'green shoots' as more and more companies look to avoid redundancy payments by simply bulldozing their surplus workers into a pit.

He added: "From a distance it could actually be very reminiscent of a fresh spring meadow. The only difference will be the unbearable stench of death."

I warned of crisis ten years ago then did absolutely nothing about it, says Brown

GORDON Brown yesterday said he warned of the financial crisis ten years ago but did nothing to stop it because, quite frankly, he wants us all dead.

In a speech to the Foreign Press Association in London, Mr Brown said: "At any point I could have stepped in and made the necessary changes that would at least have protected the UK, what with me being chancellor of the exchequer and everything. But then I thought 'where's the fun in that?'.

"I was watching that new *Batman* film the other night and there's a bit where Michael Caine – he plays the butler – says that 'some men aren't looking for anything logical, some men just want to watch the world burn'. That's me, that is.

"Now some people are saying that my bank bail outs aren't working and if I'm not careful I'll end up destroying our entire financial system and bankrupting the country. Well, d'uh!"

Mr Brown added: "I'm not right in the head. I've been setting fire to stuff recently. Just small stuff. Books, furniture, cats.

"They keep giving me these little yellow pills, but I don't think they're working. If anything they make me even angrier and I just want to start bigger and bigger fires.

"I guess it's only a matter of days now before I set fire to a car. Then it'll be a church, a hospital, a row of quaint, terraced cottages. I'm just letting you know."

Complementary therapists to be regulated by witch doctor

STRICT standards must be applied to alternative medicine, according to the voodoo priest who will run the UK's complementary therapy watchdog.

Haitian-born Papa Limba said that his first task as chairman of the Complementary and Natural Healthcare Council would be to identify which therapists were righteous shamans and which had the bad juju.

But the witch doctor stressed the therapists would be judged not on the effectiveness of their treatments but on the strength of their mogambo.

Limba said: "There are many frauds and not everyone has as strong a connection to the serpent god Demballa as they like to make out.

"I place my hands on their head and if their spirit vibrates to the rhythm of the ocean I give them a sticker to put in the window. If not I rub them with the mashed root of the banyan tree and we never hear of them again."

He added: "Once a year I shall visit them and cast my chicken bones on their consulting room floor. If they are still there a week later I report them to health and safety."

Papa Limba is the former Lib Dem candidate for Bristol North West

A CNHC official said that all applicants would be judged on the four key elements: earth, fire, water and the age of the magazines in their waiting room. Homeopaths will be able to apply for accreditation by visualising the application form and then beaming their thoughts down the nearest ley line.

For Christ's sake just buy some helicopters, says everyone

MINISTERS were last night told to stop dicking about and just buy a load of helicopters, for Christ's sake.

People across Britain said that if helicopters will stop soldiers from being blown up in Afghanistan then ministers should really get some of them and stop being such a bunch of arseholes, all the time.

The government has so far refused demands from senior generals to buy more helicopters, insisting they are even more dangerous than the Taleban because if you don't crouch down they can chop the top of your head off.

But Bill McKay, from Doncaster, said: "When it comes to wars and stuff I'm inclined to go with generals and admirals, rather than some bloke called 'Bob Ainsworth' who spent 20 years as a shop steward in Coventry before deciding to sit around on his fat arse all day spending my money."

Emma Bradford, from Stevenage, said: "The problem seems to be bombs at the side of the road. I would suggest we build a huge network of canals, but unfortunately all the Irish are now working in call centres.

"I'm no scientist, but I would have thought that the only available option would therefore be some

'Rather you than me' said Mr Ainsworth

sort of flying machine."

She added: "I know, why don't we get the MPs to hand over the profits they made from all the houses they bought with my money?

That's got to be at least three helicopters. Probably quite good ones as well."

Margaret Gerving, a retired headmistress from Surrey, said: "I've noticed that there are lots of wind turbines just standing about doing precisely fuck all most of the time. Surely we can use some of the bits to make at least one helicopter?"

And Tom Logan, from Finsbury Park, added: "Do we want a state of the art Olympic velodrome so we can maintain our global dominance at riding a bike, or do we want more live soldiers? It's a tricky one isn't it?"

Under 15s 'should not be allowed to fly'

CHILDREN under the age of 15 should never be allowed to fly a passenger jet, not even for five minutes, according to the chief medical officer.

Sir Liam Donaldson said the advice may seem obvious, but too many parents are still allowing their child to take the family car, drive to the airport and start fiddling about in the cockpit of a Boeing 737.

He added: "We've all heard stories about people who flew 350 passengers from Heathrow to JFK when they were 12 and it never did them any harm, but there are many more who had to ditch in the Atlantic and then wait for their parents to come and clean up the mess."

Sir Liam has issued new guidance outlining all the things children are not supposed to do, including chainsaw testing, running a major clearing bank, 'crack-whoring' and 24-hour tequila snorting contests.

But Kyle Stephenson, 14, from Berwick Upon Tweed, said: "The bank thing I can understand – and maybe the crack-whoring – but I love flying planes and getting drunk. And at least when I drink I do fun things like setting fire to old mattresses and laying waste to entire communities, instead of getting a bit racist and then trying to touch my neighbour's wife on the tits."

Gemma Bishop, six, also attacked the plans, adding: "I have developed a keen palate and have a particular fondness for a late harvest merlot, especially with Coco-Pops. But I don't really like Pinot Grigio, mainly because it tastes of poo and bogies."

Wear protection during pig sex, farmers warned

FARMERS who copulate with pigs risk permanent deafness from the animals' frenzied squealing, according to latest guidelines from the Health and Safety Executive.

Best Practice For Inter-Species Coitus In The Agricultural Workplace warns that farmers should not engage pigs in intercourse without 'appropriate hearing protection' such as ear guards, plugs or muffs.

Farmer Denys Hatton, who defiles more than 400 acres near Worcester, said: "Yet more nanny state nonsense. I doubt these pen-pushers have ever even seen a pig, let alone mounted one. They actually go very quiet.

"They stopped us burning stubble, and now they want to stop us humping the bejesus out of pigs. But that is never going to happen – not as long as these 30-stone beauties are the colour of sunkissed virgins and their little brown eyes are filled with yearning."

An HSE spokesperson has denied victimising the farming industry, adding: "The high-pitched squeals of a violated sow can penetrate the inner ear and permanently damage the tiny hairs that allow us to hear.

"One alternative to ear protection is a 'glory hole' style arrangement, where a small aperture is made at groin level on the side of the sty thereby allowing intercourse to occur without the farmer entering the enclosure.

The guidelines also recommend checking that tuberculosis jabs are up to date before going at it hammer and tongs with a badger.

Seven million people downloading stuff you wouldn't pay for if there was a gun to your head

SEVEN million people in the UK are illegally downloading the sort of music and films you wouldn't pay for even as you heard the ominous click of a gun being cocked.

According to the Strategic Advisory Board for Intellectual Property, illegal downloaders are accessing material that could be worth up to £120bn a year if it was any good.

A spokesman said: "Entertainers would be facing genuine hardship if it was not for all those people whose lives are so devastatingly empty that they will hand over good money to watch Daniel Craig do

some of his own stunts."

But experts stressed that while seven million people may be getting free Katy Perry, there are 53 million others who would gleefully hurl themselves in front of a train rather than listen to a single, quirky note.

Dr Tom Booker, of Reading University, said: "I was astonished to discover there are websites where you actually have to pay to listen to Leona Lewis.

"And when I read that Shia LaBeouf has moved into a luxury villa, high in the Hollywood Hills, I begin to tremble with rage at the thought that someone,

Do it, you coward!

somewhere has given him money."

Dr Booker said that out of the top 10 illegally downloaded films, 'some-

where between nine and eleven of them are utter fucking rubbish'.

"The most popular film download this week is something called *Fired Up*. It tells the eternal story of two high school football players who sign up for cheerleader camp where they discover the true meaning of friendship and bras.

"Apparently it makes *Transformers* look like a freshly discovered folio of charcoal sketches by Leonardo da Vinci."

He added: "Pass me a train timetable and a map. I have an appointment to keep."

Brown engulfed by expenses scandal as power passes to Joanna Lumley

GORDON Brown was prime minister in name only last night as the machinery of state was transferred to actress Joanna Lumley.

Ms Lumley has now set up an interim administration in the drawing room of her Chelsea townhouse as she waits for the formality of a general election.

Mr Brown is expected to be finally dragged from office later today after it was revealed he has been paying his own brother £65,000 a year to dress up like a cleaning lady.

It also emerged that Jack Straw, the justice secretary, claimed thousands in council tax for houses that he would quite like to live in, while communities secretary Hazel Blears used public money to buy tiny furniture for her vast network of burrows.

As the government disintegrated like cheap toilet paper, Ms Lumley was huddled in talks with the close-knit group of deadly Gurkhas who carry her about in a chair.

A source said: "One of her first jobs will be to visit every family in the country and tell them just how marvellous they are. Of course, once we take charge there will be no further need for political parties, or silly little things like elections and parliament. I'm warning you all now – do not fuck with Joanna Lumley."

Meanwhile, Sir June Whitfield has been made Commissioner of the Metropolitan Police, while the leader's former *New Avengers* co-star Patrick McNee will finally take charge of MI5.

VORDERMAN HIRED TO HELP PEOPLE WORK OUT IF FIRST-PLUS LOANS ARE A GOOD IDEA

CAROL Vorderman is to head a Conservative Party taskforce to help people work out if debt consolidation loans are really such a good idea after all.

The Tories said the former *Countdown* star was ideally suited to the post as one of the country's leading experts in lots of big, confusing interest rates.

Vorderman said: "Let's say you have £20,000 in outstanding credit which, if you just stopped buying shit you don't need, you could pay off in around six years with interest payments of about £7,000. But if you rolled it all up into your mortgage and paid it off over 20 years you could continue to buy the shit you don't need and pay interest of just £14,000. £14,000 divided by £7,000 equals £2 which you then multiply by 10,000 to get the number you started with. Maths is so much easier than you think."

"Of course the simple answer to all of that is to make sure you built up a large fortune selling expensive loans and pointless detox diets while earning even more money by doing sums on the telly."

Tory leader David Cameron said: "Interest rates are incredibly important. For instance I am particularly fascinated by media interest rates. So if I needed someone to head-up a taskforce about maths teaching, I suppose I could ask a professor of maths or someone who had actually taught maths in a school, but then the interest rate would be very small indeed. Do you see?"

BBC to screen Gaza appeal if it includes phone-in scam

THE BBC has agreed to air a charity appeal for the stricken people of Gaza, as long as they can include a fraudulent phone-in contest, it emerged last night.

The Corporation is finalising the details but insisted it needs time to develop a phone-in scam that is both horribly dishonest and completely impartial.

A BBC spokesman said: "Obviously we are looking at ways of skimming five, maybe ten pence off the top of every donation.

"But we'd also like to set up a fake competition to run alongside the appeal that would then be won by a member of staff posing as one of the plebs.

"We could maybe offer a two-week trip to Israel and the question could be something like, 'how do you spell Gaza?' Is it a) Gaza, b) Gazzzza, or c) fyjyplymp?'"

The BBC had earlier refused to screen the appeal claiming it would face accusations of being biased towards not dying horribly.

The spokesman added: "Screening a humanitarian appeal which most people are going to ignore anyway would have destroyed the BBC's reputation, just as if it had been hit by wave after wave of indiscriminate air strikes."

Tom Logan, professor of communications at Reading University, said: "It's a difficult one for the BBC.

"It has to weigh up a lot of very complex factors before surrendering five minutes of airtime that would otherwise be filled with some vapid, unoriginal shit."

The BBC appeal will be introduced by Jonathan Ross, the jumped-up researcher, who will highlight the suffering of Palestine's 80-year-old grandmothers, many of whom he would like to have sex with.

You're just too pretty to be a judge, Cowell tells Brook

SIMON Cowell has told Kelly Brook she was dropped from *Britain's Got Talent* because she was just too pretty.

Cowell said the four-judge format was never going to work with someone as 'staggeringly beautiful and sexy' as the 29-year-old brunette.

BGT was to be Brook's biggest TV job since Channel Four dropped her from *The Big Breakfast* for being too gifted.

Cowell added: "It's hard enough for TV viewers to cope with Kelly's stunning good looks never mind the people who have to be in the same room as her.

"And I hope she doesn't take this the wrong way, but she's also too kind and generous and funny and clever to be on the judging panel.

"And then there's all that bubonic plague we've had in the studio that for some reason only affects lovely young women with brown hair whose

Fellow judge Amanda Holden said Brook was 'too good for ITV'

boyfriends are famous rugby players."

An ITV spokesman said Brook was also being hunted by an international assassin who has filled her dressing room with dynamite.

He added: "So it's really for own safety that she's been sacked for being rubbish."

Grandparents advised to gay it up a bit

ELDERLY couples who are hoping to adopt their grandchildren are being advised to gay it up a bit.

Experts claim grandfathers will have greater success if they wear bright pink lipstick, talk like a hairdresser and make flamboyant hand gestures.

Tom Logan, an assistant director of social work in Birmingham, said: "When it comes to the interview, grandad should be as nancy as possible.

"Granny can either dress up and pretend to be his Latino lover-boy or just pose as a lesbo fag-hag.

"Either way most social work departments would rather give the children to a couple of weird, bi-curious transvestites than some old Tory with a Rover 200 and a bag of toffees."

The guidance comes as new figures reveal that most British children are now being raised by gayboy lesbians.

In Nottingham the local council is taking children from stable, traditional family homes and placing them with any old homosexual who walks in off the street.

Meanwhile in Gloucester an all-male *ménage à trois* has been allowed to adopt 48 children who they like to dress up in little leather shorts and play a game called 'hot gay disco'. But family campaigners say they have amassed a huge amount of made-up evidence which proves that children raised by gays will turn into violent morons and drug addicts, just like the heterosexual parents they were taken from.

Bill McKay, director of Families, Families, Families, said: "Invariably these children are placed with two men who are not only gentle and sensitive to the needs of others, but also highly educated, prosperous, and in a long-term, stable relationship. They don't stand a chance."

Give it some Abba grandad

NEWS BRIEFLY

RBS IMPLODES LIKE HOUSE AT THE END OF 'POLTERGEIST'

"This once again demonstrates the folly of building a major financial institution on top of an old Indian burial ground," says economist

WOMEN HARD-WIRED FOR CAKE

"If you're ever in a café and you accidentally move between a woman and a profiterole you should drop to the floor, curl up in a tight ball and lie perfectly still," says expert

WOULD YOU LIKE TO SEE OUR BALLS? ASK JAMAICANS

As researchers linked long-term marijuana use to testicular cancer the Caribbean island's male population said anyone who doubted the vigour of their balls should board a plane to Kingston immediately and cup them

TACTICAL GENIUS POCKETS £15M FOR SEVEN MONTHS WORK

"Pro-rata that's more than Paul McCartney. I'm not quite up there with Tom Cruise, but there's always the Arab chap at Man City," Luiz Philipe Scolari

TEDIOUSNESS OF CLIMATE CHANGE PUNDITS UNDERESTIMATED

New data points towards Monbiot and Monbiot-fuelled activity forcing millions of people to leap from high buildings while battering themselves to death with a heavy frying pan all the way down, just to make sure

Barclays clearly not run by bankers

BARCLAYS has finally admitted it is no longer run by bankers after posting an annual profit of £6bn.

The bank said that it had replaced most of its executives about 18 months ago after realising they had no idea what they were doing.

Chairman Marcus Agius said: "During a boom, any arsehole can run a bank. But unlike our competitors we noticed quite early on that our chaps didn't have the faintest idea.

"We made the decision there and then to replace the senior management team with people who weren't utter cretins.

"Fortunately, I had just had my bathroom refurbished and the plumber was fantastic. It took him less than a week to strip out and replace the old fittings and redirect much of the existing pipework.

"When he'd finished I brought him a cup of tea and said to him 'excellent work, I don't suppose you fancy running Barclays do you?'."

Agius added: "Polish apparently. I think his name's 'Lech', or 'Lev'. Or maybe it was 'Lenny'."

Lech Warislavski, the plumber

Barclays Bank has been run by a Polish plumber called 'Lech' since August 2007

turned banking executive, said: "It very easy. You are lending moneys to peoples who can pay back and charging as much of the interests as can get away with.

"At same time you no go round buying up load of rubbish debt when market about to go down what we plumber call the 'shitbox'.

"It no take big brain. All you need is calculator, pencil and 12 metre of good copper pipe."

Worthless, ill-informed opinions in every home by 2012

EVERY home in Britain will have access to an endless stream of worthless, ill-informed opinions by 2012, under new government proposals.

The Digital Britain strategy, unveiled yesterday, will mean no-one will be able to hide from the jibbering mess cascading from blogs, chat rooms and inexplicable newspaper comment threads.

The drive for universal broadband comes amid claims there are still too many homes across the UK where people are forced to read books and have actual, fully-formed thoughts which they then keep to themselves.

But from 2012 every consumer will be able to use the internet to pick up a random falsehood and weave it quickly and efficiently into their own offensively bizarre world view.

Tom Logan, of the Institute for Studies, said: "The technology is rather complex but basically what we're talking about is a big pipe full of nutcases shoved through your front door.

"Not only will you be able to gape in horror at their unsettling combination of wide-eyed naivete and poisonous bigotry, you'll also be able to spit your own half-chewed mince back at them."

He added: "You will experience the joy of watching a perfectly harmless chat forum about Subarus degrade into a series of furious, expletive-filled exchanges about why everything these day is run for, and by, Jewish homosexuals."

Culture secretary Andy Burnham stressed the internet can also be used to order useful products, invade your privacy, manage personal finances and access millions of photographs of Swedish vaginas.

NEWS BRIEFLY

FIRM OFFERS 'TWATS-ONLY' ACTIVITY HOLIDAYS

"Think of all the stories you will be able to tell at your twat-filled dinner parties, as you pass round photos of you in a woolly hat and a pair of wraparound shades looking like such an unbearable twat," says spokesman

RBS EXECS TO REV THEIR FERRARIS VERY LOUDLY OUTSIDE YOUR HOUSE

When you come to the window they will wave and shout 'thanks for all the money' before tooting the horn and driving the car the 20 yards to your neighbour's house where they will then repeat the process

BATMAN URGES BATWOMAN TO DO IT WITH CATWOMAN

"If the girls did want me to watch them then I'm sure that would also be okay. And I do have my bat camcorder if anyone wanted me to make a bat souvenir video, for instance," says caped crusader

SUNNY DELIGHT LOSES TASTE TEST TO INDIAN COW PISS DRINK

The vitamin-packed drink, first developed by the CIA to destroy huge swathes of vegetation in South East Asia, is now produced in a disused zinc mine on the outskirts of Gdansk

LABOUR POLITICIANS DO NOTHING WRONG AGAIN

"Asking for money to perform consultancy tasks that may or may not involve tabling amendments may not be right, but that doesn't mean it's wrong," says party spokesman

Michael Sheen to play Red Rum

TONY Blair actor Michael Sheen is to extend his repertoire of real-life characters by playing Red Rum in a BBC mini-series.

Sheen will play the gangly brown foal, who gave up a promising medical career to pursue his dream of winning the Grand National twice in a row and then once more a couple of years later.

Horse Face will chart Red Rum's stormy relationship with trainer Ginger McCain including their explosive row on the eve of his third National victory in 1977, when Rummy stormed out of his stable threatening never to race again.

It will also explore the legendary steeplechaser's brief and ultimately doomed affair with Elizabeth Taylor.

The Welsh actor, who has played the former prime minister on TV, the big screen and at a school parents' evening, said: "Rummy was a hero, a joker and an artist, but above all he was a fairly large horse."

Sheen, whose other famous characters include Brian Clough, Brian Cant and Billie Holiday, added: "I've asked John Hurt to help me prepare for the role and he has very kindly agreed to dress up as Bob Champion and ride me over a hedge."

Sheen as David Frost in *Frost/Nixon*

The actor, famous for portraying both Kenneth Williams and Hattie Jacques, will also work closely with the now retired McCain who will feed him sugar cubes and smack him on his rump until he reaches top speed.

Sheen's next project will be a remake of the Charles Lindbergh biopic *The Spirit of Saint Louis* in which he plays the eponymous single-seat aircraft.

Kinnear accidentally calls team 'Shitcastle'

NEWCASTLE United boss Joe Kinnear was left red-faced yesterday after accidentally calling his team 'Shitcastle'.

With the club just two points above the drop zone and without a win in seven games, Kinnear said morale was low but he was certain that 'Shitcastle United' would avoid relegation.

Following Wednesday's defeat at Manchester City, the manager told Sky Sports: "We face a tough couple of months after injuries to Michael Rubbish and Joey Criminal. We're just lucky no-one has made a decent offer, as yet, for Shay Over-Rated."

Kinnear then added: "It is difficult being the manager of Shitcastle. There's

a lot of pressure from the fans who look back on the days of Kevin Mental with so much pride.

"They remember players like David French-Ponce, Alan Tedious, Peter Steptoe-Face, and of course David Batty."

Kinnear later corrected himself and confessed that he had a habit of mispronouncing names, adding: "I did exactly the same thing before when I was manager of Wimblethugs, Luton Trounced and Nottingham Fuckwits.

"Sadly, this just smacks of a desperate attempt by me to finally get the sack."

Millions flee in terror as the Earth almost collides with its celestial partner. Now scientists are asking...

IS IT TIME TO DESTROY THE MOON?

BAIL OUTS? I SHIT 'EM
by Mervin King, Governor of the Bank of England

SO I barrels into the back room of No 11 and that swivel-arsed sock-banger Darling is sitting there in his nappy as usual, and the Mad Jock is standing over him with a cosh, looking for all the world like he's moved himself back in permanent. Cock. Thought I'd seen the last of him, the shitting twat muffer.

"Merv, Merv," says Darling. "The markets have gone totally shit titters. Something called HBOS is off three billion while the Royal Bank is worth less than my MP's pension pot. What are we going to do?"

"Calm down, calm down," I says all soothing like. "I've totally got it nipped. Big Larry and Steve the Psycho are, as we speak, in a van on the A1 and this time tomorrow they'll be on the side of Leith Dock frying up the last of that jocking shit tickler Goodwin and feeding it to a pit bull.

"Fat Ron and Reg the Butcher are in the Jag heading for Halifax. That jumped up shelf-stacker Hornby has eaten his last can of baked beans. He'll be propping up the foundations of some swanky flat development, assuming the boys can find one that isn't totally arse pumped already. Sorted."

"Shitting fuck tits Merv," says Darling, "we asked you to bail 'em out. Not take 'em out. Can't we just stick £500 billion into them like we said and make it all go away?"

"Five hundred bill?" I says, all slow and deliberate. "You really want me to pump five hundred large of my own money into the same pair of knobbing piss flappers that got us into this cocking shit fuck? What are you, a titting minge monkey? If they'd listened to me in the first place and stuck their money into whores and drugs instead of hillbilly mortgages we wouldn't be in these beef curtains in the first place.

"And where I'm supposed to get five huge today? I'm up to my flaps in IOUs already; if it's not the slanty eyes on the phone asking for their money back, it's the rag heads. When the phone rings now I put on a foreign accent and tell them they've got the Star of Bengal, or get fat Sandra to tell them I've broken my wrist and can't sign cheques for a month.

"It's not your money,

Merv," he says, and he's got that look in his eye you normally only see if you mention that bum humper Mandelson. "It's taxpayers' money."

"Oh," says I all calm. "Well that's alright then. I know, after we've shit the five bill down the plugger why don't we cock a few hundred mill of this taxpayers' money to those robbing puffin fuckers and they can give it right back to our taxpayers who they stole it off in the first lace."

That told him. Titting shit flapper.

Any road up, better get myself spruced. Speaking to a bunch of hedge funds at the Mansion House tonight. Fanny dribblers.

YOUR ASTROLOGICAL WEEK AHEAD
with PSYCHIC BOB

Aquarius
Nobody likes a crybaby. Nobody likes you. You are a crybaby. Is any of this sinking in yet?

Pisces
Your ability to remain positive in the face of adversity and always express yourself with enthusiasm has never been more annoying. I may have to kill you.

Aries
Piles!

Taurus
After a sluggish start to the year, things are about to slow down before eventually grinding to a complete halt.

Gemini
You can tell yourself you are just washing it quickly, but in God's eyes it is still a sin.

Cancer
However you define 'creativity'– artistic skill, business nous, or just successfully raising a family of bright and well-adjusted children – you don't have it.

Leo
There's always someone who will offer a warm smile and gentle hand, but if you're looking to be held down and beaten by a severe looking woman in a school uniform that'll be fifty quid.

Virgo
Don't imagine things to be bigger and better than they are. Measure it in centimetres if you must, but you're fooling no-one but yourself.

Libra
Ooh-huh-ooh-hah-ooh-HAH-OOH-HAH-ooaaaa-ha-HEEEEEEEE!

Scorpio
Venus hovers opposite, then follows you down the street and onto the bus to your job in the hairdressers and books in for his fourth shampoo this week. Creepy tit.

Sagittarius
Cautious progress has always been your *modus operandi*. This is precisely why you keep being hit by cars.

Capricorn
The next two months promise to be unusually fruitful but very low on potatoes. There will be eggs though, and cheese. Heaps of cheese.